Tortoise Crossing – Expect Long Delays

And other satirical, cynical and just plain snicker-inducing essays

———————

Mike Murphy

CreateSpace
Independent Publishing Platform

Identifiers: ISBN-13: 978-1545297070
Subjects: Humor, satire
Printed in the United States of America

Contents

Chapter 1   Animals

Chapter 2   Exercise, Health, Sports

3

Chapter 3   Holidays

Chapter 4   Politics

Chapter 5 Travel

Chapter 6 You Name It

Chapter 1   Animals

Gay chickens in a stew over ban at fast food chain

Chickens have been in the news a lot lately. Animal cruelty complaints, fears over hormone-treated meat, and some chickens are just afraid to reveal their tax returns.

In fact, controversy first swirled around the chicken community way back in the 17th century when clandestine chicken and rabbit intimate relationships caused an uproar as rabbits were discovered laying eggs then attempting to conceal them from the public under the guise of celebrating Easter.

In addition, there is the ongoing mockery of moral decency every time a naked rubber chicken makes an appearance at a party or as a prop for the 'fowl' humor of a standup comedian.

The most recent chicken controversy evolved from comments recently made by the president of a quick-service U.S. chicken restaurant which really ruffled the feathers of gay chickens as he announced that the chain would only cook chickens that are involved in a rooster/hen relationship, no more rooster/rooster or hen/hen chickens will be chopped up and deep-fat fried.

Of course the LGBT chicken community immediately raised a squawk and asked why they were being pecked on. Over at KFC the chickens were madder than a wet settin' hen and insisted that the fast food industry had laid an egg on this sensitive issue. When asked his opinion Colonel Saunders, replied, "Chickens is chickens."

"The sky is falling!" cried Chicken Little, a gay spokes-hen who last spring was accidentally outed by Big Bird whose fashionable head feathers, flamboyant eye makeup and rainbow-colored leggings have brought into question the super star's own sexual orientation. Critics feel that his/her appearance points to a giant silkie chicken in drag, though so far he/she has attempted to maintain a somewhat androgynous image for the general public.

Although chickens who agreed with the new anti-gay chicken policy were scarce as hen's teeth, a small minority stated that they understood the public's concern about eating gay chickens and they were willing to stick their necks out and even exhibit solidarity by joining customers in line to eat, of all things, chicken! In an attempt to explain her stance, one hen said that the gay chickens are like scrambled eggs—all mixed up.

Chickens that support the pro-heterosexual chicken eating ruling are led by none other than that symbol of masculinity himself, Foghorn Leghorn. Foghorn's homophobic attitude came through loud and clear in his attempt to explain the gay chickens, "These boys are more mixed up than a feather in a whirlwind." He went on to declare that this is what happens when chickens cross the road to get to "the other side."

But later, when pressed for more discussion of his own radical stance towards eating only straight chickens, he told the male reporter, "Ah say, ah say, now cut that out boy, or I'll spank you where the feathers are thinnest." Hmmmmm.

It's still too early to tell which side will prevail in this game of chicken. The gay chickens warn the corporation to not count their chickens before they are hatched. "They have placed all of their eggs in one basket and soon will be walking on eggshells as the public tide turns," said Chicken Little.

The gay chickens were certain that the restaurant chain owners would end up with egg on their face and regret such an insensitive stance. Young chickens in the brood that we interviewed clucked that they were cock sure that they would prevail in the end. "We deserve equal rights. Why should we be denied the privilege of being devoured by millions just because we birds of a feather flock together?"

One particularly poetic chick expressed a similar sentiment in a piece of 'poultry' that she scratched: "Hot wing, drumstick, or thigh; Gay, straight, transchicken, or bi; it's all finger-lickin' good."

The company, on the other hand, says that the protestors are disorganized and just running around like chickens with their heads cut off. An anonymous CEO predicted that the company will rule the roost in the end and will really have something to crow about as it racks up record profits. "As Henry Ford said, 'Business is never so healthy as when, like a chicken, it must do a certain amount of scratching for what it gets.'"

As usual, celebrities rushed to support the gay chickens protest, including Mike the Headless Chicken also known as Miracle Mike (no relation to the author). According to the Guinness Book of World Records, Miracle Mike holds the record by surviving for eighteen months after his head was chopped off by a farmer. When asked his feelings about the gay chicken ban, Mike had no comment.

The gay chickens had planned to stage a "gay kiss-in" but had to cancel at the last minute as their lawyer reluctantly informed them that chickens do not have lips.

My pit bull can beat up your honor student

Every time a dog-fighting operation is uncovered it seems to be big news, but, really, the problem apparently is rather wide-spread. What I'm waiting for, and what would be a headline grabber for sure, is a cat fighting bust. It's one thing to round up some bedraggled, appreciative, face-licking dogs, but just try to round up a pack of peeved pussy cats! Personally, I wouldn't enter that compound unless I was wearing a suit of armor.

Recently we have seen the best and worst of the canine world. First, we have the lowly pit bulls sentenced to a life in the murky world of UFC (Ultimate Fighting Canines). These dogs are in that 47% of mongrels that will always select the president's first dog Bo as the best in breed just because he is black and an immigrant (Portuguese Water Dog), and this, despite the fact that he is neutered. Whereas, Mitt Romney's dog Seamus would never even get so much as a sniff.

The pit bull was created by interbreeding an alligator with a Chihuahua. Like many breeds its job was to do man's dirty work for him. Ancient Roman soldiers would sic dogs on any enemy that had not already been stabbed, hacked, or boiled. Today, dogs are used to sniff for illegal drugs and bombs, always in that order since once they get a nose full of cocaine, they don't really care what's in the suitcase making that ticking sound.

Obviously, the catchphrase referring to dogs as "Man's best friend" is a classic example of propaganda devised by some PR firm and is about as absurd as putting the words George W. Bush and library in the same sentence.

Men take great pride in teaching dogs to sit, lie down, rollover, beg, etc. Often the dog's master will demonstrate each feat first then the dog imitates him. So I can't figure out why my dog likes to roll in his own urine. I simply don't recall ever doing that.

A pit bull who asked to remain anonymous—we'll call him Spike—shared a typical story. "I wasn't born with a silver dog bone in my mouth being the runt of the litter. Ever since I first bit the hand that fed me, I've been in and out of the dog pound nearly all my life. When my owner would throw a ball and yell 'Fetch' I would chomp on his ankle and drag him to the ball and growl, 'Pick it up and hand it to me.' And I wasn't the wimpy type that just bites the mail man; I bit the mail truck.

"Life is tough in the dog pound. Me and my bros would sit around and dream of escaping while listening to 'Who Let the Dogs Out.' But every time we tried digging our way out we would get confused and bury a bone. Then, of course, we had to start all over. Once a big lab named Quasimodo caught a Frisbee and just kept running to freedom, but such good fortune was rare.

"Once I was paroled, I lived in a card board box for a dog house. I learned to beg on my own with no one around to teach me. You think I like doing that? I have some pride, you know. Finally, a guy took me in and trained me to be tough. He combed my hair with a barbed-wire brush. Instead of the dog whisperer, he was the dog screamer. I got so mean that I started wearing this shock collar for kicks. Some nights I even stack two or three on to get a real charge. Heck, I'll even turn it on myself. Don't believe me? Mine's turned on right now as we speak, and I can't feel a th . . . Aargh!! Oops! Sorry I peed on your shoe."

The other side of the dog world is much brighter as evidenced by the recent showing of the Westminster Dog Show. Here you will find the privileged 1%. These are the dogs that have millions of Milk Bones stashed away on the Canine Islands.

When asked about the less fortunate breeds, dogs like Spike, this year's best in show, Banana Joe V Tanni Kazari, scoffed: "Disgusting mutts! Always scratching and licking themselves. I have a human to do all that for me. Curs chained in a back yard get fleas and worms, and when they throw up, they turn right around and eat it! I only do that that if it's canine caviar. Hey, could we cut this short? I'm scheduled for a sani-trim this afternoon."

Later, back at the pound, I asked Spike, the pit bull, "Do you sometimes wish that you had been born a Shih Tzu?"

"Gesundheit," was his reply.

No trapping while driving—it's the law

Wearing a coonskin cap, alligator skin boots, and an ostrich skin cape, an Idaho legislator recently introduced a bill to add a right to hunt, trap, and impale night crawlers amendment to the state constitution. The senator also emitted a strong essence of skunk odor which forced a number of legislators to sit farther back than normal.

Now if trapping is such a big deal in Idaho that we need this amendment, how come no one so far has trapped Bigfoot? It would seem pretty obvious that if anyone was going to get caught because he couldn't resist the aromatic scent of fish guts and cow's blood it would be Bigfoot just by the very implication of the name "BIGfoot." How could he miss stumbling into a trap set anywhere in his neighborhood?

The trapping aspect of the amendment has created controversy. However, in defense of trappers, the senator stated, on the topic of making animals suffer, "that's just not something we do." Or, as Elmer Fudd once said, "I'm sowwy, Mr. Wabbit. I hope I didn't hurt you too much when I killed you."

In a related item, a while back The Wolf Street Journal ran a picture of a grinning wolf with a trapped sheep in the background standing on blood-stained snow. A large number of sheep wrote in that the photo was in baaaaad taste.

There are regulations in place to make trapping a pleasant outdoor experience for both the trapper and the trappee. All of the rules are published in a handbook for trapping, but a legitimate concern is how many trappers will actually take the time to have someone read it to them?

For example trappers are required to check their traps every 72 hours. My questions are what kind of day job do these guys have that they can take off every three days to play Jeremiah Johnson and slosh around in icy streams checking for trapped muskrats turned stiff as giant, hairy popsicles, with orange teeth frozen in a hideous grin? And are there any openings where they work?

Just so you won't end up accidentally caught in one of the rusty traps set by some senile, half-blind old mountain man who kept forgetting where he put them and even got caught and died in one of his own traps that he set in his outhouse thinking it was a cave, and so you won't end up like Jacob Marley wrapped up in chains, stumbling around in the forest praying that a descendent of the bear whom the trap was originally intended for doesn't show up, here are some tips.

First of all remember, when you are out hiking in the woods, if the smell of beaver gland seems too good to be true, it probably is.

Secondly, I recommend that Idaho's governor stay clear of the Idaho Panhandle from November to March since it is legal to trap Otter during that season.

To get back to the role of the Idaho senate in all of this, I think that I speak for the majority of Idahoans when I say that the proposed trapping amendment does not go quite far enough. It seems unconscionable to me that while Idaho has made texting while driving a crime, no one has thought to make trapping while driving a crime!

As dangerous as texting while driving is, still it usually will only result in placing your fingers on the wrong keys creating more misspelled words than normal or a completely nonsensical message which is normal under any circumstances from what I have seen.

On the other hand, trapping while driving could result in the painful whacking off of those very same fingers if you should happen to swerve as you are sprinkling mink urine on a trap to catch . . . uh . . . some sicko mink.

Likewise picture this: you are trying to haul in a trap containing a wolf while steering your minivan down the highway— and the wolf is not dead, but he is very, very ticked off. It does not require much imagination to see the danger this presents for other drivers, not to mention the two children in the van despite the fact that they are snuggly strapped in their child safety seats.

Another connection between texting and trapping is that people who text frequently develop discomfort and muscle pain called "text neck." Similarly, animals that get their neck caught in a trap develop a rash and tingling sensation which, if not immediately treated, could result in decapitation.

Finally, I am sure that all that trapping will result in the removal of most of the wolves and coyotes in Idaho, but I am afraid there will still be lots of skunks lurking in the state capitol.

Pet suicides on the rise

We've all seen the sad headlines: "Dog accidentally squished while chasing steam roller" "Cat accidentally drowns in milk bowl" "Parakeet accidentally gets head stuck between cage bars." But now a recent report reveals the shocking truth: many of these pet deaths are not accidental at all, but are more evidence of a recent epidemic of pet suicides.

I realize that this is topic that is difficult for people to confront and discuss openly but discuss it we must if we are going to have any success at ending this disturbing trend.

The first and most obvious question is "why?" Why would Slobbers the faithful dog, Cuddles the feline slug, or Flopsy the completely worthless bunny decide to end their seemingly utopian existence?

After all, wouldn't any human love to live a dog's life? A life filled with chasing sticks, slobbering on children who actually seem to enjoy it, pooping anywhere he pleases and then melting his owner's heart and getting off the hook with that "Oops, I did it again" hangdog expression.

Even more of a mystery is a cat deciding to end it all when the "all" consist of licking itself, turning its nose up at food, licking itself, disgustedly walking away from different food, licking itself, appearing insulted by new food offered, and licking itself some more.

What motivates these creatures to end it all? Maybe we need to take a closer look at the truly pathetic lives of pets to find an answer.

People dress pets up for the holidays thinking that's real cute. Look on the Internet—they're all over the place. But look closer. Does that pink Chihuahua carrying a handbag with a Paris Hilton doll in it look happy to you? Does that dachshund dressed up like the Wienermobile appear particularly amused? Of course not. They are humiliated. They are depressed. They need a belly rub.

They say that owners begin to resemble their dogs over time. But when it comes to obesity just the opposite happens. After a steady diet of sharing pizza with its owner even a svelte greyhound could resemble Elvis before he blew up due to an enchilada overdose. Ever seen an obese dog try to squeeze through one of those doggie doors? And get stuck? Or a cat that resembles a hairy bowling ball and requires a tiny crane to lift it in and out of the litter box? Obviously their self-image is not good.

Mugly, a Chinese crested, recently won the World's Ugliest Dog title. And his prize? No crown, no sash, no sappy song, just a measly bunch of dog cookies—that's it. But the winner of such a title will no doubt wear a crown of shame which will result in lifelong mental scars for Mugly. You don't see a World's Ugliest

Human contest, do you, and heaven knows there are lots of candidates for that title.

Just imagine being forever cursed with a hurtful dog name like Pecker, Goober, Stinky, etc., to the extent that they put it in writing on your collar so all the neighborhood mutts can join in on the joke. Even worse is the stream of degrading tags such as "Here, boy" "Atta boy" "Good girl" that you must endure despite the fact you are 90 years old in dog years! Cats certainly do not have it any better. Whether their name is Frisky, Fruity, or Flippy, everyone calls them "Kitty."

With all of the publicity related to wolves, their wild ancestors, domestic dogs must certainly suffer from an inferiority complex. Just think how ashamed Twinkie, a pampered poodle with magenta manicured claws tastefully done by her personal pedicurist Changpu, must feel as she watches a wolf on YouTube howling at the moon. And how depressed is the family pet Lardo the Labrador as he waddles into the kitchen for a bedtime snack of ice cream and doggy truffles after watching wolves stalk an elk on Animal Planet?

Whereas human magazines discuss politics, entertainment, business, etc., dog magazines feature stories like Dog Anal Sacs, Dog Parasites, Submissive Urination, Tail Chasing, Drinking From the Toilet, Rolling in Yucky Stuff, Crotch Sniffing, etc., which results in animals who take on the image of a breed of hairy degenerate psycho pets.

Then there is a macho-sounding dog like Boris the Russian Wolfhound whose very name should send shivers down the spine of less manly breeds, but, no, because, quite often, he has been neutered. A neutered Russian Wolfhound sounds liked an oxymoron. And to add insult to injury the dog's owner will carelessly say this out loud so everyone knows—including the dog himself. "Did he say neutered? Me??"

And spayed I am not even going to get into since my kitty Princess Yum Yum is listening at this very moment.

Q & A with Bigfoot

So, I'm sitting around the campfire having a chat with Bigfoot, albeit a one-sided conversation since I can't get a word in edgewise due to the fact the big hairy guy hasn't had anyone to talk to for fifty years apparently, so he's blabbing on and on about what he's been doing all that time.

"... and I look back just before I step into the woods to take a whiz when this guy snaps a photo of me, and here I am, hair's a mess, and, yeah, sure, I had shaved that morning, but I grow a full beard in, like, five minutes and , boy, that dumb expression on my face, like, 'What, me worry?' as if to make me look like Alfred E. Giganto, and that was way before YouTube, else, if it happened now, I could cash in and make millions. Now, that was back, I believe, in 1967, then the next year. . . ."

Blah, blah, blah he rambles on, only taking a break when he jumps up to snatch one of the mice which scurries out from under one of the logs we're sitting on and pops it into his mouth without even bothering to dip it into the jar of salsa first.

Despite his incessant talking and annoying habit of picking his nose with his big toe, this is certainly a rare opportunity. I mean I'm just sitting here enjoying the tranquility of the forest primeval when all of a sudden a seven-foot tall Rambo in a ghillie suit comes crashing out of the brush and asks, "Say, are you, by any chance, going to eat those night crawlers you got there in the coffee can?"

And that marked the beginning of this strangest of conversations and an opportunity which I planned to take full advantage of as a proud charter member of the BS (Bigfoot/Sasquatch) Club.

Sasquatch has been part of folklore worldwide for ages. For many years people have reported seeing giant, hairy, smelly man-like creatures deep in the forests around the world as well as on football fields in this country on Sunday afternoons.

According to scientists, these creatures which have evolved alongside humans "became astonishingly adept at avoiding human

16

contact through a process of natural selection" and by not renewing their cell phone service contracts.

When they feel their territory is threatened, they are said to harass humans by screaming, breaking and crashing things, throwing rocks, passing gas, etc., which sounds exactly like my neighbors back in North Omaha on a typical Saturday night.

The first question I wanted to ask him was what that awful smell was. Then I recalled that some experts say that Bigfoot smells like sticking one's head into a pile of dirty diapers.

So I started off with a less offensive question: "How did you get the name Bigfoot?" He replied, "Well, it sounds better than Big Tootsie, wouldn't you say? I'm just glad it's my feet that are extraordinarily huge and not some other body part, say my nose or my butt. For a better answer to your question, just take a glance at this," as he swung a foot up, knocking me off my log and crushing a Styrofoam cooler.

When asked what his favorite sport is he answered, "Football—duh. I tried playing soccer but the ball blew up every time I kicked it. However, I had to discontinue playing all sports because if I get athlete's foot, it's all over for me."

At that I point I decided to probe deeper: "Do you ever get any visitors?"

"Once, these two nice young men showed up at my cave. They were riding bikes and wearing small backpacks and asked me to join something. But when I asked if I could pay my tithe in grubs and maggots one fellow said, 'Say, we've got to be going 'cause we have a 4:00 appointment to meet with The Creature from the Black Lagoon.' Other than that, I just do a lot of chattering with the chipmunks."

"However, lately I have this feeling that I am constantly being watched and all of my grunts and roars are being recorded, and, I swear, one evening I saw what looked like a drone on steroids hovering overhead. I mean, does the government think I'm some kind of terrorist, Osama ben Yeti or something?"

I decided to conclude our talk by solving a mystery which has perplexed Bigfoot experts. That is, what about female creatures and reproduction so as to produce Little Feet. So I just came right out and asked if he has had any relationships with a female Bigfoot. He pondered deeply how to respond for a moment then replied with a sly grin, "Does my scat stink? Hee, hee."

Save the bipolar bears

Boy, this has been one hot summer, don't you think? I know it's hot when I see the hummingbirds hovering around the backyard feeder wearing tiny sweatbands on their heads. Some people believe the increased heat is a result of global warming.

To warn us to take action to combat the threat of global warming there is an ad showing a polar bear sitting on an ice flow staring longingly at the mainland which is just a bigger chunk of ice. The bear appears to be thinking, "How the heck did this happen when all I did was get up in the middle of the night to take a whiz and the next thing I know I'm starring in a remake of Cast Away except I don't have a volleyball named Wilson to play with?"

I don't know about you, but when I see that picture I just have an uncontrollable urge to reach out and save that pathetic polar bear, but I'm afraid if I do he will rip off my face, and I would end up needing one of those fancy masks like the Phantom of the Opera, which ladies swoon over, only I can't afford that so I'd have to get a discount artificial nose which is attached with Velcro, and then, when I'm eating at a fancy restaurant, since I have allergies and am allergic to everything including just plain air, I would sneeze, dislodging the prosthetic schnoz which would fly off and land in my minestrone soup embarrassing my wife so badly that she would toss her napkin over my head resulting in the other diners mistaking me for an Arab, causing someone to shout "Terrorist!" and due to the fact that half of the guys in the place are packing heat . . . well, you can just imagine the tragic outcome of that scene.

So to avoid all of that trouble, I'll just change to fluorescent light bulbs instead.

As concerned as I am about the polar bear that is sitting on the floating chunk of ice, I am more worried about the bear that we

18

do not see, the one clinging to the bottom of the ice flow. Yes, I'm speaking of the endangered bipolar bear.

In a state of confusion, the bipolar bears, driven by a diminishing food supply, have already started to migrate south. The black and brown bears of the Lower 48 say that the white bears are welcome to share their berries and rotting carcasses, but they will be required to present a photo ID to vote.

Penguins are attending flight school in record numbers so they can eventually leave Antarctica. One penguin chick commented, "This would be much easier if we didn't have wings resembling fuzzy artichoke leaves. But we can't survive here by just being so darn cute anymore."

Migratory birds continue to move south for the winter, just not as far as previously. That is why we are seeing whooping cranes working in the oilfields up in North Dakota.

If skeptics need more proof that we are experiencing global warming, there was an amazing photo posted this summer on YouTube which clearly shows Sasquatch with a Mohawk haircut the entire length of his body to help stay cool.

Am I worried about the effects of global warming on me personally? You bet I am. Did you see the horrible effect of ultraviolet rays on Mitt Romney's face a day prior to his appearance before a Latino audience on Univision? His tan actually began to melt under the hot studio lights creating sort of an Alice Cooper with a crew cut look.

As a result of that experience, Romney vowed that, when he is president, he will fight global warming with a two-pronged attack. First, he will lower taxes on everyone who has a summer home in Nantucket Island; second, he will provide an air conditioner to everyone except for the 47% of the population who live in card board boxes because the units would just fall out of the plastic wrap windows and possibly crush one of the rats that these people depend on for food.

The drought has been so bad that I recently saw a jar of rain water listed on eBay. Last I checked the bidding war was fierce.

And if you're even thinking about bidding for that snowball, forget it.

As the drought lingers on, it will affect our food choices. Sand will become a common ingredient in many of our favorite dishes resulting in the term 'sandwich' taking on a whole new meaning.

Finally, we are not alone. The effects of the heat and drought are being felt around the world. For example, the entire country of Iceland will soon be turned into the world's largest water park.

Shoot and release—it's the sporting thing to do

I used to go fishing, but my conscience finally got to me. I became so soft hearted that I spent a lot of time trying to explain to a worm why I had to impale him with a barbed hook. "Look, your life in the mud and slime isn't exactly a bed of roses, is it? And every time you poke your head out of the ground some ruthless robin is just waiting to peck you to death. So I'm, like, doing you a favor."

Tried fly fishing but felt sort of devious. At least with a worm the fish gets the real thing and not a hunk of horsehair disguised as a mayfly.

I also became somewhat disenchanted with the elitist caste system that fish have been placed into. I mean how would you like to be a member of a fish species with "no limit"? Do you realize what a blow to one's ego that must be? Say you're having a conversation with your son and he tells you that his fish buddies are "catch and release" fish or endangered species fish or trophy fish, and he asks you, "Dad, what type of fish are we?" Alas, you must respond, "Son, we are fish with "no limit." How demeaning that must be! I'm sure that fish with no limit have all sorts of psychological problems caused by low self-esteem. They probably struggle in their schools and due to depression sometimes become so obese that they actually drown!

Recently I was talking to a friend who described an incident in which he saw a fisherman "fighting" a fish to get it to shore. After a brief bout duking it out with a trout, the guy's partner netted the fish. So it takes two grown men to secure a 12-ounce trout which was probably raised on a "farm," an achievement comparable to "Rowdy" Ronda Rousey pummeling a chicken in a UFC cage match.

Now "fight" is an interesting verb in this context, don't you think?

"Hey Fred, how did you get that black eye?"

"Oh, down at the lake this morning I was fighting a rainbow trout."

After snapping a photo with a cell phone for display on YouTube and wrestling the hook from its lip, they tossed the obviously distressed fish back to its home apparently believing that it would swim merrily on its way, sort of a scaled-down version of Free Willy. While conversing with my friend, they said that they didn't like to eat fish so they "catch and release" them.

Since many people agree that the "catch and release" concept is a great idea, why don't we expand the philosophy a bit? I say what's good enough for a scrawny trout is good enough for the mighty deer, elk, lion, even a bear. What I propose is a program similar to the "catch and release" fishing movement called "shoot and release" so that hunters can join their fishing brethren in the spirit of sportsmanship. After hunters shoot their prey, hold up its limp, dangling head for a picture to immortalize the feat, they mercifully release the animal.

Can you imagine the exuberant joy of that moment as the recently shot deer springs to its hoofs and prances back to its forest home flashing a touching glimpse of "thanks" back at the hunter? Granted, the tinge of pain from the hole in its flank the size of a softball will take a few moments to shake off but will soon be superseded by an eternal bond with its new found blaze orange-clad friend.

Or after a duck is blasted from the sky, thuds to earth, and is gently released from the fanged embrace of a retriever, the hunter tosses the bird skyward and with tears streaming down his face shouts, "Fly away my one-winged feathered friend!" then revels in the Pintail's circular hovering three feet above the blind.

But wait, you're probably asking, "What about our veggie and fruit friends?" Not to worry. We could add "pick and release" to the movement. Experience the satisfaction as you pat your lettuce on the head and fling it like a bowling bowl back into the garden. Or imagine that magical moment when you place a freshly picked red orb on the ground and whisper, "Roll, little tomato, roll back to your vine."

Why not "milk and release" dairy cows or "pluck and release" chickens? Of course you may notice a slightly deflated feeling as you stare at the empty plate that evening at dinner. In fact, the only real drawback to all of this that I can see is that the entire human race will probably die of starvation in, oh, say about a week—but a small price to pay in the name of good sportsmanship.

He's 'bawk'! Prodigal chicken returns home

Early this past week, I was enjoying a delicious chicken dinner that my wife had prepared, and as I bit into a drumstick it gave me pause for thought: How can I casually sit here and eat this while a local chicken that many of us know and love is out there somewhere and possibly living under difficult, even dangerous conditions?

Briskly wiping away a tear, I finished the leg and speared another with my fork. Still I wondered how it was possible that a 7-foot-tall chicken could simply vanish into thin air without a clue?

Of course other communities have their crises to deal with such as contaminated water, toxic spills, floods, etc. But this. . . this topped them all.

Well, we can all breathe a sigh of relief as Foghorn has safely returned after nearly a week on the lam. Yet, questions still remain about his disappearance.

First of all, there is something very suspicious about this whole affair. It's not reasonable that an obviously healthy chicken which lives in a lovely spot with easy access to food and a nice little pond to splash around in would just wander off without leaving a note or at least a forwarding address.

One possible explanation is that Russian agents kidnapped Foghorn. Despite the fact that there were no offers of a prisoner swap during his absence, this is still a strong possibility.

Any foreign government that condones hacking into computer systems to reveal to the world that our political parties are up to all sorts of sneaky, underhanded, back-stabbing behavior which I always thought was simply the definition of 'politics' is certainly capable of stooping so low as to sneak up on Pocatello's own 'Big Bird' and toss an extra-large plastic garbage bag over the sleeping chicken's head. That is assuming that chickens ever sleep.

And if the Russians were involved, then one can naturally assume that presidential hopeful Donald Trump had a hand in this dastardly deed also. After all, it is a well known fact that Trump likes things that are HUGE, and a 7-foot tall chicken certainly qualifies. Plus, he could get some hair styling tips.

Another feasible explanation for the extremely tall chicken's disappearance is that it was drafted by the NBA and whisked away to Las Vegas where Foghorn could help an NBA Summer League team win the championship.

In addition to his 7-foot height, as a chicken he should have a pretty impressive vertical leap. Plus, he would be the only player in the league whose impressive wingspan actually consists of wings.

Besides, even if he failed to cut it as a basketball player, he would no doubt be a shoo-in as some NBA team's mascot. For example, with just a little cosmetic surgery, like getting implants for beak augmentation, he could represent the New Orleans Pelicans.

After going through some intense soul-searching, it pains me to consider the possibility that the iconic chicken would simply up and leave us on its own accord. Why? Was it something that we did or said? Did mischievous kids leave Popeyes trash where the chicken could see it? Perhaps they teased the chicken with hurtful jokes like "Which day of the week do chickens hate most? Fry-day!"

It is quite unsettling to imagine our chicken feeling rejected, all alone, hanging out on a busy street corner in some strange city. To think of Foghorn, who never had to face the cold, cruel world alone since the day he and his fellow peeps hatched, suddenly a

23

homeless chicken with a disheveled uncombed comb, strutting wearily holding a sign: "Will work for chicken feed."

Heaven knows that our area has had its share of negative animal news what with abused dogs, starving horses, and abandoned kittens. Maybe Foghorn simply decided that this is not a chicken friendly community but more of a 'finger lickin' good' community.

No, we are better than that. It is far more likely that Foghorn simply wanted to sow some wild oats before settling into a life of pecking seeds.

Accustomed to living outdoors, it is easy to believe that Foghorn headed to a cattle ranch in Wyoming and signed on to become a free-range chicken. There he could wear a cowboy hat, smoke Marlboros, and sit near the campfire—but not too close— singing, "Oh give me a home, where the brood hens roam. . . ."

My biggest fear was that he would get in with the wrong flock. I imagined that, with Foghorn's size, he was being groomed to become the Incredible Hulk of cock fighting somewhere in South Carolina.

Or that he hooked up with the Angry Birds to form a mixed martial arts team. I have to admit that a KFC vs. UFC cage-free match would be a huge draw. With 20 billion chickens in the world, think of the potential pay-per-view revenue!

So far Foghorn is not talking about where he was last week. Regardless, we're all glad that he decided that life away from home for a chicken or its eggs is not all that it's cracked up to be.

So much for 'dominion' over goats

Folks down in Utah are stocking up on survival supplies as they fear that doomsday is coming sometime this month. They're not sure about the exact date, but many of them are fervently praying that it's after the Utah vs. Oregon football game. The "preppers" are responding to various apocalyptic signs such as a "blood moon," stock market jitters, Chicago Cubs are winning, etc. For me personally, doomsday would be the day I had to move to Utah.

But I have to admit that there could possibly be something to this "days of tribulation" thing based on the recent report of mountain goats in northern Idaho attacking hikers. Then locally there is the moose that ran down mountain bikers like some sort of Lance Armstrong with antlers. What on earth is going on here? Haven't these lowly creatures been informed that man is supposed to have dominion over all living creatures?

As stated in the Book of Genesis 1:28 "God said unto them (us), Be fruitful and multiply." Well we certainly have been fruitful what with the world population growing from just two people to 7.3 billion which makes one think that Adam and Eve's last name must have been Duggar. The Old Testament also states that we humans are suppose to have dominion over everything that "moveth," or "creepeth" if you prefer.

Last I checked, goats moveth around quite a bit, so why are they acting so crazy? Well, apparently some hikers can't tell Big Billy Goat Gruff from Mary's little lamb and have been allowing goats to eat from their hands, forgetting that a goat will eat anything and makes no distinction between a cookie and an index finger. Consequently, some people have been bitten. Worse, the goats are threatening to head-butt the hikers, an act that NFL players seem to actually enjoy but the rest of us normally avoid

All I can say is that it's a good thing there were no homo sapiens knuckle-walking around during the dinosaur period. I just don't see Tyrannosaurus Rex even paying lip service to a cave man evangelist grunting, "I've got dominion over all creatures so hop onto this grill." Sure, some hairy dude armed with a club could command a steady diet of tiny lizards and an occasional pterodactyl that accidentally flew over an erupting volcano and became instant chicken nuggets. But about the time Fred Flintstone started quoting the Good Book to a dinosaur, ol' T-Rex would have had no trouble satisfying his troglodyte appetite.

Modern day hunters quite often will quote Genesis to justify their activity although I'm not sure that one's "dominion" over his subjects necessarily includes eating them. On the other hand, I would not be totally shocked to hear that Kim Jong-un has one of his uncles stuffed and on display in his den.

To continue with an analysis of some questionable Old Testament references concerning animals, what was Noah thinking when he allowed certain animals aboard the Ark, like those huge alligators in Africa that occasionally latch onto some poor guy out sun-bathing on the shores of the Congo River? Or, closer to home, how about grizzly bears? Or even Siamese cats?

With just a bit of forethought and planning Noah could have spared mankind a whole lot of trouble. I have to believe that along with God warning Noah about the Great Flood, He most certainly could have added a footnote: "Oh, and just let the grizzlies drown." Or, if not God, where was Noah's wife in all this? I find it hard to believe that she did not take one look at a great white shark and say, "Uh-uh, honey, not in my house!"

Now a word like creepeth obviously implies that man has dominion over bugs. Ha, that's a good one! Even after Donald Trump becomes president and nukes every country that refuses to build a "huge" tower with his name on it, scientists say that cockroaches will survive the holocaust and continue to thrive on a diet of neutrons and gamma rays while we humans become radioactive "dust in the wind."

In fact, man has never even come close to achieving dominion over insects. Been on a picnic lately? Some days you can have a fly swatter in each hand and one between your toes and the flies are still winning. And is there anything more annoying than a mosquito buzzing around your ear? Why, they drove Meriwether Lewis so crazy that he spelled "mosquito" fifteen different ways in his journal!

It seems pretty clear that this report of goats biting and butting hikers forces one to pause and reconsider man's dominion over animals which really does not come as shocking news to me. Heck, I can't even get my dog to sit without bribing her with a treat.

Tofu – it's what's for dinner

At a recent meeting held locally some city slicker dude from the Sun Valley area spoke on the topic of cattle grazing on public land. The gentleman stated that the cattle herds grazing on public land should be greatly reduced in numbers or completely eliminated for two reasons: cattle are destroying the natural habitat where people love to recreate and cattle are a major contributor to global warming.

Some in attendance spoke out against his proposal, and I agree with the ranchers who say that they've always lived on ranches and raised cattle and that no one has the right to deprive them of their livelihood. In fact I talked to a feller one time who said that his family has operated their ranch so long that if you look real close the next time you watch The Ten Commandments starring Charlton Heston as Moses (Or was it Moses starring as Heston? I forget.) and the Israelites are dancing around the golden calf, like a politician dancing a jig around his super PACs, you'll see the his ranch's brand on that calf's rump! Not to be outdone, this feller's buddy swore that his ancestors established their family ranch so far back that the Marlboro Man at that time was just the Marlboro Baby.

First of all let's look at the speaker's wacky theory that cattle should be banned from public land because they are destroying it. Have you ever heard such a ridiculous proposal? If we are not going to allow the cattle to trample, tinkle, and defecate on public land, where will they do it? On private land, of course!

In other words, cattle will be dumping on our chemically manicured lawns, our pampered football fields, and even on the school playgrounds! I for one will simply not stand for it! Why just the mere thought of herds of bovine bullies waddling through hordes of running, shouting, and standardized test-failing school children will inflame parents and make one want to contact MAD (Mothers Against Dumping).

In just my home state of Nebraska alone, the cattle out number the people by 4 to 1, about 6.5 million cattle to 1.5 million people. And then, of course, there are those people who have eaten so much beef that it's difficult to distinguish which group they belong to – we'll just refer to them as Cornhusker offensive linemen.

With such a number advantage, it's quite obvious that if cattle are herded from the purple mountain majesty to graze on city greenways and golf course fairways, it wouldn't be long before cattle were stampeding to the voting booths and passing amendments banning marriage between two heifers, making it a sin to use the expression "Holy cow!" in public, and changing the Nebraska state motto to "Tofu – it's what's for dinner." Next thing you know, the schools would be required to offer Moo as a second language.

Furthermore, if we ban cattle from the outdoor paradise that they currently enjoy, trashing pristine lakes, streams, and ponds, and force them into cities, an unsuspecting suburban family could have its fun-filled day at the metro swimming pool disrupted by belly-flopping behemoths and sun-tanning sirloins which would turn the sundeck into a giant shish kabob. Imagine the horror of snorkeling up to a floating cow pie the size of an oil slick!

But here is an even worse drawback to banning cattle from public grazing access. Driving the herds from nature's all-you-can-eat buffet will eventually lead to anorexic quadrupeds sashaying down fashion runways, winning a string of titles on "The Biggest Loser," or bellying up to the local Food Bank begging for their daily supply of cud. Next thing you know starving herds will be sneaking across the border to our southern neighbor which will result in their grazing in the jalapeno fields – and you think that cattle are a major source of methane gas now!

Which leads us to the speaker's second reason for banning cattle grazing—the methane gas emission problem. This claim leads to several serious questions. First, is this gas leaded or unleaded? Second, has anyone discreetly told the cattle that they have this problem? And, finally, why are the tree huggers picking on just the cattle as a source of methane gas?

If we are going to eliminate cattle from rumbling across the plains and dropping their load wherever they darn well please without even so much as an "Excuse me," how about other animals who haven't mastered modern plumbing technology? That's right, I'm referring to Fido, Fifi, and our little feline friends.

I mean, really, why is it so hard to teach a dog to clean up after itself? At those high falootin' dog shows like the Westminster Kennel Club Show one sees dogs perform extremely elaborate tricks. They do flips, walk up ladders, and even carry their food dish up to their master and growl, "Please, sir, I want some more."

If those dogs can do such complex gymnastics, surely they are capable of learning to hold a pooper scooper in their teeth, scoop up the droppings, and place them in a garbage can. It's as if dogs learn to catch Frisbees and do somersaults because those tricks are FUN! But operating the scooper is work, plus quite unpleasant, so when we attempt to teach them how to use one, they cleverly pretend to be brainless, slobbering beasts.

And what about cats? Sure, wouldn't we all love to have a little box in the corner of the bedroom that we could use in the middle of the night to avoid walking all of the way to the bathroom and not need to flush and wake up everyone else in the house? But if I did have access to such a convenient device, I would surely have enough common sense to know that I need to cover up my deposit with more than two or three litter granules.

If you ever watch a cat try to cover it up, some of them act like they are actually paying for the litter, so they daintily place a granule or two on their kitty doodoo, sort of like a kitty Scrooge.

Whereas others show a total disregard for the family budget and also a total lack of paw-eye coordination and carelessly shower half of the kitchen floor with litter without getting any on the poopoo, and then strut out of the box like some sort of King of the Jungle.

Where the deer and the antelope prey

I have been contemplating writing about a recent local news story for some time. But, quite honestly, I found the story's content so unnerving and downright alarming that for some time I simply could not find the words to properly express my concern. Now I feel that I have finally gained control of my anxiety and can calmly deal with this looming crisis.

I must caution that you continue reading at your own risk and that I am not personally responsible for any psychological damage you may suffer. Also, please do not share the ghastly details with any children.

The newspaper story that I am referring to reported that folks living in the foothills above Pocatello are being harassed and physically intimidated by—I can barely control my trembling fingers—deer!

Evidently, the deer are making the residents' lives "a living hell." Those are the words of a source who wishes to remain anonymous due to a concern for the safety of himself and his family since deer have been known to seek violent retribution towards those who complain to the authorities.

According to the complaints, deer in droves have been banging into fences, eating flowers, tomatoes, and squash, and defecating on lawns. Most concerning of all is that an Idaho Fish and Game representative stated that "we've also had complaints about aggressive deer."

I have never felt a need to own a gun for protection—until now. I get queasy at the mere thought of hiking peacefully on a local trail when I suddenly sense that I am being watched. Glancing up at an aspen grove, I notice an ungulate gang of doe-eyed demons, ears alert, noses twitching at the scent of fear—my fear!

I . . . I need to pause here for a moment to regain my composure. But I feel obligated to continue, to warn those so naïve as to think that deer are just these cute Disney characters forming friendships with bunny rabbits.

All of this terror in the hills makes me wonder about the signs posted on the eastern edge of town, signs stating "Watch for deer" and "Caution Deer." Are these to protect the deer or are they a warning for unsuspecting humans to turn back before it's too late? I just don't know.

What makes all this even more terrifying is that it is not just deer that are under the radar as far as threats to civilization are concerned. There are other fierce creatures to deal with in a world of nature gone mad.

Remember a couple of years ago when certain neighborhoods were being harassed by wild turkeys? These lawless thugs were messing up yards, blocking traffic, and attacking residents.

Since then they apparently have moved their gang activity to the city outskirts as I encountered a large gathering on a recent drive. I was not personally attacked by the turkeys, but there were several tense moments as I discerned all of their wattles were aimed in my direction.

While we experience a suspension of hostilities with local turkeys, other parts of the country are not so fortunate. A Lebanon, Oregon, police detective recently stated that the turkeys there roam in small groups and have blocked traffic. However, "Unlike 2010, these birds don't have a reputation for being hoodlums or hooligans," he said. Not yet, that is.

The Boston Globe reported in September that "flocks of aggressive wild turkeys are attacking people in Foxborough. There have been so many problems that a local animal control officer said that she has lost count of "the number of bad birds."

She went on to say two turkeys even went postal on a mail carrier. She advises the public not to act frightened and instead to "appear bold and intimidate the turkeys" by yelling and chasing them with brooms.

And what about squirrels? That's right. Laugh if you want to, but listen to these true horror stories.

The New York Times ran an article titled "Squirrel goes nuts in California." It reports that eight people near San Francisco have been attacked by a "fearless squirrel" jumping out of a tree.

People there are in a panic. An Humane Society spokeswoman said, "The fact is we want people to stay calm. It's probably just one squirrel."

Next, an 87-year-old man was attacked by a squirrel in the garage. His 83-year-old wife came running with a broom and started swinging. "I guess I hit the squirrel with it," she later stated. Based on photos, her husband was pretty banged up, either by squirrel bites and scratches or by a broom handle over the head,.

In the same area, a squirrel entered an elementary classroom, ran up the teacher's leg and bit her. She grabbed it and threw it off. The squirrel then scurried across the hall to another classroom and bit a child.

I would say that "one squirrel" is really getting around.

So far, the tentative truce with the squirrels inhabiting my backyard has held up. But who knows what they will do once the sunflower seeds run out.

Who let the cats in?

Occasionally I'll come across a lost dog ad and I am totally perplexed. How is it possible that a dog can get lost? I have personally taken my dog for numerous car rides far out into the countryside, and, after stopping and getting out of the car, attached his favorite chew toy to a gas-powered model airplane and sent him scampering after it as it soars for miles at a low level until it runs out of gas. Meanwhile, I jump into the car and drive fast and furious back home thinking that I am finally rid of him, only to be greeted on my doorstep by a panting, grinning Rover anxious to go again.

Haven't these lost dogs seen "Lassie Come Home?" Or how about "The Incredible Journey?" It is simply against a dog's nature to get lost. What if seeing-eye dogs were to get lost? Now you've got two individuals to search for. Speaking of search, aren't some canines trained as search and rescue dogs? So if the dog searching for a lost person gets lost, what next? Send a search and rescue pussy cat?

Now a lost cat ad, that I can understand. A cat steps a few feet from the litter box and begins to panic. A cat can walk around the street corner and suddenly think it has been transported to the middle of Mirkwood Forest. But, come to think about it, most people don't even bother to report a lost cat. Since, at any moment, another person's lost cat will most likely show up meowing mournfully on their front step, so it all evens out and the owners and their new cats simply start all over.

Finally, how many dogs or cats do you know who read the newspaper? So what are the chances Kitty is going to see her picture and say, "That's me! Why, I didn't know I was lost. I better call home right now."

Related to the who-gets-lost-the-most question is the age-old argument as to whether dogs or cats are more intelligent. I say cats are dumber because they will only go to bathroom in a small, designated box, whereas dogs will go anywhere in the house – no wait, maybe that makes dogs dumber.

All right, so maybe it boils down to the fact that most people feel that dogs are easier to train than cats. I'm not so sure. A current popular television show is "The Dog Whisperer." A while back I tried to put into practice some tips from the Dog Whisperer in training my dog. Yet it seemed that each time I would whisper something to my old, nearly deaf dog, he would bark "Wolf? Wolf?" (What? What?). Or, when he did hear me, no matter if I whispered "Sit", "Beg", or "Lie down", he apparently thought I whispered "Roll over for a Belly Rub, Bubba." Over time I found myself evolving into the Dog Screamer and, eventually, bottomed out as the Dog Curser, which resulted in some embarrassing moments at the public park.

Quite often while at the park, I would see proud dog owners tossing a ball for their dog to retrieve. The well trained pooch would hustle to the ball like a laser beam, streak back to the man, and politely ask, "Would you like me to place the ball here or there? Perhaps you would like me to toss it this time and save you the trouble."

So I tried it with my dog a few times. Usually what resulted was I would toss the ball, the dog would spin around like a maniac, barking madly, finally figure out that the ball was gone, take off running in the wrong direction, be blinded by a blasting lawn sprinkler, try mating with a tree stump mistaking it for a black lab, stop to investigate several piles, water a few trees, accidentally trip over the ball then proudly scoop it up, acting as though he knew it was there the whole time. Then I would chase after the dog for around five miles.

By the time I cornered him, tugged at the slobbery ball while suffering various puncture wounds and scratches, and eventually retrieved it by pointing at a stump with my free hand while shouting, "There's a poodle!" the once nice new ball resembled the center of a Tootsie Roll Pop.

I personally know some people who own dogs listed as AKC (American Kennel Club). I, on the other hand, have a dog listed as ADD (A Dumb Dog). But I guess I love him anyway. Otherwise we couldn't sit and have the deep conversations that we have despite the distraction of his licking himself here and there. Places where if I even tried scratching myself there, I would end up in traction.

Which restroom can my service chicken use?

Wild creatures are making the national news again. Stories about alligators, gorillas, and Trump's hair seem to pop up daily.

In northern Idaho, Cindy Tefft's chicken Grace was ticketed for trespassing when she crossed over the fence into a neighbor's yard. Why did the chicken cross the fence? Well, we don't know because, apparently, Grace's attorney has instructed the chicken not to cluck to the press while the case is pending in the Kootenai County court.

While Grace is out on bail, Cindy had her registered as a service animal. Now the chicken will be able to legally appear in court to represent itself and peck away at the evidence.

Another recent story involving service animals was about a passenger on a Delta flight who brought along a turkey as his "emotional support animal." The turkey even got its own seat. Airlines will allow you to bring any animal aboard a plane for no charge if you have proper documentation for a service or support animal.

But, hey, a turkey as an emotional support animal? I'm not gobbling up that malarkey. With people even bringing along horses

34

and pigs on flights for comfort, the growing problem is plain and simple: some passengers are abusing the comfort animal rules.

This whole service and comfort animal thing seems to be getting out of hand. After all, since you can buy a license for $29.95 on the Internet certifying that you're a brain surgeon, one can assume it's pretty easy to get a phony service animal certificate. Just make sure to white-out the Chinese words.

Now I'm sure that we all agree that some animals can be very comforting. When you're stressed out, there's nothing better than giving a big fluffy animal a hug. Which explains why you never see a porcupine as a comfort animal.

My own black Lab is an occasional source of comfort and service. Recently, she and my wife were surrounded and harassed by a pack of coyotes while out hiking. As the dog headed off over a hill, she barked, "I'm heading home now. Will send help. Good luck!"

Just to be fair and show my dog that it's not a one-way deal, she has a comfort human whenever there is thunder or fireworks.

In some foreign countries, this whole concept is viewed a bit differently. For example, in Vietnam dogs are referred to as "comfort food."

Far as cat owners are concerned, I do not recall ever seeing a service cat. I mean, think about how many times you have cleaned the litter box vs. how many times the cat has cleaned your toilet.

On the other hand, cats can provide their owners comfort. Nothing like petting a purring cat on your lap while handfuls of cat hair drift up into your nose.

If cat owners want to return the favor, they can now provide their cat comfort by using the new LICKI silicone brush shaped like a giant tongue which attaches to your real tongue so you can lick the cat—with little chance of getting a hairball stuck in your throat!

It's easy to see how all of this questionable use of service animals is going to lead to future complications. For example, when it comes to the use of public restrooms which, apparently, is a full-time occupation for a significant portion of the general population because a lot of folks sure are fired up about it.

Personally, the only reason that I can think of for even risking a trip to a public restroom is to contemplate philosophical graffiti discussions on the wall above the urinal like "Question everything." "Why?"

As a man of sound principles, I for one simply refuse to use a public restroom with a comfort chicken present. First of all, how can I tell if it is a rooster or a hen? I'm a city guy and, besides, I understand it's sort of hard to tell with chickens.

Sure, you can say, "But Mike, roosters have long flowing tails and brighter, bolder colorful feathers." Throw in a wattle and a red comb and, yeah, the chicken in the next stall could very well be a rooster, but how can one be sure nowadays?

There are lots of other disturbing questions. If I'm a man, can I take my comfort hen into the men's restroom without causing embarrassment for the other guys? If I'm a female, can I take my comfort cock along to powder my nose and the chicken's beak without causing a ruckus amongst the other ladies?

As a simple solution, I suggest that if you're a rooster in the hens' restroom, just don't start strutting around like a male mating sage grouse and crowing about it, and no one will probably even notice.

On the other hand, if I'm sitting on the pot in the men's room and hear nothing but a lot of senseless cell phone clucking in the next stall—I'm going to get darn suspicious.

Will purr for food

Dogs and cats are making the local headlines once again. Every week it seems that one or the other is stolen, gets lost, or miraculously shows up after disappearing for years, sort of like a politician around election time.

Heaven knows that I've had my share of pets that have vanished. When some have reappeared, I have to admit that I locked the front door, turned out the lights, and kept quiet until they took off again. But others I've spent hours searching for, and it certainly is a nerve-wracking experience worrying about their whereabouts. Is my pussycat stuck in a tree somewhere, besieged by rabid squirrels and deranged crows? Did Rover run off to join ISIS?

The most intriguing recent story involved a cat who wandered off, was taken in by another family, and five years later returns and is reclaimed by its original owner. Now each family has its own name for the cat and, naturally, both want to keep it.

All of which will predictably result in a joint-custody battle between the two families. The end result could be that the cat will spend alternating weeks with the two families. And you know how the cat will take advantage of that situation.

During his time with one family he will complain about his treatment at the other home, using his position to cajole both masters to shower him with treats so that they can become his "favorites." Utilizing this tactic, soon his huge cat-toy collection will become the envy of the litter. Due to overindulgence he will eventually become a catnip junkie and end up out on the street again, begging for milk and seeking shelter in a discarded shoebox. It's a sad tale, told and retold countless times.

Certainly, none of this comes as a surprise to us who have experienced even a casual cat companionship. Only a cat would show up at a strange family's door and attempt an almost immediate coup.

If you let a lost dog into your home, his friendly face cries out "Just tell me what you want me to do for some food scraps. Sit? You want me to sit? Got anything easier I can do? How about giving me a belly rub and we'll talk this over?"

Whereas a cat, within minutes of strolling into a new home, appears to be saying "Look, you can feed me if you want, but chances are I won't eat that slop that you call gourmet cat food. And if you even think of touching my belly I'll remove all the flesh from your hand quicker than you can say 'Nice Kitty.'"

In contrast to cats, dogs make sacrifices for others. They rescue people who are in danger such as drowning or lost in the woods. Remember Lassie? Or Old Yeller? You never saw Fluffy the pussycat saving Timmy from a trained circus bear trying to act ferocious, did you? No, of course not. A cat would more likely think "Bye, Timmy, it's been nice knowing you" before scampering up the nearest tree to wait until the coast is clear.

You never see pictures on the Internet of a cat grieving for its owner after he or she has passed away. In contrast to a dog that will lie on the grave, sadly resting its head on its front paws, refusing to budge for days, a deceased owner's cat is more likely to treat the freshly-dug grave as a large litter box.

Some animal experts say that it is unhealthy to leave a cat alone at home for an extended time. Cats will become bored when alone so owners should scatter toys for them to bat around, set up various scratching poles, and erect towers to climb. But I say, if a cat is alone how do we know that it is doing any of these things? My guess is that, after wondering why the humans left all this junk lying around, a cat is more likely to find a warm spot and sleep the entire time.

Cats do not seem to develop much emotional attachment to their owners. It's easy to imagine that a cat reuniting with its owner after five years away would be pretty cool about the whole thing and act like nothing happened. But a dog in a similar situation would spin in circles, jump up on you, lick your face, and get so excited that it would pee on its favorite table leg—now that's real love.

So it's only natural that when a cat gets lost it would take for granted that the inhabitants of the next house it comes upon will find it simply adorable after a small dose of purring and leg rubbing. Why not just hang out there for five years before deciding to head home?

After all, a cat has nine lives, might as well live each one at a different home.

Chapter 2   Exercise, Health, Sports

And the gold medal goes to . . . .

In a nod to the 2014 Winter Olympics, it is time to hand out medals to the 2014 Idaho state legislature for its efforts in providing leadership for the people of Idaho so far this session. Believe me, it is not easy wading through the mind-boggling array of high level, well thought out bills for which our elected officials surely spent countless hours gathering facts, surveying constituents, discussing with experts, weighing both the pros and cons of, etc.

Only problem is if you skim the list of bills and resolutions on the state legislature website, it becomes immediately clear that their wording is anything but clear; instead there are reams of governmental gobbledygook obviously written by some sadistic ex-Internal Revenue Service tax form designer with the sole purpose of giving common ordinary citizens an instant headache so they will never again risk sticking their noses into state law makers' business.

Nevertheless, I did slog my way through the list and discovered that there are so many bills worthy of being recognized on the medal podium that some outstanding candidates will regretfully be omitted. Here are the Honorable Mention laws.

Senate Bill 1332 which shields Idaho law enforcement officers from confiscating Idaho citizens' weapons if so ordered by any federal decree written after January 1, 2014, is a bill certainly worthy of recognition. Only problem is what if those sneaky feds actually wrote the order prior to this date and "accidentally" misplaced it until a later date?

Otherwise, this law is noteworthy since it should put a stop to any fantasized confiscation of Idahoans' personal arsenals. Or at least until a military drone comes knocking and, after you open the door, having fallen for the old SNL "Land Shark" routine, proceeds to completely annihilate you, your house, your pit bull chained in the backyard, etc. After which there is mop up duty involving the National Guard/Air Force/Army/Navy/Marines/ Boy Scouts/ Girl

Scouts/ Gay Scouts, etc. Then see how much good the Second Amendment does you.

One sponsor of this bill is Senator Marv Hagedorn, who, according to his website, also wants mandatory gun safety classes in Idaho schools which should really help the kids prepare for the SAT, Common Core tests, etc. But at least if they fail the tests, they could release their anger by going out and shooting something without injuring themselves.

Next bill worthy of Honorable Mention is HB 399. This bill lowers the age to hunt big game from 12 to 10 years old. Now here's a bill that we can all sink our teeth into like a big slab of raw beef tongue. But here's a relevant question: what big game are they going to hunt? For years we've been hearing that the wolves have decimated the elk population and coyotes are preying on deer, so how logical is it to add ten-year-olds to the hunting roster? Besides, do they even make safety orange hats that small?

Another thing, is this bill fair to all of the five-year-olds who burn with desire to have their picture taken struggling to support the head of a bug-eyed deer carcass with its dangling tongue splayed out on little Johnny's leg to show off during kindergarten recess? No, of course it isn't. And what about three-year-olds? Why, any preschooler worth his weight in Fruit Loops can handle a rifle strapped to the handle of his Big Wheel. Obviously, this is a matter of age discrimination which must be rectified next session.

Now let's get to the medal winners.

Bronze medal goes to HR 38 which commemorates 2014 "as the 60th anniversary of the addition of the phrase 'under God' to the Pledge of Allegiance." Great idea, but why the 60th? Or is it possible that the resolution's sponsor James Holtzclaw, who states on his website that he is in favor of "fraking", whatever that is, as an energy source, simply missed his target by ten years?

Senate Bill 1284, recipient of the silver medal, would allow increasing the speed limit to 80 mph on certain stretches of the interstate. Granted, this means that now many people will drive 85 which will obviously increase the death toll on Idaho's roads, but better to die quickly than be asphyxiated from slowly suffering through the dairy stench emitted around Jerome on a hot August day.

Finally, the big moment is here. Winner of the 2014 state legislature bill of the year gold medal goes to Senator Janie Ward-Engelking who had the courage and time on her hands to introduce SB 1271 which proclaims the giant salamander as Idaho's state amphibian. I just hope that no one introduces the Japanese giant salamander, at 4-foot long, to Idaho. Otherwise the 7-inch Idaho giant salamander will quickly be relegated to giant sushi.

Blimey, it's time for the bloody, blooming Summer Olympics!

Let's face it, unless you get really excited witnessing tennis players fall down and cry every time they win a match or you find it fascinating watching baseball managers try to stay awake in the dugout as their heads slowly descend on the bench into a puddle of their own freshly drooled chewing tobacco juice, televised sports in the summer are a real drag.

Well rejoice, sports fans! With the Summer Olympics set to begin in London later this month, you will have even tougher choices to make. Hmmm, do I watch two-person dinghy men or mixed dressage at 3:00 AM tomorrow?

No doubt the Games were much simpler in the old days. For example, Ancient Greek athletes chose to compete in the nude because . . . uh . . . it was fun. Married women who tried to sneak a peek at the competitors could be executed. Single women could watch and often did because . . . uh . . . it was fun. Apparently, the ancient Greeks were fun-loving people.

Actually, the real reason the Ancient Greeks competed nude in the Olympics was to avoid a team uniform firestorm. For instance, it would have been a serious blow to national pride to have had the Greek team loincloths made in China.

Since the early 19th century, numerous Olympic events have come and gone, like rope climbing which two Greek athletes dominated in 1896. Unfortunately, both athletes were left stranded on the top platform as their rope was repossessed by the bank due to the country's financial troubles which continue to this day.

In fact the Greek athletes have traditionally led the grand entrance parade, but due to the ongoing Greek budget crisis, the team is taking an inflated raft to the Games this year and hopes to make it on time for the grand closing ceremony.

The Olympic Games of the early 20th century more closely resembled The Hunger Games. What with dueling pistols, club swinging, underwater swimming race, not to mention live pigeon shooting, it's no wonder voluntary participants were hard to come by—especially pigeons!

The first suspension for drug abuse was at the 1968 Mexico City Games. The drug in question was a few pints of beer consumed by a Swedish athlete and explains why the entire Irish team has virtually been permanently banned from the Games.

Speaking of Swedes, the first ever twins to win gold medals at the Games were Gustaf V. and Gustav E. Carlberg in the 30-meter dueling pistol event. At the awards ceremony, their medals were placed on top of their coffins.

Of course this year's Olympics are not free of controversy. A few weeks ago, Saudi Arabian officials reported that no female athletes had taken part in their Olympic trials. This was possibly due to the fact that it is against the law for Saudi women to leave the house unaccompanied by at least one male, three goats, and a talking camel. As a compromise to avoid future sanctions for sending no women to London, a Saudi male weight lifter has agreed to wear a Dolly Parton wig and a sports bra, but he refuses to shave his beard.

In addition, the IOC has ruled that USA swimmer Michael Phelps must wear all 16 medals that he has won in previous Olympics while he is competing "to give everyone else a fair chance."

One positive fact is that athletes who stay in the Olympic Village have access to free condoms with around 150,000 available this year. I could not find any reference as to which Olympic event requires this equipment, but there must be a large number of athletes in it since they used up all 70,000 in less than a week during one previous Olympics.

Some final notes: The London Philharmonic recorded the national anthems of 205 nations to be played when medals are presented. Uruguay's anthem is six and a half minutes long so many fans are praying that they do not win any medals.

Over 3,000 ping pong balls will be used this year, not simultaneously, although the Chinese players could probably handle it since they won every medal available in Beijing four years ago.

And, finally, the team representing Mexico will be there if any of the members other than the pole vaulter can make it over the wall.

If you are fortunate enough to attend the Olympic Games in London, keep in mind that it is against the law to be intoxicated while in charge of a cow, to ride a bus while one has the plague, and for a cab in London "to carry rabid dogs or corpses."

So leave the corpses home and have a great time in London!

Buddhist coach's self-immolation ends team's losing streak

Can you believe it? As soon as assistant coach Joe Kennedy at Washington's Bremerton High School gets suspended from coaching the team for praying on the 50-yard line after games, that nasty Satan fixed it so the Bremerton football team racks up a rare win the very next game. Of all the lowdown dastardly devilish deeds!

Just to show that the team will win now that the coach isn't allowed to pray where everyone can see him, old Beelzebub himself was out on the field goosing the opposing team's quarterback as he attempted to pass and tickling his receivers as they reached to make receptions.

Why is it that, out of all the sports, only football coaches and their players make the news for praying at school events? You never hear about coaches of other sports publicly praying. I wonder what Coach Kennedy would do if he were a swim team coach. Would he dive off the high board after meets and shout "Praise the . . . glug!" as he does a belly flop in the deep end?

And then there are all those coaches who privately call on the Lord in a variety of ways during practices and games. Some thank him for their success while others plead "why hast thou forsaken me?" At the other extreme, I've known coaches who would start taking his name in vain before the pep band even finishes playing the national anthem—and some of those coaches won a lot of games and state titles.

Of course, it's not all about praying to win. I know that I sure did a lot of praying during my 20 seasons as a high school girls basketball coach, although I do not recall ever jumping up and hanging on the rim shouting "Alleluia!" when one of my players actually made a free throw. I must confess that years when my teams were really struggling I'd pray for itsy-bitsy miracles like, "Please, Lord, make it snow real hard so the game is canceled," or "Is it too much to ask for a little divine intervention to cause our opponent's team bus to break down?"

One problem with public displays of silent prayer by coaches is that you never can be sure what people are actually saying in their prayers. Oh, they'll tell you it's an expression of thanks for the players, the game, the under-inflated footballs, etc. But how do we fans know that's all they're praying about?

Let's take the Bremerton assistant coach's case for instance. The Bremerton Knights football program has not been very successful, especially over the last three seasons. Plus, the school has never won a state football championship. So . . . maybe Coach Kennedy is offering up a somewhat selfish appeal, like praying that the entire coaching staff doesn't get fired.

It's possible that all this losing was Kennedy's downfall because it seems that when it comes to coaching you can get away with about anything as long as you are winning. If you're winning championships, you can pray, scream, cuss, and throw chairs onto the basketball court. But you can't get away with murder. Well, not unless it's murdering the English language like Southern coaches who say stuff to their players like "Y'all fixin' to get down to bidnis' and do sumpin' so w'all can beat jawjuh?"

I knew a highly successful coach who kept a voodoo doll with pins stuck in it on the volleyball team bench during games. It freaked out the opposing players, but never a complaint from his fans or administration. Another coach had no trouble holding pre-game séances in a dark locker room, until the losses started to mount.

In a way I hope that Coach Kennedy wins his appeal and is allowed to continue praying after games. Such a ruling would open up the door for a wide variety of public displays of religious fervor which could possibly help some other struggling sports programs in several ways.

Take our local college sports programs, nearly all of which could use a boost in attendance and heavenly help in achieving success on the field and the court.

How about hiring a Hindu football coach who practices the spiritual ritual of Garudan Thookam in which he sticks a hook through the skin on his back, attaches it to a rope and swings from an elevated spot? What a great halftime show that would be as he swings from Holt Arena's rafters while the marching band plays "Hang on Sloopy"!

Of course, allowing coaches like Kennedy to pray on the football field could result in a complication if a school hires a Muslim coach. I mean, if we have to stop a football game several times so he can kneel down at midfield and turn toward Mecca to pray, we fans will never get out before the bars close.

Dennis Rodman—ambassador of weirdness

There has traditionally been a connection between politics and sports. One can go clear back to boxing champion Joe Louis proclaiming that the USA would win WW II because "we're on God's side" which doesn't quite sound right. Or during the Vietnam War when Muhammad Ali protested the draft saying "I ain't got no quarrel with those Vietcong . . . ." taking the words right out of my mouth along with millions of others back in 1967.

In the 1970s, the USA table tennis team helped open the diplomatic door with China by visiting and playing the Chinese team, an event labeled by Time magazine as "The ping heard 'round the world." Needless to say the Chinese smoked the Americans, similar to if today's USA basketball team played a team of pygmies from Borneo.

More recently we've been kept up to date on two examples of the politics and sports link: former NBA player Dennis Rodman visiting North Korea and Russia's preparation for the Winter Olympics next month.

During a recent overseas trip, Rodman upset some people when he stated that Kim Jung-Un "is a great dad." Maybe, but not such a great nephew since, according to some reports, he recently had his uncle Jang fed to a pack of starving Chihuahuas and his Aunt Kim just sort of "disappeared."

There's no doubt that Rodman himself had a rough childhood. When he was three, his father deserted the family due to embarrassment from dropping off the only three-year-old at daycare sporting tattoos, orange hair, a pierced nose, and sucking on a spiked pacifier. Later, his mother kicked him out of the house for tearing her pantyhose every time he squeezed into them.

Rodman was a rebounding machine during his colorful NBA career. Colorful based on the fact that he dyed his hair during timeouts. At one point in his career, Sports Illustrated wrote that he was "a sort of basketball genius" which, in the NBA, means that you know which end of the basket the ball goes through first.

Now retired, he has decided to use his basketball star status to improve diplomatic relationships with North Korea. For example, during a game there last week he sang happy birthday to Supreme Leader Jung-Un then, caught up in the joy of the moment, grabbed little Kim and slam dunked him. The soldiers in attendance didn't know whether to applaud or 'let the dogs out'.

Rodman said that he was honored to share his basketball skills with the Korean people and referred to the event as "historical", but a more accurate term would probably be "hysterical."

Despite fondly calling Kim his "best friend", Rodman, as yet, has failed to convince Kim to dye his black hair with a white stripe down the middle, or to join Dennis in wearing bridal gowns to the next public execution of all those citizens accused of not buying Jung-Un personalized basketball jerseys.

The second story involving politics merged with sports dominating the news is the Winter Olympics in Russia this February which, by the way, will be the first Olympics to present special medals to all spectators who simply survive due to imminent terrorist attacks. In fact, the terrorist team is the odds-on favorite to compete with Norway for the most gold medals. However, it may be difficult for an Islamic extremist dressed in a turban, pajamas, and sandals to pass himself off as a member of the Iranian hockey team.

A second Olympics issue concerning organizers is the question as to how many people will actually show up to watch the Winter Games since they are being held in a location more difficult to reach than the Andromeda Galaxy which, if you left for it in a rocket ship today as a newborn baby, you would not arrive there until you were as old as Keith Richards.

Another problem is the Olympics are just too expensive for the host country's sports fans. For example, an Olympic t-shirt is $93, or half a week's salary for the average Russian. That's significant considering that most Russians already spend half of their earnings on vodka for their daily intake of anti-freeze since, according to every TV image that I've ever seen of Russian citizens, they appear to spend all day outdoors in eternal winter weather, exhaling clouds of steam, wearing goofy fur hats, and milling around in mukluks simply trying to keep from freezing to death.

Added to the cost of tickets for various events, attendees must also find money to buy bullet-proof vests, shatter-resistant helmets, bomb-sniffing dogs, etc. due to the terrorist threat mentioned earlier.

President Vladimir Putin has vowed to "annihilate" all terrorists. For some reason, annihilating suicide bombers just doesn't seem like that serious of a threat.

Drivers, plug in your power packs

I was shopping at Wal-Mart recently trying to decide amongst HD, LCD, DLP, etc. When I asked the salesperson if he had a TV, he seemed confused and said that he would check. (And I thought ordering a cup of coffee at Starbucks was complicated). The experience made me think back to when all the kids bought jeans and there was just one kind – the dark blue, stiff ones. In fact, I believe that one pair that my mom bought for me was the original pair that Levi Strauss himself had worn which he would occasionally remove and use a pants leg to break up rocks in his pursuit for gold.

Anyway, at the store I just happened to be watching NASCAR on about 100 screens simultaneously when the question popped into my head "Why is gas so darn expensive? Is it possible that people are needlessly wasting it?" But for the life of me, I could not think of any examples of waste.

In fact, whenever I drive my F-250 4WD turbo quad cab pickup truck across town to pick up a Snickers, I don't notice people wasting gas. I myself am so conservative that, while in the store, I always make a point to only leave my truck running if the temperature is over 70 degrees (for the air conditioner) or below 69 degrees (for the heater). Otherwise, I shut it off – unless, of course, I'm in the middle of Desperate Housewives Season One which is showing on my dual DVD screens. In which case, I'll leave the engine running so I can record it on my dashboard TiVo to avoid missing one scene; otherwise, you know, the viewer would be lost.

As my attention was drawn back to the summer homes on wheels, otherwise known as 'campers,' which average 4 mpg on leaded gas, I still could not think of one obvious example of fuel waste in this country. It's not as if our elected leaders aren't trying to help solve the fuel crunch. President Bush recently commented that he would look into the problem "... just as soon as I fix up this war thingy." Now that should inspire confidence in the hearts of concerned citizens.

Furthermore, the average person is certainly aware of the problem and is not going to do dumb things to waste fuel. On the contrary, one need not look far to see U.S. citizens making sacrifices to reduce the demand. Why just yesterday, as I drove my ATV across the neighbor's lawn to retrieve my dog's fetching stick which I threw a wee bit too far for the old boy to track down, I saw a football-field long RV with a swimming pool on top towing a Hummer H2! You know, the "green" Hummer which gets up to 10mpg going downhill with the wind at its back. Now that's a prime example of what I'm talking about when I point out that people are making sacrifices to conserve fuel.

Some radical conservationists have suggested changes in NASCAR such as switching to unleaded fuel since the race cars are currently exempt from federal guide lines. Oh sure, how manly would that be? Next thing you know the drivers would be drinking light beer or smoking filtered cigarettes.

Another suggestion is that NASCAR switch to electric powered race cars. That would be just great! Thirty-three cars going 200 mph for 500 laps – imagine how tangled up they would get in the cords! And every time a dad blamed car came unplugged out comes the yellow caution flag! Then just when the race is reaching its climax, some guy down the street pops a Hearty Man frozen beans and franks TV dinner into the microwave and suddenly all of the cars slow down to 40 mph! And what if it rains during the race and a cord has a short—next thing you have a massive barbeque of southern fried Earnhardts.

Of course, none of the proposed changes would be as radical as that made by the innovative Ray Harroun in 1911. Ray added a rearview mirror to the race car and was the first driver to race without a passenger to tell the driver about oil pressure, oncoming drivers, etc., sort of like having your mother-in-law along on a trip to Salt Lake City.

No sir, I say leave good old gas-guzzling NASCAR just like it is. If some fan who's so big that the oval track sags in his direction wants to watch the race from a chaise lounge on the roof of his RV while sipping on a keg of Bud and barbequing Hogzilla, then let him. That's the American way. Who knows? Maybe someday there will be NASCAR in Iraq. Then they'll know for sure that democracy has arrived.

Drop the weenie! You're under arrest

One recent evening I returned home after attending a local college basketball game where I enjoyed a delicious two-course dinner, starting with a home-style micro-waved-to-perfection hot dog perfectly centered on a soft light-brown bun and decorated in a dazzling display of yellow and red zigzags.

This was followed by a scrumptious serving of lukewarm and slightly limp corn chips smothered in melted gourmet cheese called Velveeta which I believe is French for "velvet glue " and is normally only found in high-end New York restaurants.

Soon after arriving home, I checked the news on the Internet and a frightening headline smacked me in the face like a slab of raw bacon. It was another public health warning, this one stating that processed foods are not good for us and can cause cancer.

Isn't it bad enough that I already have to worry about trans-fats, high fructose, gluten, lactose, sodium, sugar, and a new species of giant tape-worm that can grow up to 82-feet long in our intestines and is actually considering running for the Republican presidential nomination?

I'm so worried about germs that I wash my hands BEFORE I go to the bathroom. Plus, I suspect that whenever I sneeze into my elbow people think that I'm actually sniffing my arm pit.

Along with all that, now I can't even eat a hot dog with a clear conscience. It's just no wonder that so many people are suffering from depression these days. Did the government ever consider that public health warnings are unhealthy for public health?

Sure, I admit that I've always been a bit suspicious when it comes to hot dogs. Any food that is cooked inside a casing made from small intestines of sheep can't help but raise the question

"What are they hiding in there?" Besides, the very name "wiener" just sort of screams "Unfit for human consumption!"

Health-conscious grocery shoppers do have the option of vegetarian hot dogs which are made from some sort of soy protein. In addition there's something called Tofurky which, maybe it's just me, sounds somewhat obscene, like, "Hey, if you don't like it go tofurky yourself!"

To add to the weenie's image problem, the World Health Organization recently listed it as a carcinogen, placing it in the same category as cigarettes which, of course, could possibly lead to an even greater health risk: lighting up and smoking a weenie.

It's just darn lucky that someone came up with the idea of placing the weenie in a bun. Otherwise its consumption would even be more dangerous because, in its early history, hot dog sellers supplied customers with gloves to avoid burning their hands. But customers kept running off with the gloves so the peddlers were losing money, thus, the bun was born.

Another story is that the hot dog was originally called a "Dachshund sandwich" which, if you used that name today and ordered one cooked "rare" at a restaurant in Vietnam or Korea, it would actually arrive on your plate while still barking!

Seems as if the corn dog would be a healthy alternative to the hot dog since at least its name gives the appearance that you are getting a vegetable along with the processed meat. However, to completely eliminate any risk, it might be helpful if manufacturers added a warning label stating "Eating the stick may be hazardous to your health."

Along with the hot dog, other possible cancer-causing foods are donuts, cookies, chips, and bacon; all of which, if deleted from my grocery shopping list, leaves just dental floss.

Avoiding bacon is becoming increasingly difficult in our country. Along with the regular breakfast staple food, there is bacon vodka, bacon popcorn, and bacon toothpaste. There are even bacon mints which I had to quit using since they sent my dog into a face-licking frenzy, resulting in an even greater health hazard than the bacon itself.

Bacon sales in the U.S. climbed over 9% in 2013 alone. A recent survey indicated that 65% of Americans would support bacon as their "national food" which, I suppose, could lead to a flying pig replacing the bald eagle as America's symbol.

There is a healthier alternative, something called "vegetarian bacon," an oxymoron if I ever heard one. It has no cholesterol, is low in fat, and is made from strips of tofu, and probably tastes pretty good if buried between two quarter-pound hamburger patties topped off with a large slice of raw onion.

Since it is a harmful processed food, I think one way to reduce bacon consumption is to simply change the name. So instead of ordering two eggs with bacon, the restaurant menu would list "two eggs with the cured belly of a swine carcass."

My wife and I are already taking steps to reduce consumption of processed foods. We have vowed that we will only eat bacon on special occasions—like breakfast.

Fantasy ex-coaches league now forming

The unemployment rate bumped up last week as many NFL coaches received a lump of coal and a contract buyout check in their Christmas stockings. But it's no big deal since it seems there is always a worse team clamoring for their services (see "Chiefs").

On the bright side, New Orleans coach Sean Payton, despite the fact that several of his Saints' players' lockers were decorated with shrunken heads dyed in various teams' colors, was apparently unaware that his players were getting paid bonuses for head-hunting opponents on the football field. He was suspended from coaching the Saints for a season, yet recently was welcomed back with a new $8 million a year contract, along with NFL commissioner Roger Goodell's shrunken head, making him the highest paid coach in the galaxy and once again proving that ignorance is bliss.

During the suspension, while Sean's wife found his obsessive drawing of x's and o's on the wallpaper, furniture, children, etc. cute at first, his spiking of the family Xbox console while playing

Madden NFL 2013 was the last straw. She eventually filed for divorce, once again proving that familiarity breeds contempt.

The Saints under Payton have won a Super Bowl, an event which regularly sets records as the most watched television show in history, not because of Montana, Marino, or Manning, but because of Madonna, Minaj, and Malfunctions. Also the clever ads are a big draw, such as one last year that featured Clint Eastwood talking to an empty Chrysler. Will someone please get this guy some professional help?

Thank goodness we have college bowl games to fill in the dead time between NFL announcements concerning fired coaches, suspended players, steroid-induced ED (no, not education), etc. I watched every play of every game over the holidays until my eyeballs were dangling from my head like two Slinkies. Well I have to confess that I did miss one play when my dog "accidentally" stepped on the remote and switched channels to watch his favorite pinup pooch Kim Kardachshund on Animal Planet.

I calculated that in the time I spent watching football I could have instead earned my PhD in nanophysics while simultaneously building a full-scale replica of The Great Wall of China out of Legos. On a positive note my right arm now resembles Popeye's due to pushing the remote buttons; however, the rest of me looks more like Wimpy.

After viewing so many bowl games, here are my recommended changes. The first new rule I would consider is banning all bowl games from locating on the East Coast, in the Midwest, the Great White North, and Idaho.

I once attended the then Humanitarian Bowl, a misnomer since sitting through such weather conditions was anything but humane. One poor fellow froze solid while doing the wave resulting in fans shouting "Sit down!" the entire second half. No doubt, any bowl game at which more hot cocoa is sold than cold beer and the cheerleaders have to wear galoshes should be axed.

Next change required is to shorten the games. What with officials' conferences ("How embarrassing! If I'd known you guys were wearing stripes I would never have . . . ."), reviewing out of bounds plays a hundred times ("You put your left foot in, You take your left foot out"), and recruiting the entire marching band to help lift up a 360-pound player stuck on his back like a giant cockroach, fans get about 5 exciting minutes.

Also, we need to get back to simple bowl game names. It was a heck of a lot easier to know the New Year's Day bowl schedule when I was a kid: Cotton Bowl, Sugar Bowl, Rose Bowl, Orange Bowl—and notice, no more than two syllables per word, much easier for men to read and remember. None of this San Diego County CU Poinsettia Bowl stuff. As if a real man would even know what a poinsettia is, let alone how to spell or pronounce it correctly.

No, I say let's bring back the now defunct Bacardi Bowl, Salad Bowl, Raisin Bowl, and the Oil Bowl. Mix that up with the Famous Potato Bowl and you have one heck of a casserole bowl. But, please, don't bring back the Poulan Weed-Eater Independence Bowl. It doesn't fit on a t-shirt.

Finally, I feel that 3D football broadcasts are just too darn dangerous. For example, during one play I dove out of bounds to avoid a hit and accidentally tossed the entire popcorn bowl into the air, angering everyone except the dog. Another time I told my wife that I could not shovel the walk due to multiple concussions suffered during three bowl games the previous night.

To 3D's credit, however, an official review clearly showed that I had grabbed the last nacho before my wife.

Happy holiday flu season

Now here is a recipe for disaster: We live in the most obese nation in the developed world ("developed" meaning that we floss) and the hottest fashion currently in the U.S. is slim-skinny jeans—for guys, nonetheless! I just hope that I am not standing between two Rick Majerus look-a-likes wearing skinny jeans in the checkout stand who simultaneously decide to inhale. Speaking of Majerus, he was one tough guy. Think you could coach over 500 basketball wins while suffering nearly as many heart attacks? As a nice gesture, at a recent home game Utah University honored Coach Majerus by leaving three chairs empty at courtside.

Other than fashion and sports, other recent headlines deal with the start of flu season. Flu season—sort of like saying it is the football bowl season without the constant play reviews, thank goodness.

There are three types of flu virus: A, for Awful; B, for Better reserve the bathroom for the entire week; and C, for Cancel your cable, phone, and Internet contracts—you won't be needing them.

Ancient Greek physician Hippocrates first noted flu-like symptoms when he described an albatross flying overhead with a thermometer in its beak, thus, the first case of bird flu.

In the 1700s, some doctors thought that the illness was spread through sexual intercourse which, I guess, could explain why guys get the flu more frequently prior to marriage. Or, possibly, they were confusing the Spanish flu with Spanish fly which, by the way, is not the present tense of the illness.

Later, during the 1940s, gargling was promoted as a preventive measure. Try to imagine using that dispenser in the work place versus the modern day hand sanitizer—Yuk!

Today, one can get a flu shot. Some people refuse due to religious beliefs. Their reasoning is that they claim that "On the 8th day, God created nausea, vomiting, and diarrhea." Others feel that the shot is a government conspiracy to track people. That is why you see certain people on the Internet so frequently; they are being tracked. For example, Kim Kardashian, whose CIA secret code name is 32-DD.

Personally, I have come up with a theory that the best flu prevention measure is to have oneself hermetically sealed in a giant plastic baggie sometime in October and not come out until around the 4th of July.

Throughout history, major flu strains have originated in the Far East, such as the Asian flu, the Hong Kong flu, the King Kong flu, etc. There have also been flu outbreaks which originated in animals such as the previously mentioned bird flu which was spread through direct contact with bird droppings which sounds like a sequel to the Alfred Hitchcock classic.

Then there is the swine flu, first detected in 2009, which actually consist of bird, pig, and human genes combined which conjures up a rather bizarre Big Bird, Miss Piggy, and Kevin Clash image, and, is variously referred to as pig flu, hog flu, and, in Arkansas, Hogzilla flu.

A distant cousin of the flu is the common cold which, of course, is "common" only when anyone else gets it besides me. When I get a cold everything else in the world becomes meaningless. Fiscal Cliff? Show me where it is and I will be the first in line to jump off. Egyptians holding their monthly riot? Hand me a Molotov cocktail and I will guzzle it. I just don't care. The only thing that matters is the stuff resembling leftover turkey gravy after having sat in the frig for two weeks that is slowly navigating around inside my head.

I simply have to be the worst patient in the world, a nurse's nightmare. Now my wife is a medical professional and has worked in nearly every possible setting, from metropolitan ICU to rural hospital graveyard shift. She has dealt with people suffering every imaginable injury and ailment. But she has never put up with someone as miserable as me to be around when sick. You've seen those zombies in Night of the Living Dead? That's me. I can make sounds from my mouth, nose, even my ears, that resemble a cartload of chimpanzees on meth.

When I have a cold, I normally stay in bed with a large array of cold medicine guaranteed not to work spread out on a nearby table. Although some cough medicine actually does work because by the time you finally manage to remove the foil cover from the bottle, you will most likely be cured.

While in bed, I spend my time writing my obituary, making sure that it includes a reference to my bucket list which I misplaced years ago and unknowingly replaced with a grocery list which I have diligently fulfilled many times over.

♫I'm beginning to look a lot like a Christmas tree ♫

Well, the big-three holiday stretch has come and gone, yet some reminders linger. Like that huge bulge that blocks my view as I attempt to look down at the scale. One researcher reported that the average American adds one pound to his body weight during the holidays. How on earth did they arrive at that miniscule number? Did the poll include skeletons in the grave? Did they only survey ultra-marathon runners? People I spoke to said that they added at least five pounds, and that was just from looking at the holiday recipes and accompanying photos in the newspaper.

Why, just the other day I was standing in the checkout line at the local grocery store trying to figure out which of the figures ahead of me was the customer and which was the Norbest Butterball Turkey! Have you noticed how the checkout stands have gradually gotten wider over the years? That's not to accommodate more customers, but rather more of the customer.

Just as the holiday shopping season kicks off earlier each year, so does the calorie-loading season. It starts several weeks prior to Halloween. Oh, it's very subtle at first, to be sure. Innocently enough, the wife picks up a few bags of "bite size" candy bars and slyly hides them in the cupboard right behind the corroded gallon jar of wheat germ which you had planned to add to a five pound bag of oatmeal, which also has long ago rotted.

But, of course, it isn't long, say five minutes, before the kids uncover the secret hideaway and begin to pilfer tiny bar after bar, leaving a telltale tinfoil trail. So, of course, Dad has to step in and cut off the gravy train, only to make a mental note of the location and soon undertake his own stealthy sugar heist.

Initially, he justifies a few bars to supplement his lunch at work. Next, he tops off his regular dessert after dinner with "a bite of chocolate" to satisfy his craving. Eventually he is grabbing a bar every time he passes the cupboard so that by Halloween the costumed beggars at the door have to be satisfied with one of those rock hard lumps permanently sealed with Gorilla Glue inside orange or black paper which you scratch and claw at until you eventually give up and eat the paper and candy both. Then when you try to chew the candy it pops out several fillings and by the time that happens you beg for something less torturous to eat like an apple full of razor blades.

By the time Halloween night is over and you've eaten more candy than you handed out, even stooping so low as to reach inside the kids' bags and grab handfuls of Smarties and Tootsie Rolls, you have such a sugar buzz that you're running up and down the walls like Spiderman, Batman, and Superman all morphed into Glucoseman.

Immediately after Halloween, the push begins to convince Americans that they must start early to acquire adequate stuffing for Thanksgiving. During this period, the grocery stores face a frenzy of salivating shoppers who often fill a grocery cart per family member.

Doesn't it seem that the average Thanksgiving turkey today has been somewhat artificially enhanced, sort of a Nip/ Tuck Tom? Wild turkeys always look so swarthy, so lean and mean with a James Cagney–type swagger, while poultry farm turkeys waddle around pale and bloated, like Elvis late in his career. It's possible that while ripping apart a turkey one could come into contact with more chemicals than you would hanging out in a major league baseball dugout. But all of those chemically-enhanced trimmings are necessary to fortify us for the caloric climax of Christmas.

One of the great aspects of the Christmas season is that one can quadruple his calorie intake without spending a penny on food. Everywhere you go there is free food. People I've never even seen before will stop me on the sidewalk and shove jars of cashews and mints in my face. At work, platters of homemade goodies mysteriously show up in the office and quickly disappear.

In fact, I have discovered that fellow employees will eat absolutely anything. It can be hard as a rock, burnt black as coal, or melted into a slimy jelly-like substance that one must eat with a straw – doesn't matter. I can place the most hideous looking, teeth jarring stale baked goods in the office, turn my back for a second, and they're gone. Not only will someone eat it but quite often the gleefully grinning victim will even compliment the beneficent donor. "I can't believe your family wouldn't eat that green meatloaf; it was deeeeelicious!"

I believe that one even has to question the sanity of eating some of the classic Christmas fare. Would we actually eat a lot of this stuff if it wasn't for some spirit of the season obligation? Can you see yourself sitting down to an eggnog shake and a dish of divinity on a stifling hot July afternoon? No, certainly not. This is stuff that people in their right minds simply would not normally ingest. And how about soaking up some rays while lying on the beach and biting into a sticky green popcorn ball with a hunk of fruit cake for a chaser? You can't be serious. Yet during the Christmas season, which is nearly approaching the NBA season in length, we think nothing of eating this stuff.

So as we look back at the ghost of Christmas past and notice a ballooned appendage dragging behind us in the snow, let's all resolve to shape up and make room for some green beer and corn beef on the menu in March.

My bulge is winning the battle

January is normally the time of the year when couch potatoes actually begin to take root and grow those ugly brown sprouts all over their bodies. As the football season winds down, many of us dedicated sports fans will soon need to make an appointment to have a doctor surgically remove our posteriors from the couch in front of the television. My rear end has sunk into the cushion so deeply that in a couple of more weeks my feet will be hovering over my head and my chin will be nearly touching my knees.

Just like the football players that we catch brief glimpses of between commercials, I too am determined to get "bigger, faster, stronger." Okay, scratch faster and stronger, but bigger I can do if I really set my mind to it.

In fact if it wasn't for watching the home workout equipment ads on TV, I wouldn't be getting any exercise at all. Obviously I realize that my physical conditioning has been deteriorating over the last few weeks, but I must admit that I was a bit shocked to find myself hyperventilating and sweating profusely at the conclusion of simply watching a 30-second Ab-Cruncher sales pitch recently.

Let's face it, you know your situation is not good when the weight-loss commercials depict the before and after pictures, and you would sell your soul to look like the person in the before shot!

Another thing that I have noticed is that the people demonstrating these miraculous exercise devices are already in tip-top condition and can roll around endlessly on a tiny rubber ball without their hands or feet even touching the floor while you or I suffer a lower back injury just reaching for the remote to change the channel to a burger commercial!

If I was that toned and tanned and good looking, I sure as heck wouldn't be worried about paying $29.95 for a steel bar to do pull-ups in the doorway. What I mean is those people don't need to buy a Flab-Flinger or a Butt-Buster. They are beyond that stage. I doubt very much that a bronze Adonis who has more muscle in his left eyebrow than I have in my entire body is going to gain much by rolling around on a beach ball!

And why do they offer two Bun-Blaster Balls for the price of one? Are they implying that I need one for each cheek? Or that I most likely will break the first one when I sit on it? I've known some people who, when they roll around on the huge rubber ball, they just sort of blend together, and you can't distinguish amongst the belly, butt, and ball!

It is actually very shrewd for the companies to run an endless tandem of exercise/weight-loss ads during the holiday season. I must admit that I paused briefly during a recent Lard-Liquidator ad while pondering the wisdom of finishing off an entire box of chocolate-covered cherries, but after a loud, reassuring belch, I remembered that "quitting" isn't in my vocabulary, along with most words of more than one syllable, so I finished the job.

One trend I do find quite frustrating and torturous is that the exercise/weight loss commercials seem to alternate with food ads composed of 50-inch, high-def, and 3D, double-decker bacon/cheeseburgers with grease oozing out and dribbling down the screen onto the DVR.

Or they depict a delivery guy dropping off a stack of door-mat size pizzas, one of which would not only feed an entire African pygmy village but the villagers could use the empty box for a new town hall. Besides, what good does it do to have a pizza delivered if I still have to get up from the couch and open the door!

Usually it's only a matter of time before all of the home exercise devices mysteriously disappear. Chin-up bars become handy clothes hangers. A variety of plants hang from the weight machine bars. Stationary bikes collect dust in the shed. While, and I can certainly sympathize, the giant ball rolled off on its own and is hiding in some dark corner cringing in fear and hoping that it isn't found.

One inevitable bonus result of all of those exercise device ads and the countless Christmas gifts that they result in is that come around, oh, say, April or May, as sure as the dandelions spring up after the spring rain, there will be a huge increase in want-ads advertising great deals on "barely used" or "still in the box" treadmills and stationary bikes.

Plus, driveways during summer garage sales will be overflowing with inexpensive equipment. So if you have any money left over after buying some of those doughnuts they're selling for a quick breakfast while you shop, you just might get a heck of a deal on a seriously discounted giant rubber ball in mint condition, other than the fact it's flat.

Oprah trains for next Tour de France

It is now becoming quite clear that Andy Warhol was correct in predicting that "In the future everyone will be world-famous for 15 minutes." But it seems to me that celebrities the likes of Taylor Swift, Kim Kardashian, Justin Bieber, etc. are running way overtime on their spotlight allotment. Swift's wardrobe malfunction at the recent Golden Globe Awards made a splash in the media which I felt was totally unfair since, after careful analysis of her photos with a magnifying glass, I couldn't see a darn thing.

Just to be fair, why do you never see a wardrobe malfunction involving a man? Okay, other than the plumber bending over while working beneath the sink.

Furthermore, I doubt that Warhol ever dreamt such fame could be lavished on a kid who's even whiter than Michael Jackson, has a hairdo like a rooster, sounds like a singing chipmunk, and looks like he should be sitting in a desk in junior high memorizing state capitals instead of dancing in front of five black guys who all dance better than he does and can probably sing better too.

Finally, I am not sure why the media is so obsessed with celebrities' baby bumps or extreme diets. No, give me the old days when Babe Ruth could light up and smoke a Camel in the dugout after a ball game, or even while trotting around the bases during a homerun, without a bunch of paparazzi hovering nearby.

In a related matter, I am also wondering why Lance Armstrong is getting more publicity for his recent interview on Oprah than he did during his incredible string of victories in the Tour de France. Really this whole doping thing is blown out of proportion. Why, back in 1904 all of the stage winners were disqualified for the illegal use of cars and trains! At least Lance maintained contact with his bike! In 1937, the whole Belgian team withdrew when a French rival was towed uphill by a car. Over the years riders have used alcohol, ether, strychnine, cocaine, chloroform, horse ointment, etc. Compared to that, a little blood-boosting EPO doesn't sound so bad, now, does it?

In hindsight, there were early clues as to the source of Lance's super-human athleticism. Workers at his day care center where he stayed as a baby were mystified as to why smoke and sparks flew from his baby bottle filled with "formula." While the other babies were fed with bottles, his "milk" was injected. Needless to say, the other babies were duly impressed.

When Armstrong was a two-year-old, neighbors watched in wonder as little Lance pushed his parents around the block in a baby carriage. At four, he stunned the NASCAR circuit by winning the Indy 500 while pedaling a Big Wheel.

Honestly, Armstrong's confession does not surprise me. I was suspicious throughout his Tour de France racing career as each year the victories became more mind boggling. First, there was the year he won despite the fact he did wheelies while climbing Mount Ventoux. The next year, he flaunted tradition by riding a unicycle to victory. Then, in 2004, he was inspired to success by Sheryl Crow who sat on his handlebars—I mean his bike's handlebars—jamming on her guitar during the race. Unquestionably, his most stunning victory was in 2005. While the other competitors rode hi-tech racing bikes, Armstrong rode a stationary exercise bike and blitzed the competition.

The Oprah interview was certainly painful to watch as a great American hero, a man who, for years, was a symbol of courage as a survivor of testicular cancer, which resulted in the removal of one testicle, and who once boldly claimed, "Testicle! I don't need no stinkin' testicles!" dealt with the humiliation of confessing to cheating.

You have to admit that, if you didn't know any better, as you view Lance sitting next to Oprah, you might guess wrongly as to which one was pumped up on steroids? Which one would you want to grapple with in an MMA cage match? Well, after Oprah sat on Lance's racing bike in a moment of levity and smashed the bike, it left no doubt in my mind--I'm taking on Lance.

Oprah stated that even before Lance directly confessed to using PEDs she thought it was suspicious that he had to change his shirt during the broadcast due to the fact his neck size doubled midway through the interview.

No doubt, she added to the shock value of the interview show by announcing that, with Lance officially out of the picture, she has begun training and will be ready for the Tour in June. Not to be outdone, Lance vowed that he will unofficially enter the race, and will win hopping backwards on one foot while blindfolded. Personally, I would not bet against him.

Perfect game is perfectly boring

Ah, you can tell baseball season is well under way by the crack of the bat and the splat of tobacco juice on the dugout floor.

This past week a sports network has been honoring past perfect games thrown by pitchers. A perfect game is one in which one team gets no hits, no walks, no base runners, etc.—in other words, nothing happens. Worse yet, it takes about 90 minutes for that nothing to happen. Meanwhile, a fan sits wondering why he spent $40 for a ticket, $10 for a beer, and $5 to purchase a hot dog containing a wienie the size of a green bean and for which he could not get any condiments because by the time he finds the dispensers which are located in the restroom some kid has squirted out all the ketchup trying to draw a funny face on the table.

Some baseball experts refer to the perfect game as "a defensive gem" while some fans refer to it as "an offensive dud." At the conclusion of a perfect game, the winning pitcher is mobbed by his teammates in celebration whereas the losing team's players should be mobbed and held hostage while their fans demand a refund because they just witnessed a bunch of guys who earned about $10,000 per inning and couldn't get one hit!

Of course I played in lots of perfect games during my little league baseball career since we were a bunch of dweebs who were perfectly awful and only joined the team to get a "Burzinsky's Meat Market" tee shirt. We were so inept that if we accidently won a game our coach would ask us afterwards, "What went wrong?"

It got so bad that we had to find a new sponsor every summer. Believe it or not, during one of our frequent blowout losses, our Danish Dairy sponsor was so embarrassed he walked onto the field and made us hand over our tee shirts during the fourth inning, so we finished the game as "skins." It was nice having a sponsor like Danish Dairy because if we won they gave us cold bottles of chocolate milk. But a sponsor like Ajax Flea Collars wasn't so great, although I must admit I personally experienced less itching by mid-season.

I wasn't such a great player myself. Whenever I was preparing to bat, my teammate ahead of me was intentionally walked every time. I'm sure that today, this would be considered some form of psychological bullying. While most players warmed up by taking practice swings, I was down on my knees praying, burning incense, and filling out my will.

When batting, I was so afraid of the ball that I would wear a catcher's mask, chest protector, and shin guards. All I could think about was, "Why does this guy want to kill me?" My coach would always give me the same signal: he would shake his head side-to-side and clutch his throat which I eventually figured out meant "Don't choke." But it didn't matter because I would bunt no matter the situation.

I once tried pitching. However I did have some control issues. My last season, I set a league record for hit batsmen—in the on-deck circle! Over time I did develop a decent fastball and somewhat of a curve ball, but there was one pitch that I could never master—the strike.

Over the years, I played about every position, possibly because I was so versatile or, possibly, because I was lousy at all of them. The one spot I never tried was catcher. Our team's catcher was so mean that he had to wear his catcher's mask 24/7, sort of like a dog muzzle. Back then you could always spot the boy who played little league catcher because he was the only kid on the team with a beard.

Kids playing little league ball today show up for games sucking on fancy water bottles filled with an assortment of expensive energy drinks. Their parents sit in the stands with coolers full of high-fiber, gluten-free, antioxidant packed snacks like soy crisps, raw asparagus with hummus dip, and bamboo shoots. At our games, we just hoped that the park's water fountain was working, and even then we first had to scoop out nasty stuff that the 'greasers' and 'hoods' had hacked into it.

We played our ball games in a rough neighborhood with a very high crime rate. In fact, if during a game someone "stole a base" we would have a delay until it could be replaced. If a fan would inadvertently shout "Kill the ump!" we would all hit the deck expecting a shot to ring out any second.

So, fans, root, root, root for the home team—unless they lose a perfect game.

Happy Nude Year!

Two recent incidents triggered the topic for this article. First, on a recent trip we stayed in one of those motel rooms that has a full-length mirror on the bathroom wall placed where you can't avoid staring at it when stepping out of the shower. That was fine when I was in my twenties and all parts of my body were located where they should be. But now some regions have headed south and I can't hold my breath long enough to permanently relocate them.

When I first opened the shower curtain and saw my reflection I screamed, thinking that we must be sharing the room with attendees of a senior sumo wrestlers convention. For future showers I dried and dressed while still behind the curtain.

The ultimate solution is to simply not turn on the bathroom light during my stay which also can be a bit hazardous at my age since the motel toilet seats are located approximately two inches above the floor creating the possibility of completely missing the runway as I attempt an instrument landing in the dark.

The next experience occurred while I was doing some serious academic research on the Internet when suddenly up popped nude pictures of Kim Kardashian! I was never so shocked and embarrassed in my life and had no idea how this could have happened simply by my accidentally typing "totally nude pictures of Kim Kardashian" on Google when I meant to type "the Balkan crisis of 1914." I must have hit a wrong key or two.

I bet a lot of you have had similar experiences, say you're a college student doing research to find some fun things to do on your spring break trip so you Google "50 weird things to do in an elevator" and, bingo, suddenly you're watching Lady Gaga wearing an outfit consisting of three slices of strategically placed Spam, gyrating like a spastic cuckoo bird while singing her latest hit.

All of this started my thinking about why our modern day culture is so fascinated with nudity, especially when one considers how far we have come since the days when cavemen considered a porcupine-hide thong and saber-toothed tiger teeth bling-bling as formal wear. Now when we have an endless variety of clothing to choose from—I myself have a closet jam-packed with nearly three flannel shirts—we suddenly have this uncontrollable urge to be seen in public wearing nothing.

Humans first started wearing some type of clothing about 170,000 years ago. And let me tell you, that stuff was made to last. In fact I still wear a pair of oak bark socks which were all the rage back then. People who study such things were able to establish this starting date because that is when the clothing louse first appeared to join its cousin the hair louse. Both types of lice were then joined much later by the computer bug which has really loused things up.

Recently, a shoe over 5,000 years old was discovered, having been preserved in sheep dung. And here I've been wasting money on expensive shoe polish to protect my footwear all these years.

Originally, ancient Greek athletes wore clothing while competing. However, legend has it that, in 720 BC, an unusually long loincloth worn by a sprinter named Viagras fell off and tripped up the other race competitors, resulting in the then naked runner's victory. This was the first recorded incident of a wardrobe malfunction. From then on, Olympic athletes competed nude for some time.

Of course, females were not allowed to compete back then, nor even allowed to attend and watch the Games, which explains why Plato, Socrates, Aristotle and other famous Greek philosophers all got their start as cheer leaders.

Another historic moment in the history of public nudity was the famous ride of Lady Godiva whose husband promised to lower taxes for the people if his wife would ride a horse through the town's streets while completely nude, covered with only her long hair. Thankfully, President Obama has not made the same offer to Mitch McConnell who barely has enough hair to cover his nose.

And if he did ride, I doubt if there would be even one Peeping Tom to worry about!

In 1936, a man's right to appear bare-chested in public was made legal in the United States which, combined with the end of Prohibition, was an important stage in the evolution of the modern-day NFL fan.

Despite reports of nudity at the 1969 Woodstock Festival, it was difficult to see through all the mud, pot smoke, and "long beautiful hair."

Today there are even nudist resorts one can visit. Among other proper dining etiquette tips listed on their websites, they also suggest guests do not let the waiter serve you hot soup and that first-timers should be extra careful at the outdoor barbecue wienie roast.

When the going gets tough—have a snack

Another winter has come and gone, and if you're anything like me, your mind is full of what ifs. What if I had actually gotten out of bed these last three months? What if I had done some exercise more strenuous than watching "Dancing with the Stars" reruns?

Then there is the matter of diet. It is possible that during the winter you have eaten so many steaks and burgers that when your wife says that you woke her up last night you ask, "Was I snoring?" And she replies, "No, you were mooing!"

Or perhaps you have feasted on stuffed pork chops to the point that you seriously fret that you are the original source of the recent swine flu pandemic.

Well, now is the time to do something about it. It's summer, and along with the fact that it's a great time to develop allergies and West Nile disease, you can reshape your body with a little self-discipline and a large scalpel.

Jogging—now there is the exercise for every man. Nothing like the cool breeze flowing through your hair, a bouquet of summer scents gushing up your nose, scenery rushing by, the purr of a finely tuned engine ... OK, this time we went for a little car ride around the reservoir. But next time we go jogging.

You just can't get a more basic, a more primitive form of exercise than jogging. It isn't very hard to imagine our prehistoric ancestor, the caveman, running barefoot across the primordial slime, and then being warmly greeted at the cave door by his cave wife grunting, "Wipe that primordial slime off your feet so you don't get it on the dirt floor!"

Of course, today we no longer run to escape some saber-toothed tiger slobbering on the heel of our Nikes. We run for fun.

Ha, ha . . . just joking. But actually there are a number of logical reasons why jogging is so popular today.

One great thing about jogging as a form of exercise is that it's so darn inexpensive. I am living proof that it is possible to pick up a pair of running shoes on the clearance rack for a measly $29.99. That is if you happen to wear a size 14EEE and think that the colors turquoise and beige go well together. But, heck, for that price I'm willing to risk being arrested for impersonating Bozo the Clown.

Along with shoes, all a runner needs for clothing is a tank top and shorts. That is, of course, unless you live in southeast Idaho. In which case, it is advisable to add long underwear, mukluks, mittens, a parka coat, stocking cap, thermal face mask and a GPS in case you get lost in a blizzard. And that's in July!

In addition to proper jogging clothes, you will want to add some optional items that will officially label you as a serious runner.

Such things as a pair of cool wraparound sunglasses, an iPod full of snappy tunes to pump you up ("Weeeee are the champions—my friends"), and a fanny pack with those cute little water bottles and a pocket to hold essentials such as keys, energy bars and a whistle in case of a mountain lion attack.

Add a few final accessories like a heart monitor, pedometer, odometer and an Obamater which will compare your pace to the President's during his first 100 miles jogging while in office, and you are all set.

Now comes the hard part—stepping out the door and putting one foot in front of the other somewhat quickly. This is the juncture where most people falter. For many recreational runners this is their version of "hitting the wall."

Suddenly, I have to go to the bathroom (again!). Better check my shoelaces one more time. Boy, I shouldn't have eaten that third enchilada for lunch. The middle toe on my left foot feels odd. Now it's my right foot. Maybe the blue shorts would look better. Is that a cloud I see coming this way?

The birds outside appear to be gathering in an ominous manner.

And on and on the litany of excuses rolls through your mind endlessly until you realize it will be dark sometime soon within the next two hours so better wait until tomorrow.

But don't get discouraged. Every baby has to crawl before it can walk, and that's exactly what you will end up doing—crawling—if you jump into this running thing prematurely. So grab a copy of Runner's World, curl up on the couch, and get a vicarious workout. Just be sure to stretch well before you start.

Winter fun is an oxymoron

Recently some publications have come out with their winter recreation guide. Such guides usually feature action shots of snowboarders screaming down a mountain, dodging trees, displaying big grins on their faces, as if that could actually be "fun." It's a type of activity that, if I tried it, would result in the placement of a flowery memorial including a note saying "Here is where Mike was last seen with his face intact."

Or they show a scattering of brave souls sitting on a frozen lake hunched over tiny fishing poles, staring at holes drilled in the ice, like a couple of stoners staring at a painting on the wall and wondering why the remote won't work. Of course, you have to keep in mind that ice fishermen are the same guys who DVR chess tournaments.

Then there is the annual photo of Yellowstone National Park snowmobilers crawling along in bumper to bumper traffic, their machines struggling under the weight of buffalo which have hopped aboard for a lift, the drivers' faces shrouded in a gaseous cloud of mountain fresh air.

But what about us poor saps who cannot partake of such exhilarating winter wonderland activities? What about us lesser souls whose noses start dripping at the sign of a single snowflake? Just because the very sound of the word "outside" conjures up images of a death sentence and sends chills down our spine and a rash down our legs, doesn't mean we must be completely omitted from the winter recreation conversation. Au contraire! I have put together my own list of choices we winter wimps have available to escape cabin fever during the cold, dark winter months.

Let's start our winter fun with sledding, a traditional favorite. Nothing like dragging a sled up a slippery slope for ten minutes just to feel the exhilarating thrill of bouncing downhill for thirty seconds while experiencing the pleasure of children diving out of your way, dogs growling and leaping at you, the sled flipping over an embankment, you smacking down on your back, and the sled leaving tread marks on your chest. Now add to your glee gloves and boots full of refreshing, freezing snow and it's no wonder you're blubbering like an idiot, "Let's do that 100 more times!"

Now here's an activity that is obviously a new concept in Idaho: it's called "Shovel the Sidewalk." I can sense a lot of head scratching and confused looks coming from many of you. In fact, often when I propose this idea to people I receive responses such as "Do what to the what?" Or, as if a revelation has occurred, they ask, "I have a sidewalk? Where is it?" But the most common reaction is "Can I get it in Wii?"

But if hoisting a shovel full of snow from your sidewalk and tossing it onto your neighbor's is a bit too sedate for your adventurous taste, then how about the most dangerous game known to man at this time of year: winter driving!

I don't know about you, but, personally, I don't really mind driving on the Interstate in the dark at 6:30 AM as long as there are road blocks strategically set up so that no other cars can enter the same stretch that I'm occupying. That's because I'm totally convinced that all the other drivers out there have formed a conspiracy with one specific goal: to kill me.

How else can one explain the fact that as soon as I enter the freeway in my tiny station wagon—which was made in Japan where it only snows during the occasional nuclear winter caused by tsunamis drowning some rods which glow an eerie green—an armada of semi-trucks mysteriously appears out of the mist, surrounding me as if we're all competing in an Indy 500 race for produce delivery trucks?

My wipers cannot move fast enough to keep the windshield clean so I have to lean out the driver's window and attempt to help them by stretching a brush as far as I can. Next thing I know the brush is jerked out of my hand by a wiper blade which proceeds to fling the brush at a passing semi's fender, and the driver reacts like the Wicked Witch of the West when she sees Dorothy's house has crash landed on her sister.

If I'm lucky enough to finagle my way out of that mess, I still have an array of gargantuan pickups to dodge, not to mention deer that are illogically attracted to identical snow and sagebrush on the other side of the road and moose that want to hitch a ride on my windshield.

Of course, none of these hazards hold a candle to the ultimate winter driving threat: any vehicle with the word "Utah" on its license plate.

Yin, Yang, Yaks, and the Summer Games

The response to my last column about Yao Ming and China was overwhelming. In fact, one reader even wrote "wǒ hěn gāoxìng gēn nǐ jiànmiàn" which I believe means "Write more about China or face exile for life in Utah." Eek! So here goes.

Besides cranking out people so tall that they must bend down when walking beneath wind turbines, China is also in the news because of the upcoming Summer Olympics in Beijing. In fact, it is only 137 days, 17 hours and 58 executed Tibetan monks until the

Olympic torch arrives at the stadium. And as you are probably aware, China—frequently governed by a man named Ho, which distinguishes it from some U.S. governors who frequent hos—is trying to clean up its political image prior to the Games.

In reality, totalitarian China has loosened up a bit. For example, all citizens are no longer required to wear black clothing. Recently I have seen pictures of Chinese donning wild and crazy charcoal colored jackets with even an occasional sexy grey popping up. However, efforts to eliminate the state-mandated Moe hairdo for both sexes were stymied with a televised prisoner execution for "first-degree public display of a curl."

An additional monkey wrench was thrown into the image improvement effort several weeks ago when unrest broke out in China-controlled Tibet. Those wild and crazy monks were at it again as they took to the streets demanding the release of earlier jailed fellow monks. Nothing more terrifying than berserk monks snapping prayer flags with reckless abandon at Chinese tanks. After the ensuing violence, ten local people were burned to death. However, the official government news release stated that no shots were fired and no foreigners were killed. Whew, close call!

So what sort of changes can we expect once the Olympic Games actually begin? It just so happens that Beijing does have some fresh ideas for competition in the 2008 Games. Some new sports that the Chinese have considered proposing are Yakkity Yak Racing, an entertaining combination of karaoke while riding the large, shaggy oxen; Fireworks Catching which is usually won by the player with the hot hand; Hold the Mao; Synchronized Kung Fu Swimming; and the controversial Yang Your Yin.

But the only official addition is Olympic Water Boarding. This is a sport in which the Chinese have a huge advantage due to centuries of tradition and the fact that they are not even aware of the existence of the Geneva Convention. However the American team has made great progress, especially over the last eight years, and the recent addition of Donald Rumsfeld as the U.S. water boarding team's honorary coach has certainly speeded up the training process. Although new to the Olympic Games, water boarding as a form of competition has been around since the Spanish Inquisition. One witness at that time described it this way: "In one case, the torturer (read "referee") applied water three or four times successively until the victim's (read athlete's) body was swollen twice or thrice as big as before, his cheeks like great bladders, and his eyes staring and strutting out beyond his forehead." Should look really great on HD!

Americans have sought to even the playing field concerning new Olympic sports by petitioning to add dog fighting. This would be a competition in which they feel they have the upper hand. In response, the Chinese have made a gallant effort to quickly put together a dog fighting team, but, unfortunately, the trainers have been eating the dogs as fast as they can obtain them, so the IOC has nixed the proposal.

Besides political unrest and the rush to add new competitive events, the Chinese must also deal with the negative impact of air pollution on the competitors. For example, who in their right mind would want to be out on the track measuring the javelin throws in the zero visibility smog? One bold move by the government was an edict proclaiming that the 350 million Chinese smokers would be allowed to continue inhaling but banned exhaling. This should help.

There are a number of other concerns surrounding the Chinese hosting the Olympics. What about the possibility of cheating? Who can forget the emotionally charged incident in the 2004 Games when Zhou threw the badminton semifinal match to Zhang, a fellow countryman? Badminton purists worldwide still sob uncontrollably when viewing replays on YouTube. Add to that the fact that the U.S. team must ship over 25,000 pounds of meat to feed its athletes because chickens in Chinese markets are so full of steroids that one big clucker named Foghorn Leghorn has actually won a spot on the Chinese weightlifting team, and you begin to get the picture.

So grab your oxygen mask, lock up your dogs, and head to the Olympic stadium – let the games begin!

Rolling into the New Year on a big rubber ball

January is normally the time of the year when couch potatoes actually begin to take root and grow those ugly brown sprouts all over their bodies. As the football season winds down, many of us dedicated sports fans will soon need to make an appointment to have a doctor surgically remove our posteriors from the couch in front of the television. My rear end has sunk into the cushion so deeply that in a few more weeks my feet will be hovering over my head and my chin will be nearly touching my knees.

Just like the football players that we catch brief glimpses of between commercials, I too am determined to get "bigger, faster, stronger." Okay, scratch faster and stronger, but bigger I can do if I really set my mind to it.

In fact if it wasn't for watching the home workout equipment ads on TV, I wouldn't be getting any exercise at all. Obviously I realize that my physical conditioning has been deteriorating over the last few weeks, but I must admit that I was a bit shocked to find myself hyperventilating and sweating profusely at the conclusion of simply watching a 30-second Ab-Cruncher sales pitch recently.

Let's face it, you know your situation is not good when the weight-loss commercials depict the before and after pictures, and you would sell your soul to look like the person in the before shot!

The latest shape-up craze involves rolling around on rubber balls of various sizes. This exercise routine was accidentally developed by Pontius Pilates, an ancient Roman governor, who tinkered with the idea of replacing camels with the balls as a means of transportation but gave up on the idea due to the fact that the Roman soldiers' swords kept puncturing the balls.

Have you noticed that the people demonstrating these miraculous exercise devices are already in tip-top condition and can roll around endlessly on a tiny rubber ball without their hands or feet even touching the floor? While you or I suffer a lower back injury just reaching for the remote to change the channel to a burger commercial!

I seriously doubt that they need to buy a Flab-Flinger or a Butt-Buster. They are beyond that stage. A bronze Adonis who has more muscle in his left eyebrow than I have in my entire body is not going to gain much by rolling around on a beach ball!

And why do they offer two Bun-Blaster Balls for the price of one? Are they implying that I need one for each cheek? Or that I most likely will break the first one when I sit on it? I've known some people who, when they roll around on the huge rubber ball, they just sort of blend together, and you can't distinguish amongst the belly, butt, and ball!

It is actually very shrewd for the companies to run an endless tandem of exercise/weight-loss ads during the holiday season. I must admit that I paused briefly during a recent Lard-Liquidator ad while pondering the wisdom of finishing off an entire box of chocolate-covered cherries, but after a loud, reassuring belch, I remembered that "quitting" isn't in my vocabulary, along with most words of more than one syllable, so I finished the job.

One trend I do find quite frustrating and torturous is that the exercise/weight loss commercials seem to alternate with food ads composed of 50-inch, high-def and 3D double-decker bacon/cheeseburgers with grease oozing out and dribbling down the screen onto the DVR.

Or they depict a delivery guy dropping off a stack of door-mat size pizzas, one of which would not only feed an entire African pygmy village but the villagers could use the empty box for a new town hall. Besides, what good does it do to have a pizza delivered if I still have to get up from the couch and open the door!

Usually it's only a matter of time before all of the home exercise devices purchased during a phase of temporary insanity mysteriously disappear. Chin-up bars become handy clothes hangers. A variety of plants dangle from the weight machine bars. Stationary bikes collect dust in the shed. While, and I can certainly sympathize, the giant ball rolled off on its own and is hiding in some dark corner cringing in fear, hoping that it isn't found.

One inevitable bonus result of all of those exercise device ads and the countless Christmas gifts that they result in is that come around, oh, say, April or May, as sure as the dandelions spring up after the spring rain, there will be a huge increase in want-ads advertising great deals on "barely used" or "still in the box" treadmills, stationary bikes, large (flat) rubber balls, etc.

Chapter 3   Holidays

Already broke my resolutions—and proud of it

It seems that when most people make their New Year's Resolutions they commit the common error of choosing things that are just too darn hard to do. For example, last year one of the top resolutions was to exercise more. Based on the number of treadmills and stationary exercise bikes that I saw at garage sales this past summer, I'd say that resolution didn't work out so well for a lot of folks.

Oh, and I also saw quite a number of those exercise mats going for cheap. You know the comfortable cushions that you lie down on to stretch, do sit-ups, etc. I had one but would more often than not fall asleep while lying on it. Though I do believe that I burned a few calories from aerobic snoring.

And how about that perennial favorite resolution of promising to watch our weight? I'm sure that most of us do not have any difficulty "watching" our weight. I can do that while lying back in my recliner right after devouring a pint of Ben and Jerry's Chubby Hubby ice cream and gazing at my belly as it expands before my very eyes. But losing weight? That's a whole 'nother thing.

Relieving one's stress during the upcoming year is also high on resolution lists. So why make resolutions that will no doubt increase one's stress? My solution is to simply make resolutions that are either extremely easy to keep or they are so bad for me that I'm better off breaking them as soon as possible. Makes for a win-win situation.

Here's an example of how my strategy works. Many people vow to quit smoking during the new year. Now this is a very difficult resolution to keep. So I take the opposite track and resolve to START smoking which is really easy to do. However, it is not good for me and very expensive. So I'll have one cigarette then vow to quit smoking. Heck, I can knock off two resolutions in about five minutes. Let me share some of my other resolutions.

I resolve that by the end of 2016 I will have less hair on my head and more hair on my nose and ears. I have made this resolution for at least the last ten years and have carried it out faithfully each year.

To become more socially active I vow to Skype with myself by taping my picture over that tiny camera hole on our two computers and running back and forth to speak . Also, I will spend less time watching television simply by falling asleep in front of the TV even sooner than I did last year.

For health reasons, during the new year I will only drink beer on Saturday nights. Oh, and Friday nights too if something special is going on, like some sort of rare natural phenomena such as a sunset. Most likely I'll have to drink beer on Thursday nights since there's always the possibility that Friday may be canceled due to the fact that TGIF violates church/state separation. I swear that I will not touch beer on Wednesdays—unless my wife needs the room in the fridge. No beer on Tuesdays, but if I do drink some it will be gluten-free. I'm not sure what gluten is, but it just sounds unhealthy. On Mondays, beer only if football or baseball or basketball is on TV, so no beer during curling season. That leaves Sunday, a day of rest, except I may need to have a beer to recover from all that stressful resting.

I resolve to start using my credit card more often when shopping instead of my spare-change collection. Mainly because credit cards have really helped to reduce unemployment since there are apparently thousands of hard-working people totally dedicated to stealing credit card numbers. I know this because recently my credit card company notified me that I had charged fifty cents to a catering company in Mexico. Now my memory isn't quite as sharp as it used to be, but I'm pretty sure that if I had recently hosted a party in a place called Zihuatanejo and ordered one pint of refried beans for all my guests to share, I'd probably remember it.

Related to using my credit card more, I resolve to practice writing my name at home with the plastic handle of my toothbrush so I can get better at signing the screen at the checkout stand with that chunky high-tech pen which doesn't let you see what you're doing and when I ask the clerk if my signature looks okay she giggles and says, "Sure."

A final interesting fact about resolutions is that the percent of people over 50 who achieve their resolution each year is the lowest of any age group at 14%. That's probably because, if they're anything like me, they forgot to write their resolution down, or, if they did, they forgot where they put the piece of paper.

Haunted by the holiday spirit

Thanksgiving has come and gone but turkey issues remain. According to recent local headlines, some turkeys in here in the city have gone rogue and formed street gangs. Reports of turkeys "harassing schoolchildren" along with "destroying property and being rowdy" have alarmed readers. Personally, I was so intimidated that I did not purchase a frozen turkey for Thanksgiving this year, fearful that I would be seen carrying it from the store and accosted by a turkey gang. So instead I put on my camo and went hunting for a Tofurky which I easily bagged using a large fork and spatula.

While strutting down the sidewalk, flaunting his dreadlocked snood and wattle and brandishing an "Eat More Beef" tattoo, Lil Tom, leader of the turkey gang, explained his flock's 'tude by saying, "It's a gobble or be gobbled world."

The neighborhood wild turkeys are suspected of drawing in relatives from outlying areas to join them, spreading the word that life in town is much easier than in the wild. Conservatives fear the possibility of amnesty by the mayor so want to hunt and eat the turkeys. Meanwhile, liberals held a candlelight vigil outside a local butcher shop.

Nowhere is the true holiday spirit displayed more clearly than at Black Friday sales. Deals like "Buy one at the regular price and get a second for the same price!" proved too good to pass up. Shoppers nationwide came together as one big dysfunctional family: shoving, kicking, pepper spraying, and stabbing one another for parking spaces as Salvation Army bell ringers cried out, "Have a good day!" then ducked for cover.

Prices for 60" televisions were so cheap on Black Friday that homeless people could afford to buy them just so they could have a bigger box to live in. Also popular with shoppers was the "Normal Barbie." It is much more like the average American female than the original svelte Barbie Doll. This new Barbie has a fuller figure, skin blemishes, and earns 77% of what Ken makes for the same job.

Lots of new smartphones on the market this year with a variety of useful apps such as the free "Is it cloudy or sunny?" app, guaranteed to be nearly as fast and accurate as looking out the window.

Black Friday also marks the start of the holiday shoplifting season when retailers lose billions of dollars from theft. Most popular item stolen nationwide is alcohol which I would guess is being consumed by the millions of dads who have to suffer through another elementary school performance of the Nativity.

Our family already drew names for the annual gift exchange. Danged if our black Lab didn't draw my name again, and here I haven't even finished gnawing on the bone she dug up in the backyard and gave me last year!

Christmas shopping is one of my least favorite chores. Nothing more uncomfortable for me than walking into the ladies department with all that flimsy lingerie hanging around which I avoid even glancing at, afraid I'll be caught on video and show up on the evening news. And I just happen to be the only male present at that particular moment, with all the female shoppers giving me a wary glance.

Add to that the fact that I just left the cosmetics counter and spray-tested eight new fragrances including Dessert Beauty Deliciously Kissable Love Potion Perfume by Jessica Simpson, all of which combined create a sort of Pepe Le Pew aura, nearly suffocating customers that I pass.

Naturally, being the dutiful husband that I am, I watched my recording of the annual Victoria's Secret Fashion Show three times just to get an idea as to what is super sexy hot . . . uh, I mean the current style, before going shopping for my wife's gift. Luckily, I was able to pick her up some Duck Dynasty flannel pajamas on clearance.

Of course, my shopping woes pale in comparison to polygamists back in the 1800s. Can you imagine having to buy presents for 40 or more wives? Plus, those men were darn lucky credit cards had not been invented yet. Besides, I can't see any advantage to having so many wives. It would be just my luck that all 40 wives would "have a headache" the same night.

Christmas season around here seems to have some unique hometown touches. The season kicked off with the annual Old Town parade creating a dazzling nighttime scene on a chilly night with reports of spectators suffering only three minor injuries from frozen popcorn balls thrown by sinister looking elves riding on a float.

And once again I'm organizing a troupe of Christmas-caroling mimes to ride through local neighborhoods on a hay wagon and perform all the old standards, giving "Silent Night" a whole new meaning. Hopefully, we won't encounter any turkeys.

I'm dreaming of a neutral-color Christmas

There seems to be a lot of current discussion about political correctness. People today who are concerned about omitting or even upsetting certain individuals choose their words more carefully than when I was growing up.

It does seem that sometimes people get carried away with the political correctness thing. Like the Nebraska school district that suggested avoiding the terms "boys" or "girls" and instead use "purple penguins" when telling first-graders to sit down on their rugs. An obvious drawback to such gender-neutral words is that the kids could grow up thinking that they have to breed in large colonies.

Then a few years back, a teacher in Michigan replaced the word "gay" with "bright" in the carol "Deck the Halls" because the kids giggled when they sang it. Parents were not gay (happy) about the switch, so the principal told her to use the original wording at the school concert.

On the other hand, with Christmas season comes Christmas carols and, boy (or purple penguin), this is an area where the song writers could use some intense sensitivity training.

Before I get to the lack of political correctness in Christmas carols, I have to say that I feel sorry for people who work in businesses that provide constant music for their customers, thus subjecting the employees to the torture of listening to Christmas carols while on the job. One store I was visiting last week played the entire Burl Ives Christmas CD, and by the looks on some of the stressed faces of customers and employees, I'd say we were real lucky no one was carrying a concealed weapon.

Then there is that one guy in the neighborhood who thinks he's providing his neighbors with a real treat by blasting carols from speakers strategically located in his yard behind giant inflatable elves and angels. One can't help but wonder who this jolly fellow's intended audience is? People driving by in cars with the windows rolled up? That daily jogger trudging through the slush wearing earbuds and listening to Guns N' Roses? It certainly can't be his neighbors who have been wearing ear plugs since the day after Thanksgiving.

Above and beyond the fact that mere over-exposure to these songs, along with the omnipresent bell ringers at store entrances, can drive one to "red-kettle rage," my main concern is that many of these songs' lyrics seem to come close to crossing the line in today's politically-correct climate and run counter to the true spirit of the season.

For example, who is the line "Do you hear what I hear?" mocking? Well, me, of course. Sure, I do have some trouble hearing these days, like when my wife hints that a fungus is forming in my toilet bowl that rivals The Blob and I should consider cleaning it. But I can clearly hear a song "with a voice as big as the sea," especially if the singer is Burl Ives. And, yes, I "see what you see," it's just a little bit blurry.

What about "Here We Come A-Wassailing"? Sounds innocent enough, doesn't it. But I would argue that singing about a pre-Christian fertility rite encouraging folks "fortified by copious quantities of alcohol" to head off into an orchard and threaten the apple trees to produce fruit "or else" is clearly inappropriate for joyous holiday background music at the grocery store and is precisely what Bill O'Reilly is referring to in his annual outrage against the War on Christmas.

The song "Little Drummer Boy" is first of all quite blatant in its ridicule of vertically-challenged people and, secondly, upon close inspection, unquestionably contains a hidden black-magic incantation involving the repeated mesmerizing chant of "Pa rum pum pum pum," with the worrisome result of more than one spellbound listener's face plopping into a bowl of plum pudding.

"Frosty the Snowman" is politically incorrect pretty much from beginning to end. Along with the title character being plain sexist, it also promotes smoking ("With a corncob pipe") and violates the recent Paris climate control agreement ("And two eyes made out of coal").

I'm sure that, like I did, dads today turn off the radio whenever "I Saw Mommy Kissing Santa Claus" plays. Any responsible parents would not let their children hear this lurid tale of Mommy smooching and tickling a stranger who sneaks into the house. Even more shocking is that the child witnessing this scandalous affair has the gall to think it would have been funny if his dad saw all this! I am turning red with anger just thinking about such indignity.

Finally, I feel that residents of the Deep South receive enough ridicule without the addition of an entire Christmas carol for that purpose. How else can one possibly interpret the intent of such cruel sarcasm as in the pitiful plea "All I Want for Christmas Is My Two Front Teeth"?

It's Father's Day—where's the remote?

I always find it interesting how the store ads differ between the build up to Mother's Day vs. Father's Day. For Mother's Day the stores push products that, of all things, are aimed at making mothers more attractive to fathers! Such things as cosmetics, perfume, hair products, fetching apparel, beauty salon certificates, etc. I thought the whole idea was to give Mom a day off. Isn't that approach simply making mothers work even harder than they already do?

Or, to take that concept a step further, for mothers the stores run ads featuring stoves, washers and dryers, and vacuums. Gee, I wonder who's going to get the privilege of enjoying such gifts! Of course , a fancy washer is sure better than sending Mom down to the river with a shiny new rock to beat the babies' diapers clean with, but something still seems slightly screwy about this whole picture.

Then there are the Father's Day ads published over the last few weeks which attempt to create the illusion of the hard-working family man. Ads loaded with gas grills, power washers, lawn mowers, etc. which, quite honestly, makes me laugh since, when I look around my neighborhood, I see women using these items at least as much as men!

It's probably a more realistic portrayal of the modern American Dad when the stores feature fishing gear, duck decoys, golf clubs, and big-screen televisions to purchase for his special day. It's even feasible that wives pitch in to help the kids buy Dad these items so that he will use them and stay the heck out of the way so the rest of the family can get some work done around the house!

That's actually the way it pretty much works worldwide if you study various cultures. Take the early Native American tribal culture for instance. Females gathered firewood, tanned hides, cooked food, raised kids, etc. while Dad went hunting, beat on drums, and then took a break to smoke his pipe. Boy, things certainly haven't changed much in this country, have they?

A contemporary example of a gap in family gender labor roles would be Saudi Arabia. Once again, mothers pretty much carry the workload on their backs although it's hard to see them doing it since they are forced by men to wear recycled nuns' habits. Meanwhile the fathers sit around comparing camels, smoking hookahs, and fantasizing that they rule the roost

Furthermore, I've never been able to figure out why women waste so much time, money, and energy on fancy hairdos, makeup artistry, and sexy attire. I'm pretty darn sure that Eve and her leaves had no problem luring Adam into a relationship despite stiff competition from such manly enticements as abundant hunting prey, ravenous fish, and an entire private orchard of trees to take naps under.

If I were a female, I would gather all of my universal sisters together via the Internet to sign a pact swearing that none of us would ever again take steps to make ourselves more attractive to men or else face punishment of being immediately "unfriended" by 3 billion females, a fate worse than death for most women.

It seems to me that such an attitude is only fair when one considers how little trouble men go to so they can attract the opposite sex. Young guys today think they're over dressed if they wear their ball caps with the bill pointing forward.

But it's not all guys' fault. Whereas Mother's Day clothing ads display beautiful fashions that allow Mom to transform into Cleopatra, Father's Day clothing gift choices, such as steel-toed boots, hard hats, and utility belts, are so dull as to result in his appearing as a member of The Village People.

There are other obvious commercial discrepancies. Stores display a variety of hair shampoos, blow dryers, and leg razors for moms only to be later replaced with deodorant, Rogaine, and nose and ear hair trimmers for dads.

Restaurants offer elaborate brunches including prime rib, Champaign, and chocolate-dipped strawberries for Mom's Day while pizza-delivery coupons and sales on 2-liter soda pop dominate Dad's Day ads.

Mother's Day observers are enticed to attend a symphony concert of romantic classics while, for their special day, fathers receive a discount to an Elvis impersonator show.

I guess the people that I feel the most sorry for this time of year are the kids adopted by a man and his male life partner. Just how in the heck is little Johnny suppose to know which one gets the chainsaw and which one the fresh fig bubble bath?

The year in review, including the last twelve months

It's always interesting reading various lists of the top stories for the past year. However, you soon discover they are all pretty much the same, leading readers to the conclusion that "Okay, I get it, we need the Affordable Care Act to protect us from perils in life like Malaysian Airlines, Ray Rice, Ebola, etc."

In some ways I'm glad to see the year end. Since I've been accidentally writing 2015 on checks all year anyway, I'll look smarter after next week. Also, there are some national and regional news topics many of us certainly will be glad to see fade into the sunset.

Kim Kardashian was in the news quite often this past year for reasons that I don't understand, other than that one incident when she accidentally knocked the Washington Monument off its base by twerking too close to it during a nude photo shoot for Paper Magazine.

Russian President Vladimir Putin took the 2014 Sochi Winter Olympic spirit a bit too far by subjecting Ukraine to a crushing defeat in ice hockey, using Crimea as a puck.

Televised World Cup Soccer matches set records for most watched games ever. Not surprisingly, at the same time, millions of insomniacs worldwide were miraculously cured.

The Secret Service caught a lot of heat over people sneaking into the White House. Security guards eventually became suspicious something was wrong when they heard sneezing, yawning, and laughing sounds coming from a closet only to find upon opening the door that the Seven Dwarfs were hiding inside.

After initial questioning, all seven were then handed over to the CIA to face an interrogator, code name "The Evil Queen."

South African Olympic athlete Oscar Pistorius was sent to jail for shooting his girlfriend four times through the bathroom door after he repeatedly told her that he had to go and would she please hurry up. Pistorius was denied early release from jail because he could remove his artificial legs along with the electronic monitoring ankle device, although one has to wonder how far he would get.

National midterm election results reaffirmed that the GOP is the Party of the South. You know, all those southern states which lead the nation in worst poverty rates, worst health care, most cigarette smokers, most uninsured people, most violent crime, most executions, highest obesity rates, highest divorce rates, highest teen birth rates, etc. But southern states are also the most religious, so they'll probably be okay.

Hopefully, we'll elect a Republican president in 2016 to work with the Republican-controlled Congress so that the entire nation can have the same high quality of life enjoyed by residents of Toad Suck, Arkansas.

Also during the midterm elections, more states voted to legalize marijuana which is understandable since we are all going to need something to help us maintain our sanity if the above scenario plays out over the next couple of years.

The President moved to normalize diplomatic relationships with Cuba. This will allow American couples to vacation in such romantic locales as the Bay of Pigs and Guantanamo Bay Prison.

North Korea's leader Kim Jong-un, the Pillsbury Dough Dictator, forced Hollywood to cancel the release of another totally stupid comedy film, something Americans have consistently failed at due to the fact they actually waste millions of dollars on such garbage. Maybe now they will spend money on something more culturally enriching like a Miley Cyrus concert.

In Idaho, cows corralled headlines this past year. First, the state legislature passed a law requiring all dairy cows to wear XXXX-L t-shirts printed with "Hooves up! Don't shoot videos of my mistreatment!" Later, in Pocatello, several cows on death row escaped and surprisingly eluded capture for days in an area teeming with wranglers, rustlers, and trappers. Despite access to a mine-resistant ambush protected armored vehicle (MRAP), a military surplus armored personnel carrier, a Bearcat or armored SUV, and a SWAT team, local police were stymied in their efforts to locate and capture all of the bovine fugitives.

Wildlife poaching stories also made regular appearances in the news. Penalty for "flagrant" poaching cases includes revoking the criminal's hunting privileges which is like revoking one's driving privilege for driving without a license—probably won't stop them.

Sherri Ybarra won the state superintendent of schools position in November despite lying about her endorsements, personal life, and education, plus plagiarizing her opponent's website and admitting to hardly ever bothering to vote in past elections. Regardless, GOP voters figured the new "Chief of Schools," as she refers to herself, would be an improvement over the previous Republican state superintendent.

Finally, in a northern Idaho local election for county coroner, voters mistakenly elected a potato. Reason given for the embarrassing mishap is that GOP voters thought the "R" next to the candidate's name stood for Republican when it actually stood for Russet.

These are the ties that try men's souls

"Peace on earth, good will towards men . . . and with every gun purchase you'll receive a free gift." It's no doubt ads such as this that drove holiday shoppers to set a new one-day record for background checks during gun purchases last Black Friday.

Many times we have heard good Christian folks express a concern that the true meaning of Christmas is dead in this country. Well, I think it's safe to say that the over 185,000 background-check requests processed on Nov. 27th prove that nothing could be further from the truth. Just imagine the smile on dad's face on Christmas morning when he picks up his gaily wrapped package marked in large letters "Do not shake—may go boom!"

When it comes to Christmas gift-buying, it's lucky for dads that times have changed. Remember when the running gag about Christmas gifts for dad was the annual ugly-tie purchase that he received from his kids? Well, I can vouch for the fact that it was not a joke. I fondly recall forcing myself to wear a new tie to work just to make my boys happy and facing a barrage of inquiries from fellow employees throughout the day as to why I was wearing a tie covered with neon-orange pizzas.

If you don't believe me, go look at your tie collection in the closet right now. Notice the ties covered in dust buried behind the ones you regularly wear to work? There's the tie with three scantily-clad women that says "Ho, ho, ho," or the black one sporting a snarky looking creature stating "I'm a Grinch before coffee."

Today there are so many other options for Christmas gifts, and shopping for them has never been easier. It's not like the old days when a kid had to ride the bus clear across the city to reach downtown. Then he had to actually "go outside" into the cold and snow to tussle with bustling crowds on the sidewalk.

Once inside a department store, a kid still had to make his way through the line of parents and children waiting for Santa to reappear right after his ten-minute cigarette break that he took every hour. Considering the hassle of shopping back then, it's no wonder that boys grabbed the first necktie that caught their eye. Besides, that way they could get to the toy section quicker.

Thanks to technology, those days are dead and gone. Now on Cyber Monday kids can purchase about anything for dad with just a few clicks on the keyboard. And things are cheap! Why, by saving his paper-route money for a year, a boy could buy a huge 4D HDTV with a life-sized picture so sharp that dad will feel like he's PLAYING football, not just watching it.

In fact, I'm sure that a number of guys who experienced football games on their high-definition TVs this past weekend called in sick on Monday due to concussions, pulled muscles, or large bruises from chest-bumping the screen after throwing touchdown passes! Plus, I'll wager that more than one accidentally swallowed his mouth guard while wolfing down a leftover turkey sandwich, which explains why now he can't find it anywhere.

Based on what we all saw this past weekend, the pace of TV ads for the next few weeks will be coming at us faster than football's "hurry up offense." There are even new ads specially produced for holiday shopping. For example, what is with these TV ads suggesting that I buy my wife a new Mercedes-Benz for Christmas? Really? As if the cheapskate who neglected to replace the wiper blades on her '96 Dodge van before winter set in, will suddenly swell up with Christmas spirit like a giant goiter just because I hear the Chipmunks singing "Jingle Bells" and order her a $90,000 car!

Probably the hottest holiday gift idea this year supplanting the necktie for dad is the drone. Stores claim that they cannot keep them in stock because they are soaring off the shelves so fast. Drones range in price from around $90 to over $4,000, just depends on what use dad has in mind.

For example, if he simply wants to video some bunny rabbits scampering across the yard, you can get by pretty cheap. But if dad is more the Rambo-type, get him the very high-tech model with teeny-weeny missiles that dad can use to take out the pesky squirrel that keeps invading the bird feeder.

If you're still thinking about a necktie for dad, another hot option is the Fifty Shades of Grey DVD which is on sale and makes a perfect stocking stocker for dad to watch on Christmas eve. I just have to warn you that, if he's my age, I'm pretty sure that dad will be sound asleep and sawing Yuletide logs after just one shade.

It's that time of year when turkeys are flocked

As the cold winter wind generated by 33 million Canadians simultaneously inhaling and blowing with all their might in a southerly direction signals the start of the holiday season, it warms one's heart to hear the honking of fleeing geese and the gobbling of terrified turkeys. Yes, it's that time again when birds of every feather head south.

During this migration I often wonder who the real "bird brains" are as the birds head for sunny climes while you and I hunker down for three months of ice, snow and NBA games filled with balding Italians who get a standing ovation if they even make so much of an effort as to point at a loose ball and shout "Mama Mia!"

Some of our feathered friends are simply going on vacation to soak up the tropical sun and preen for the annual mating season, sort of like single senior citizens going on a Caribbean "Love Boat" cruise each winter and then returning home for an eleven month nap. But others, such as turkeys, have a much more urgent mission: to escape execution. It is a time when the border with our southern neighbor is crawling, rather waddling, with illegal fowl applying various tactics to cross the Rio Grande.

They use a variety of clever ruses. Some of the big birds attempt to cross in rented trucks marked "Piñatas" which are filled with turkeys safely dangling from strings attached to the ceiling, staying perfectly still, not a waddle waddling, and decorated with bright, colorful strips of paper. Others swim the river pretending to be albino duck decoys on steroids.

Unfortunately, many have discovered it is very difficult to cross the border on foot. First off, commercially bred turkeys have such large breasts that they keep falling forward which makes for slow progress. There are even drawbacks to clever disguises consisting of sombreros, which often fall down over their eyes so they become lost, and the phony black mustaches which are no good since they tend to slide down their beaks and on past that slimy looking red thing that hangs from their chin, so the mustaches end up looking more like bow ties. Thus, despite their best efforts, the illegal Butterballs often end up as an easy KFC bucket for the coyotes.

And are they welcomed with open ovens to their new home? Of course not, since they will now compete with the other birds for access to birdseed, birdhouses, birdbaths and government protection for endangered species. In addition, none of the native birds can understand all of that gobble-gobble gibberish.

Naturally, their presence fouls up the resident bird society pecking order, and the once dominant squirrel cuckoo now must compete with these bloated, pale gringo gobblers. Despite their efforts to conceal their identity beneath 3XL serapes, eventually the unwanted migrants will be caught, caged, and shipped back to the US where their gruesome fate awaits.

Which brings to mind this question: why is the turkey so maligned here in its native country today? How did the word "turkey" come to be associated with something dumb or senseless? The connotation actually evolved due to a series of failed attempts by turkeys to behave like other birds. First, one patriotic bird attempted to fill the role of a carrier pigeon and deliver a top-secret military message during WWI. But since he needed to rest after every flight of about 20 feet, he failed to deliver the important document until midway through WWII.

Even more damaging to their status was when families tried to keep turkeys in living room cages as pets, similar to a parakeet or a canary, but the little wooden swings kept breaking from their weight, the bottom of the cage required a fresh copy of the entire New York Times newspaper each day, and neighbors' cats were getting the crap knocked out of them when they attempted to grab the birds.

Other attempts were made to establish respectability for the hulking bird. Ben Franklin once proposed making the turkey the United States National Bird instead of the eagle. If our culture ever does follow through with the idea of having the turkey and the eagle exchange places, I would certainly hate to be the first person to attempt to put stuffing in a full-grown bald eagle for Thanksgiving – it could get real ugly.

Let's put the X back in Xmas

Well, Christmas is right around the corner; I mean literally since I hear those obnoxious Christmas carolers heading towards my house at this very moment. But this year I'm prepared to hand out cups filled with hot chocolate that has sufficiently cooled to the point that a thick layer of scum has formed on top, just right to gag them.

When they arrive, I will recommend to them that next year they should consider forming a mime troupe to go Christmas caroling.

For some reason, during the Christmas season everyone suddenly thinks that they can sing—even people who are so bad that when they are singing alone in the shower, the water will stop running and not resume until they cease.

In many ways the holiday has certainly undergone changes since I was a kid. Understandably, parents today worry about giving their kids too many violent video games, games like the new one in which Mary and Joseph give the innkeeper a serious beat down.

Just think of the three Wise Men trying to cross those countries' borders today, they would be spotted on radar and disintegrated by a drone, what with various armies in that region blowing up people to see who can rule the land of the Prince of Peace. And Santa entering Syria's airspace would definitely be toast!

In some ways Christmas use to be just as violent in the old days. As little tykes, we would get those paddle balls and use them to bop each other in the back of the head until the ball completely flew off then Mom would use the paddle on us, so the gift was sort of a mixed blessing.

For years, my mom always said, "I'm not going to buy you kids BB guns 'cause you'll shoot out someone's eye." But one Christmas she finally broke down and bought some, and, sure as heck, within a few hours there were eyeballs rolling all over the basement floor.

Of course, we had the usual snowball, ice ball, golf ball-inside-the-snowball fights, and, the ultimate Weapons of Mass Destruction, month-old divinity and fruitcakes.

Our worse holiday experience was the year Dad fed the pet rabbit some dog food, and it died. But, we all agreed, Old Floppy sure made a delicious Christmas dinner.

94

We kids loved it when the cat would grab hold of the Christmas tree's tinsel and pull down the entire tree, lights and bulbs crashing onto the floor, bringing Mom running brandishing a broom which she once accidentally swung wrong and cracked the handle on the cat's head, resulting in kitty walking sideways the rest of its life and doing peculiar things in the litter box.

Today, people go to the mall and buy a tree made out of some high tech tinsel that changes colors, plays music, and will even put itself away in its box upon command. In contrast, in the old days, Dad and us kids would trudge out on a frigid, moonlit night and chop down a family Christmas tree, hoping that the neighbor didn't spot us until we had stealthily dragged it into our house.

Also, I don't understand why people's real Christmas trees that they buy at some lot are always catching on fire and burning down the house. I mean you're not supposed to smoke the darn thing. When I sold trees one winter in a grocery store parking lot, I would only show customers the side of the tree that actually had branches then rotate it as they walked around it, careful not to spin it too fast or the dried up needles would fly off.

After I stood outside in the freezing cold and snow all evening I would return home looking like Bob Marley's ghost, all pale and crusty. No, wait, that's Jacob Marley. Bob Marley's ghost would be red, yellow, and green, with dreadlocks and singing "I Shot the Sheriff." But either ghost would be wailing.

We always opened the presents on Christmas Eve. Afterwards, the floor would be knee deep in torn up wrapping paper, and, with so many kids in the family, occasionally one of them would end up missing and not be found until New Years Eve.

It seemed like every year we got an electric football game, the kind where the field vibrated and made the figures bounce around like miniature players going through nicotine withdrawal, but I'm pretty sure that some of those teams could beat this year's Kansas City Chiefs.

Aunt Weasel would always give each of us a popcorn ball that apparently formed during the Pleistocene period and was perfect for removing fillings from your teeth.

Overall, I will always have fond memories of Christmas as a kid because without it I would not have had any socks or underwear.

Season's Greetings from our family to yours

It's that time of year again when distant relatives and friends that you sort of remember send you the notorious Christmas letter. You know the type that summarizes the activities for various family members during the nearly completed year. Generally, it seems that older people focus on trips and surgeries while young parents brag about their kids. It just seems that people are not completely honest and forthcoming.

This year for the first time I put together a family yearly review holiday letter for 2011. Here are some excerpts.

January: Our blind nineteen-year-old sheepdog Slobbers who gets around on two legs and an implanted skateboard led by a seeing-eye cat finally caught that pesky squirrel he's been chasing for months. Come to find out it was only because the squirrel froze solid overnight so wasn't moving real fast. But we didn't tell the dog 'cause it would break his heart—he was so proud. You can see him holding the squirrel (that flat, blue thing) in the family holiday picture card.

February: Uncle Lester is slowly recovering from that nasty fall around Christmas when, after too much spiked egg nog, he climbed up on the roof while shouting, "Ho, Ho, Ahhhhh!" He slipped on the ice and landed head first in the frozen bird bath down below. Ever since then we just use him to hold the yarn while Grandma knits pot holders.

March: One joyful evening in mid-March Bobbie Sue stood up at the dinner table and proudly announced that she was going to have a baby. We all clapped and cried tears of joy. After the rejoicing quieted down, I had two questions. Who is the daddy, and who in the heck is Bobbie Sue?

April: Aunt Maggie, the one we all call "Silence", was recently abducted by aliens. When she returned she seemed perfectly normal except now she talks a lot about tubes, laser beams, and tentacles. Also I've noticed that she can roast marshmallows by just staring at them which comes in real handy on family campouts.

May: We enrolled our youngest (at least last I checked) Little Jimmie Joe into the Jihad Pre-School which recently opened down the road. I'm not sure what jihad means, but the alphabet sure has changed since I was a kid and Little Jimmie is always talking about "virgins" which is another word I need to look up.

June: We all took the Greyhound down to Sucker Springs, Arkansas, to attend our step-niece's foster grandson's half-sister's child Emmylou's graduation from that special school they have there for kids who like to burn things. Her senior quote was, "May the flaming torch of wisdom ignite an inferno of blazing knowledge that leaves this school and my fellow students smoldering charcoal briquettes." Very deep.

July: Uncle Darwin shocked the family by undergoing a transgender operation. Most of us thought it was a waste of money for a 68-year-old man to have breast implants since most men that age already have breasts! However we all agreed his lip augmentation and wig sort of give him an Angelina Jolie look and he is now dating Uncle Rufus.

August: Loaded up the '58 Studebaker pickup for a family picnic. Grandma's rocking chair fell out of the truck when I backed over the curb which would not have been a big deal 'cept she was sitting in it. Grandma was still able to go. She just had to eat her sloppy Joe and potato salad through a straw.

September: It's been a roller-coaster year for us dirt farmers. First the weather was bone dry and we got more dirt than we can sweep up so invested in extra brooms. Next would come some rain showers forcing us to keep a close watch on the mud pie market. Another hot, dry spell and dust prices spiked so bought more dustpans. The fall monsoon hits and the price for a barrel of sludge plummets.

October: "Batty" Aunt Hattie finally had that cosmetic surgery she's been insisting on forever. She came through the surgery fine although the nurse mentioned that while in the recovery room a still sedated Hattie kept screaming, "No, Pa, I ain't marryin' no penquin!" Come to find out the "hideous" lump they removed from her face was her nose.

November: Had the family Thanksgiving dinner at the farm this year. It was delicious although some thought the turkey looked and tasted a bit peculiar. On a bright note, we ain't seen that pesky skunk under the porch for quite a spell.

December: A lower family income means a bleak Christmas. We discover that Great Aunt Nimrod has been teaching the kids to "collect the eggs from the cows and milk the chickens"! In addition, Pa's scheme to plant Cheerios and start a donut farm fell through.

Squanto and the Pilgrims revised version

That darn Rand Paul is at it again. Did you see his holiday CD of "All original" Christmas tunes which he "wrote, arranged, and performed"? However, with such titles as Jingle Bells, White Christmas, etc., I'm a bit suspicious.

Yes, the holidays are upon us, and I could not be happier. At last I am receiving real mail from real people, not phony inheritance notices from lawyers in Ethiopia who can't spell.

Now I get thoughtful season's greetings from people like Harry and his life-long partner David, Eddie Bauer, and a Mr. Figi. I do not know who these people are, but I appreciate the fact that they always think of me around this time of the year.

Halloween has come and gone and I'm nearly finished with my supply of black and orange wrapped pieces of cement glob candy, and a good thing too since I only have a few fillings left!

If this holiday season follows the same order as in previous years, and I see no cause for change since the switch from the BCS to a playoff system in college football is not due for another year, Thanksgiving is next in line.

On Thanksgiving we celebrate the first sit-down dinner for the Pilgrims after they had spent an entire year in America eating while standing up since it took that long before someone thought of the concept of a table and chairs. Plus, we are even more thankful that 60" LCD-HD-3D-STD-ADHD TVs are once again on sale for $879!

It was really a miracle that the Pilgrims even crossed the Atlantic safely.

First of all, some voyagers complained because they happened to be standing on deck downwind from some thoughtless people who emptied their chamber pots. In addition, a lot of the passengers on the Mayflower were really ticked off and demanded a refund because they thought that they had signed up for one of those swinging singles Caribbean cruises.

Most of us know that the Pilgrims landed on Plymouth Rock. What isn't so well known is that they intended to land on Chrysler Rock.

Soon after docking the ship, William Bradford's wife jumped overboard and died due to the stress caused by having run out of recipes calling for shoe leather and ship caulking.

A Native American named Squanto quickly became enthralled by the fact that when these strange visitors removed their pointy hats, their heads were exactly the same shape, so he befriended them.

Or did he? Some modern day historians have shown that Squanto was using the invaders to secure his own position of power within the Indian nation by playing one side against another—sort of a 17th-century Hamid Karzai.

Unaware of this, the English valued Squanto as an interpreter while trying to convince the Indians that they should not align with the French because they talk funny and eat sissy food like soufflés and truffles.

Once the pilgrims did figure out what Squanto was up to, he tried to make peace with them by offering free drink coupons at the local casino. They refused but did throw the first Thanksgiving dinner to celebrate all that they were thankful for in the New World.

They were thankful that their ship was called the Mayflower instead of the Chrysanthemum which was a lot more difficult to spell and would not fit on the commemorative t-shirts that they were hawking.

Also they were thankful that they already had universal health care since, no matter the health problem, everyone was treated with beer and amputation, hopefully in that order.

Unfortunately, they did not have forks, only knives, which resulted in a very long dinner since eating the peas alone took hours.

After dinner the Indians and Pilgrims obviously had no football games to watch so they played a Native American game called "run the gauntlet" where one lucky participant, which somehow was always a Pilgrim, got treated like a human piñata. It was a lot of laughs but did mark the beginning of the sports-related concussion issue.

They had no idea of the brain damage being done but became concerned when, afterwards, Miles Standish, the military leader, started twerking the minister.

The Indians who attended were thankful that John Smith was not with the Pilgrims. You may recall that they tried to execute him years earlier because they were tired of his practical jokes like pulling feathers out of their headbands and replacing them with lit sparklers, or lifting warriors' loincloths, snapping photos, then posting them back home in England as selfies.

This probably explains why Pocahontas saved John, signed a huge contract with Disney, and then immediately dumped Smith for another settler, John "Long Rifle" Rolfe.

Personally I'm thankful for cranberry sauce because it makes the dry white meat go down a lot easier.

Santa replaces reindeer with drones

Looks like the School District Morality Police are at it again. They recently posted updated rules for local schools to follow as they celebrate the holiday season. First of all, all references to nutmeg, chestnuts, Nutcracker, Yule log, etc. are banned due to obvious sexual innuendo.

No district school chorus can perform censored songs such as "I Saw Mommy Kissing Santa Claus" "I've Got My Love to Keep Me Warm" "Baby, It's Cold Outside" and South Park's "Chocolate Salty Balls" for obvious reasons. Also on the naughty list are "Ding Dong Merrily on High" and "Angels We Have Heard on High" for blatant illicit drug references, and most certainly banned is the classic "White Christmas" since it is clearly a racist song.

Finally, all depictions of Baby Jesus posted on Facebook must be fully clothed, none of this swaddling stuff.

Nowadays it just seems like it's getting harder to celebrate the holidays in the old-fashioned way. Take Santa Claus for instance. Use to be he would load up on calories all year to be prepared for his exhausting trip around the world to deliver toys. By Christmas Eve he would have a supply of body fat to draw from for energy needed to round up the reindeer, pilot the sleigh, and personally navigate rooftops, enter homes, and deliver packages.

However, after one bucket of Christmas pudding too many, his weight problem got to the point where people were constantly confusing Santa with Frosty the Snowman or, worse, Chris Christy.

In today's health conscious society, Santa's lists contain food additives to avoid along with who's been naughty or nice. No artificial sweeteners for Santa which eliminates nearly every holiday treat known to mankind resulting in an anorexic Santa who simply does not have the stamina to deliver toys the old-fashioned way.

Enter the drone. There are proposals to use drones for everything from farming to spying on one's spouse. Soon personal drones will be as common as cell phones—yikes! Not only will people be trying to drive cars while chatting on the phone, texting, checking the GPS, searching Pandora, ordering pizzas, etc., now you can add to the list controlling an overhead drone to pick up the pizza for them.

Drone rage will be as common as road rage. Can't wait until one of those cute little drones gets fresh with a bald eagle, could get real ugly.

Guess it's only natural that Santa will soon use drones in place of his beloved reindeer. Now, instead of kids leaving unhealthy milk containing lactose and chocolate chip cookies for Santa, they can leave a plate filled with batteries.

Sounds like a fairly harmless switch. But what about the effect on one of the most popular Christmas standards "Rudolph the Red-nosed Reindeer"? The revised version referring to Santa's use of drones just doesn't have the same jolly ring to it:

You know Rockwell and Beechcraft and Boeing and Dragonfly,
Lockheed and Northrop and Teledyne and Firefly,
But do you recall
The most famous Unmanned Aerial Vehicle of all?
Reaper the infra-red-nosed UAV
Had a very shiny nose . . . .
Well, you get the picture.

No doubt the use of drones would make Santa's delivery job much quieter and safer. First of all it would eliminate all that "clatter" in the yard and hooves "prancing and pawing" on the roof which is hard on the shingles and on Dad's head after one too many Mistletoe Madness Martinis.

As far as safety, I can hardly imagine anything more dangerous than Santa stealthily entering a home in Florida, dressed in a red suit with black patent leather boots, and shouting "Ho!" at everyone he sees. Top that off with Santa snarfing down the family's holiday treats and you have the perfect storm for a stand-your-ground defense for homicide.

In addition to using drones to deliver gifts, Santa has also upgraded his Naughty and Nice List by utilizing the services of the National Security Agency (NSA) in place of relying on children's letters although he still accepts tips sent by Edward Snowden who is currently snowed in somewhere in Russia.

Certainly there are some positive aspects to the modernization of Santa's approach to Christmas. For example, there's no denying that Santa's indentured servants, otherwise known as the elves, should not be tolerated in the world today. That is, unless he is willing to move his Toy Shop from the North Pole to the former location of a handbag factory in Guangdong, China. There, the degrading green uniforms and paltry salary of fruitcake and eggnog would fit right in.

Despite such radical changes in some Christmas traditions, we should not lose sight of the season's real meaning. After all, if Sylvester Stallone (67) and Robert De Niro (70) can make one more movie about boxing, then miracles definitely can happen.

Chapter 4   Politics

Angree White Man will pick next president

The other day our next president of these united states John McKain said that Joe the plummer is who he represents because he himself is just the average joe even though he has 40 million dollars that he said he would give us if he could and I believe him! And Sara Painin also said that she is Joe sixpack, I guess cause she drinks Schlitz like me.

Then last week I heard some guy talking about the angree white man vote witch he was thinking would be big and probblee pick the next president. I agree cause that's what I am, the angree white man. Just as that guy did I two voted for the Honourable George UU. Bush both times, even the time when he lost but won!

Poles say that Obamma will win but what do people in Poland know about it?

And I just no that Olabama wont start no war like the Honourable George UU. Bush did and we need war to find weapons that those sneeky arabs are still hiding, probably under those girly clothes they wear.

Also no one will vote for obamma cause his first name was in that sicko movie about cowboys that ride side saddle and ware pink boots called Baroke Back Mountain! Yuck! And why does he get a mountain named after him anyway, he's no Marten Luther Keeng!

Someone said that this compuker would check my speling so I hope its doing good. Looks dang good too me and you?

Yes I know that Maccane has a woman VP and we shure don't need no woman telling us what to do, I been there! Butt she is hot and I would not mind seeing her head on say a quarter some day if you know what I mean, ha ha. Plus she can see Russia can you? Its time we got her in there cause she shoots moose and so do I. And she looks just like that girl on Saturday nite live who is real funny! And she is like Mccane's granddaughter or something so she could take care of him and remind him ware we should go to war next. And she said Obamme hates the usa and we all love it so if he don't like it he can go back to Hawahee.

Also nothing tics me off like illeegals who come here an wont do english. Seems somone could learn them the langwich. I had to learn it good so should they. It drives me nuts when I go to the store and they are saying things which I don't know so I think they are talking about me so I check my zipper an it is ok but I don't know so I don't like it.

I got guns too and am a proud member of NAR too! In fact one of my guns just now accidently fired and scared the crap out of me! Wait a sec, I will put it down. And you kids better shut up or i'll beat the crap out of you to!

Ok where was I, oh yeh, I to get ticked off when some smart alek in india cant tell me how to use this friggin sellfone cause he is dum as dirt or I don't know what he is saying cause he talkes like he is Mahatma Gandee and probably ways 50 pounds and rides around in a riksaw pulled by a skinnier guy who eats ramon noodles all day! Just cause he's got a pHD in compuker science dont make him smart--you think? Heck, I almost got my GDE and it dont make me smart--you think? Heck, if my pickup was runnin I'd drive over to india write now and ring his neck with my pinky!

So I think that guys like me will pick the next president of the usa which we all no will be Jon Mcclaim and even if he doesn't win for real he will anyway because there is still florida where they will hang Chad if he loses but he will win because we want to keep our guns and Obomma is a buddhist and if he wins he will make us shave our heads like munks and walk around like zombees in the movie Night of deadly living, and chant 'om, om, om' and he will take away our pickup trucks and make us jog and hugg trees and sing hip hop and ware our baseball hats sideways!

Anyway, I think that I speek for all angree white men and am typical of them and know that Maccane will kick some Olabama butt. And I would vote to if my parole bored would let me but I still say my old lady had it commin!

god bless usa,

BOO! GOP hopefuls go trick-or-treating

Like the narrator in Poe's famous poem 'The Raven,' one recent evening I was nodding and "nearly napping" when . . . I heard someone knocking. Opening the front door I was greeted by a group of trick-or-treaters including . . . Marco Rubio!

Hey, little fella, what are you supposed to be, I asked?

I'm President of the United States.

Awww, aren't you cute. So, little Marco, why do you want to be president?

'Cause I could show up for work whenever I wanted, and if I was absent and one of those mean old senators gave me crap, I could fire them!

But, Marco, aren't you kind of young and inexperienced, and didn't you . . . .

You must be part of that nasty mainstream media that hates 'Publicans and loves Hillary, that Wicked Witch of the White House who led the attack in Benghazi disguised as an Arab then sent secret zucchini- recipe emails. So either ask me something else or give me that Snickers!

Okay, Marco, it's starting to get dark, so you better run on home. Bye. So who do we have next? Hey, why do you look so sleepy? Wake up, kid. What's your name?

I'm Ben Carson, the next President of this country which is just like Nazis Germany.

Say what? Tell me, why do you think you should be president, Ben?

Well, if there were two scary creatures in Washington joined at the head, I could separate them.

Yeah, like Ted Cruz and Dracula. Any other reason you think you could win the election, Ben? Ben? Ben, are you awake behind that mask?

Huh? Oh, yeah. I can win because I am number one in the latest Republican Iowa poll. And do you know who has won the Iowa GOP caucus in the past? Great American leaders like Pat

Buchanan, Mike Huckabee, and Rick Santorum. Plus, Pat Robertson got second there, and he's a famous billionaire holy man.

Yes, Ben, but doesn't Robertson say crazy things like people die in tornadoes because they don't pray enough and kids celebrate Satan when they dress up for Halloween?

Hey, crazy's in the eye of the beholder—and quit looking at me that way. Thanks for the candy and remember, stay out of prison or you'll turn gay.

Thanks for the tip, Ben, and don't fall asleep while walking home. Well, now, this boy looks vaguely familiar. What's your name?

Trick-or-treat! I'm Jed Bush. No, wait. He's the dad in Beverly Hillbillies. I'm Jeb!

Jeb, who taped that sign on your back that says "Kik me"?

Oh, that darn big brother of mine! I'll never win president with him around. As soon as I said I was running for president, George said "Mission Accomplished" like I'd already won. Then when I dropped like a lead balloon in the national polls he told voters they "misunderestimated" me. Darn him. He just wrecks everything. It was George and Daddy's idea that I should run for president in the first place.

Awww, poor Jeb. Here, have a big ol' sucker and you'll feel better. Bye-bye. Who's next? Hi there, you sure are a big guy. You look too old to be asking for candy. And why are you carrying three bags?

Hey, put a lid on it and just dump in that bowl of candy. I'm Chris Christie, and I'm pretending to be presidential. You got any of those big Hershey's with the almonds? How about some cookies with M&Ms stuck in them? Mmmmm, I love those.

Here, you get one Tootsie Roll.

Whoa, whoa. That's it? I'll make you an offer you can't refuse. Say, you got any bridges here in the neighborhood? Kiss your Social Security good-bye. You better hope you don't have a hurricane here because . . . .

See ya. Oh, my gosh. What is that racket? Who is talking so loud that it sounds like he's using a megaphone?

I'm Donald Trump and I want to make America great again.

Yeah, I can see that by your neon pink cap. Exactly how do you intend to do that?

I will be huge. I don't wear a toupee. Oh, and Cher is a loser.

Why else should people vote for you, Donald?

Would anyone vote for Carly Fiorina? I mean look at that face. I'm a really smart guy. I'm more honest, and my women are more beautiful. My fingers are long and beautiful. I'm very rich. I'm . . . .

Okay, stop, stop! Put away that mirror and hold your Gucci satchel open so I can give you some candy.

Keep your damn candy. I got better stuff at home.

Then I woke up. Whew! Luckily, it was all a nightmare. We couldn't possibly elect such scary creatures, could we? "Quote the Raven 'Nevermore.'"

Celebrity Death Match: The Donald vs. El Chapo

Whereas GOP politicians generally wait until they are elected President of the United States before starting questionable wars, Donald Trump may end up being the first Republican to start a war while still just a candidate for President! His recent comments about Mexico and Mexicans first riled up the Mexican government, which was bad enough, but now he has angered the world's number one drug kingpin, Joaquin "El Chapo" Guzman, and that is a very big deal.

After the cartel leader's recent prison escape, Trump tweeted that whereas Hilary Clinton and Jeb Bush would negotiate with Guzman, "Trump would kick his ass." Guzman responded with a tweet filled with more bleeps than a Lil' Jon rap song, the crux of which was that he was going to get Trump. This led the real estate mogul to immediately contact the FBI and to greatly increase his personal security guard force. Hopefully such precautions will prevent Trump from being the first person tagged in the morgue as "death by tweets."

Despite the current war of words, Donald Trump and Joaquin Guzman actually have some startling similarities when one compares their lives, the most glaring of which is that both men are masters of the construction business: Trump constructs tall towers while Guzman, with just a spoon and a toilet plunger as tools, can dig a mile-long tunnel equipped with lights, an air pump, and a track on which to ride a motorcycle to freedom!

Guzman was born poor in rural Mexico. Sources say the year was either 1954 or 1957. Really, whatever year El Chapo says is okay with me. Heck, I'll say he's 18 years old if that's what he wants.

Trump was obviously born into a bit more upscale lifestyle, and about the age many boys are working on their Eagle Scout badges, both Trump and Guzman were getting into trouble. El Chapo at 15, got kicked out of the house, and started in the marijuana business. Likewise, Trump, even younger at 13, got kicked out of school "for behavior problems" which we can assume involved buying up the other kids' school lunches and reselling them for a profit.

From that point on, Guzman, an aggressive and opportunistic business man, worked his way up through the Mexican drug cartel ranks to become the boss, similar to Trump who played "the boss" on the TV show The Apprentice and would declare "You're fired!" to eliminate candidates from the show. Likewise, Guzman is known to shout "Fire!" and eliminate people from the cartel who fail to make drug deliveries on time.

I'm sure that one can assume there was a lot of backstabbing by both men, some figuratively some literally, as they climbed the ladder of success. In addition, each man has a long history of legal troubles albeit for distinctly different types of infractions. Due to good luck and money up the wazoo, both have dodged convictions and punishment many times, one by paying off pricey lawyers and the other by paying off poor law enforcement officials.

Both men reaped the benefits of their business efforts over time in a number of ways. Forbes ranks both Guzman and Trump among the richest and most powerful men in the world. Evidence of their wealth is quite visible as Trump arrived by helicopter recently for a ribbon-cutting ceremony marking the completion of his new winery, about the same time Guzman was being picked up by a helicopter marking the completion of his prison escape last week.

Their personal lives have parallel aspects also. Guzman has had "at least" four spouses and "at least" ten children which is pretty amazing since his line of work keeps him on the move from hideout to hideout. Trump trails a bit with three spouses and five children, but, despite being 69 years old, may still add to those totals since he is "The Donald."

When one compares their most recent marriages, it's like staring at mirror images. Trump married a former model who is 24 years his junior. Under eerily similar circumstances Guzman married an 18-year-old beauty queen when he was 61. However, the beauty queen title is somewhat suspect as the contest judges may have been unfairly influenced by a well armed Guzman and hundreds of gunmen who rode into town on motorcycles to support her candidacy.

Finally, both men have garnered honors recently. El Chapo was named Public Enemy No. 1 by the Chicago Crime Commission after he vanished from Mexico's most secure prison. Officials are convinced that he used his great wealth to pay for help in pulling off his second prison escape.

Donald Trump's status also reached new heights this past week. In the first major nationwide poll released July 14, Trump is the 2016 Republican presidential frontrunner.

Just goes to show that with enough money you can accomplish about anything, even become President of the United States.

CIA gone wild

Well, they finally did it. They uncovered the WMDs, the Weapons of Mass Destruction—they are the US military brass themselves. Recent news reports have disclosed the biggest US military debacle since General George Armstrong Custer declared, "Backup? I don't need no stinkin' backup!"

Mr. Former Everything Military David Petraeus now faces his most harrowing, dreaded and unforgiving battlefield foe—his wife. He describes her current frame of mind as "beyond furious." Yeah, I can see that. And tell me, how many times have you seen Hilary Clinton smile in the last twelve years? Hell hath no fury like a wife "beyond furious."

According to scientists, men who sleep around are less intelligent than average. Maybe that is why they get caught pretty consistently. An average man who is having an affair just has to explain to his wife the scent of perfume in his hair or the lipstick on his big toe. Petraeus, however, had it a bit tougher and stumbled while attempting to explain to the missus who the pink tank was for.

Obviously, it was easier to get away with this sort of thing back in BC (Before Computers) when Roman emperors could host orgies and cover them up by referring to them as Super PACs. And I don't imagine that an Indian brave in the Wild West would send smoke signals to a mistress arranging a secret rendezvous "behind the large tumble weed" and risk getting caught by his wife Warrior Whacker.

Today such risk takers not only post on Facebook what they did; they post minute-by-minute tweets while they're doing it! Thus proving the above stated scientific theory that they are not very bright.

However, in this case, the perpetrator isn't the lone dodo bird that we should wonder about. After all, CIA doesn't stand for Culinary Institute of America. Doesn't it have something to do with "intelligence"? Weren't the CIA employees just a little bit curious when they heard suspicious moaning sounds coming from the director's office, or did they just assume there was some recreational water boarding taking place?

According to Wikipedia, "The CIA was founded in part for intelligence-gathering as a means to prevent a declaration of war based on erroneous conceptions." Uh, too bad David Petraeus misconstrued the meaning of conception, but he was right on with the application of "erroneous."

It goes on to say that the agency carries out "covert operations." Okay, so a possible defense for Petraeus is that he was simply doing his job—and a darn impressive one at that since he obviously bamboozled approximately 20,000 CIA employees!

Around 20,000 employees and not one suspected any hanky-panky by the director! Not even the maintenance man or the office secretaries who, in every other institution, know everything about everybody. In fact, I use them as my major source of information while on the job.

The CIA finally became interested when they intercepted some emails from the director signed "Rear Admiral Snookums."

Well, duh, someone should have become suspicious about Petraeus and Broadwell a long time ago. I mean just look at the huge grin on his face where he is standing next to her in recently released photos! Whereas, in every official picture he has the Mr. Serious Soldier Dude face on—there's that deviously clever secret agent side coming out.

Of course, in France this sort of political scandal is accepted, even expected. But here, it's . . . it's . . . becoming pretty common place also.

If you recall, last spring there was shocking news centered on some Secret Service agents who were caught hiring prostitutes down in Colombia. It wasn't so shocking that they hired them, or that they agreed to a price of $800. What was shocking was that they were so stupid as to refuse to pay the ladies! Did they actually think that they could get away with that when "Guido," wearing his purple leisure suit and gold car-towing chain necklace with a silver hubcap medallion, is waiting outside in his lowrider1964 Chevy Impala?!

The entire CIA/FBI operations are beginning to look like real-life enactments of the Dilbert comic strip. Does anyone even know what the CIA secret agents are actually doing to justify the $50 billion budget? Okay, I mean besides flying to Florida to attend Jill Kelley's parties? Of course not—it's a secret!

There is fear that Petraeus revealed top secret information to his mistress, such as his favorite cologne. Even more sensitive security threatening documents could be clandestinely passed to our enemies, including photos of Petraeus prancing around in his camouflage Speedos.

Fortunately, the CIA is going to update its ethics policy. For example, add a section that states if your biographer wants to set up an interview at a massage parlor, probably not a good idea.

Giddyup, Trojan Horse, giddyup!

If you're thinking about traveling to Greece to take a selfie with the ancient ruins as a backdrop, better hurry up since the government may soon be loading up the Parthenon in a large U-Haul and taking it to the nearest pawn shop.

Greece, with its $356 billion debt, is so far in hock that the entire country is sort of like a giant version of the legendary Trojan Horse, chock full of people hanging around waiting for someone else to open the trapdoor of opportunity, except, in this case, the repeated bailouts may be more like beating a dead horse.

Over the years, Greeks have elected a string of leaders who just can't seem to get the hang of the concept that a loan can only be repaid if someone in the family is working. With current unemployment in Greece between 25-50%, depending on the age group, there apparently are a lot of people killing time eating goat cheese and telling jokes like "A Greek, an Irishman and a Portuguese go into a bar and order a drink. Who picks up the bill? A German."

Ha, ha. That is really funny until one of the unemployed Greeks strolls over to the ATM machine to get some money only to discover he's already used up his daily allotment of 60 euros so now must move his family out of the upscale cardboard box they've been renting.

The Greek economy was a lot simpler back in 1,000 BC when olive oil was the only currency. Olive oil was used for everything from religious rites to food. Greeks would cover themselves with oil to cleanse the body resulting in villages full of people slipping and sliding and falling down constantly. That's also how the expression "Beware of Greeks bearing gifts" originated as the gift was most likely some more oil which was the last thing anyone needed since all the guys' hair was already so slicked back and greasy that entire towns resembled Elvis impersonator conventions.

Eventually grapes were added to the economy which added some variety to the Greek menu. Of course, a steady diet consisting of just oil and grapes resulted in people spending most of the day sitting on the pot so that they couldn't work, and that's when the country's economic troubles first began.

Around the 10th century BC, Greece went through its Dark Age because other European countries took away all of its candles due to the country's inability to repay a loan of one billion olives. The Greek leaders at that time tried to work out a deal where Greece would simply give back the pits, but the offer was rejected by, whom else, some hard-core early Germanic tribes.

Soon after, things really started to go downhill for the Greek economy because the country developed money and an early form of organized government to waste it. Things got so bad that tenant farmers who could not pay their rent were sold into slavery. Modern-day Greeks just better hope that current German chancellor Angela Merkel doesn't hear about that penalty as an option.

A major development in the Greek economy took place in the 18th century when a Greek shepherd who was strolling on a hillside trail slipped and tumbled down the hill. A few hours later the soaking wet boy ran back to his village to share the startling news that the Mediterranean Sea was ". . . like, right over there!" as he pointed excitedly. Skeptical, the entire village population ran to the cliff edge and jumped off to verify his story. The discovery of the sea led to rapid growth in the shipping of oil, not the kind made from olives or by squeezing Yanni's moustache, but the kind used in cars which Greeks currently can't afford to drive.

Greece switched to the euro in 2001 because it was much easier to spell and pronounce than drachma, a word that came from the Greek verb meaning "to grasp" which is exactly what the European Union has accused Greece of doing in recent years. The term euro is certainly a cinch to say compared to the Greek sandwich called a gyro which you most likely mispronounced just now since many Greeks can't even get it right. In fact, the Greek voters were so impressed with Alexis Tsipras' ability to pronounce the sandwich correctly that they elected him their new prime minister.

Tsipras ran on the platform that he would renegotiate the Greek debt. Furthermore, he promised that he would follow that up with acquiring a new loan so his people would finally have enough money to paint some of their houses a color other than white.

Of course it might help if he would first deal with the graft, corruption, and tax evasion issues that plague the country. Otherwise, his election promises will sound as hollow as the Trojan Horse.

Give me your tired, your poor, your southpaw pitchers with a blazing fastball

Nothing like a long, boring baseball game to give political leaders an opportunity to sit and hash out their differences. Why, entire political revolutions have taken place in less time than it takes to watch a televised game when you have to patiently endure images in the dugout of players spitting gallons of gross stuff and managers struggling to stay awake.

So there were President Obama and President Raul Castro at a Tampa Bay Rays exhibition game in Cuba earlier this week sharing their nachos with everyone sitting in the stands in true communist fashion. On this historical occasion, they, along with thousands of baseball fans, were soaking up some Cuban sunshine which is pretty much free right now, but just wait until Marriott, AT&T, Major League Baseball, etc. get their greedy capitalistic hands on it.

This season a ticket for a decent seat to a Rays game in Florida costs around $40, and you'll fork over $7 for something called a

"Cuban" sandwich. In contrast, admission to a game in Cuba will run you $0.12, and it's a mere $0.80 for a ham sandwich. You can bet your bottom peso that will soon change.

On this day, the Tampa Bay Rays defeated the Cuban national team which is just a tad bit short of talented players since the really good ones are playing in the United States. Why is that, you might ask. I'm just going to guess that it's because in this country a person has the freedom to be grossly overpaid to play a game for a living.

Talented Cuban ballplayers can earn million of dollars playing in the U.S. Whereas, in Cuba all players earn $125 per month. That's why you see Cuban players here arriving at the ballpark in a Rolls-Royce or a Porsche while in Cuba the team members ride bicycles to the stadium on game day.

Or if a baseball player is fortunate enough to own a car back home in Cuba, it's most likely the very popular 1953 Chevrolet Bel-Air. Pictures of traffic on the streets of Havana give one the impression that all those jalopies traded in during the 2009 Cash for Clunkers rebate program were shipped to Cuba. That's one of the reasons that I am personally excited about opening up trade with Cuba; maybe I can get top dollar for my 1994 Dodge van.

Normalization of relations between the U.S. and Cuba will have a dramatic effect on other aspects of the island-nation's culture besides baseball, for example music. One has to admit that even a vintage 1953 Chevy looks pretty youthful compared to The Rolling Stones who hit the stage in Havana for a free concert on March 25, the first British rock band to ever perform an open-air concert in Cuba.

While visiting, perhaps the Stones can take advantage of the very highly regarded medical care system in Cuba. Medical technology there must be quite amazing when one considers that former president Fidel Castro has been rumored to be dead at least three times and, yet, he shows up again. Keith Richards, are you listening?

Speaking of Fidel Castro, the political leader of Cuba for nearly 50 years, a biographer stated that he could be "vindictive and unforgiving." That he could be "a bad loser" who would act with "ferocious rage if the thought that he was being humiliated." It was also a well known fact that Castro would throw tantrums and make "snap judgements which he refused to back down from." Overall he was "intolerant of those who did not share his view."

In addition, Castro was quite the ladies' man. One conservative calculation is that Fidel fathered eleven children by seven different women and was married at least three times.

Doesn't this description of Fidel Castro bring to mind a certain front-running GOP presidential candidate? However, there is one glaring difference: during his speeches, Castro would frequently quote and cite various documents and books that he had actually read.

Most GOP presidential candidates have voiced disagreement with the current administration's move towards renewed relations with Cuba. Asked how he felt about Cuba, Donald Trump replied that he would build a wall to stop any Muslims hiding in Cuba from sneaking into the U.S. When told that Cuba is an island ninety miles off the coast of Florida, Trump said, "So first I will build a HUGE bridge then put a wall on it."

Even Ted Cruz has spoken strongly against opening up diplomatic relations with Cuba which is really baffling since, based on his family roots, if he does not gain the GOP nomination for president in the U.S., Cruz is clearly qualified to run for president of Cuba.

Both Trump and former presidential candidate Marco Rubio expressed opinions in regard to various brands of famous Cuban cigars. Rubio accused Trump of having a Short Panetela while Trump countered that all the ladies know he has a Giant Perfecto.

GOP ponders what not to do next

Republican leaders in Congress are still reeling from the shock of President Obama's announcement last week that he is taking action on immigration reform. They are not so much distressed by what he is doing as they are by the fact that he is doing anything at all.

"The fact that the President sounds serious about doing something caught all of us off guard, "gasped John Boehner as he struggled to cease hyperventilating. "Sure, declaring wars like Bush did is fine, but this action is to help people! Why?"

Congressman Boehner went on to declare, "The 36% of eligible voters who cast ballots and overwhelmingly supported Republican candidates in the midterms gave Washington a clear mandate that they wanted to continue the do-nothing leadership of this country—the President apparently did not get the message."

When asked about his Time Magazine post-election statements "I think we [Congress] have an obligation . . . to begin to function again," and that his goal now is to "just get stuff done," Kentucky senator Mitch McConnell winked, shrugged his shoulders, and said, "Shucks, I was just joshing you folks."

McConnell went on to justify not having done anything as a Congressman over the years, outside of helping his home state coal industry, by stressing, "I've just been too busy working on various committees planning what not to do next. Believe me, my docket is chock-full of jobs to avoid doing. Besides, if I did actually do something then I would have nothing left to not do . . . which would make me appear lazy."

Fortunately, Senator McConnell does not have sole responsibility of planning what not to do next. He is assisted daily by dozens of personal staff members including directors, aides, correspondents, secretaries, assistants, etc. in thoughtfully putting together a "Not to do list." "Thank goodness for their help," expressed an obviously grateful McConnell, "or I'm sure that I would forget not to do something and accidentally do something to help the nation. No doubt my Republican colleagues would rib me to no end if I did that! "

Assumed 2016 presidential candidate Rand Paul, a leader at avoiding taking action by filibustering in the Senate, was asked if he thought that Republicans would change and actually do anything over the next two years. "Why sure," he responded, "take for example right now. I'm standing here speaking to you about all of the things that I have not done during my first three years in office.

Now, isn't that doing something? Plus, I've written up a declaration of war to carry on the time-honored Republican tradition." Paul then added, "And I did not plagiarize that response."

Of course, there is a whole laundry list of actions that Republicans in the next session could choose to not do, such as not vote for President Obama's future office nominees, not approve the budget, not fund the immigration executive order, etc. One Tea Party senator hinted, "After a lot of soul-searching, what my heart tells me is the best course of inaction is to vote for another government shutdown which I realize is sort of like doing something, but at least after all the hard work of saying "Yea" I will get another paid vacation and can resume doing nothing."

Other Republican leaders feel like it is time to end the government dysfunction. Governor Chris Christie told NBC that the new Congress needs to bridge the communication gap between parties. "You know, if the bridge isn't open, folks can't cross the river," he philosophized with a smirk.

Congressman Boehner agreed that the midterm election results show that the country is tired of years of gridlock and antagonism so Republicans must reach across the aisle in Congress, embrace their Democratic colleagues, and hand them copies of the lawsuit he is filing against the President over the Affordable Care Act. "Republican presidents Nixon, Ford, Bush all pretended to pursue health care reform laws and failed. But they were just kidding. This guy was serious!"

One newly elected Republican representative echoed those sentiments and feels that the GOP must now govern responsibly. "My first act of conciliation once I'm sworn into office will be to remove gridlock and move to impeach the President. By actually getting things accomplished he sets a dangerous precedent. Why I haven't even picked out my office décor yet, and people are already asking me what I'm going to do."

According to Time Magazine, "Change" is what the Republican controlled Congress is promising. But just like the guy in the nursing home where I once worked was told to "change" his dirty underwear and simply took them off, turned them inside out, and put them back on, one gets the distinct feeling that the new Congress is going to smell even worse than the old one.

Health care costs spur need for more health care

Boy, a lot of people sure are upset about the recent Supreme Court ruling in regard to the Affordable Care Act. Some claim that it was unfair, that Chief Justice Roberts got mixed up and thought no health care was bad when actually it is good. Other folks are certain that this ruling will result in a Nazis/Communist/Vegan government takeover. Meanwhile, Tea Partiers wonder if they can't appeal to a yet higher court, say the Intergalactic Divine Court of Wookiees.

Of course the ruling had an immediate negative effect on the stock market, which was briefly offset by good news in the dog house construction industry, which was instantly dragged back down by, who else, those economically challenged Greeks!

I have determined that, without a doubt, there is a direct connection between the bleak economic picture and health care reform based on the fact that I nearly have a stroke each month when I open my bank statement.

Within the health care debate, some people state that they fear socialized medicine which implies that they favor anti-social medicine. It seems that we already have plenty of that. Just try to strike up a friendly conversation with your physician the next time he is poking that little flashlight in your ear and wondering why the light is exiting from the opposite ear.

No one disagrees--other than doctors, insurance companies, drug companies, pharmacists, lawyers, Republican members of Congress, Charlie Sheen, etc.--that some health care reform is necessary. The situation is obviously pretty bad when Texas ranks in the top 100 in the list of places with the worst health care in the world, just one spot ahead of North Korea. However, women's rights in North Korea rank well ahead of those in Texas.

Idaho's own Governor Otter has appointed 26 people to discuss the state health insurance exchange, but the initial meeting has been delayed due to health reasons as most of the people got mysteriously ill upon learning about their appointment and can't afford to be treated.

The program that they eventually form will be known as Ottercare which sort of sounds like a wildlife rehab center.

To help these people with their task, I have a few suggestions. How about installing insurance dispensers similar to Redbox movie rentals? That way if a person is about to embark on a particularly dangerous experience like going shopping at 4 AM on Black Friday, which is comparable in physical risk to a UFC cage match with a herd of Sasquatches, he or she could simply purchase health insurance for a few hours.

Maybe the committee could recommend that the insurance companies make some simple changes in their policies. For example, it would be nice if the "Exceptions" section of a policy wasn't ten times longer than the list of what is actually covered. It is sort of like a store sale ad for 50% off all clothing. But when you finish reading the "Does not include" list all that remains on sale is a pair of red and green Santa socks.

Here are some basic medical care cost-cutting measures. During visits to a clinic patients should have the option to decide exactly what they want done beforehand. It should be like the counter at a fast food restaurant. "I'll take a strep throat check and a dozen of those generic antibiotics; hold the ear poking and testicle squeezing." I mean if the toenail on my big toe is black then I probably don't need to have my blood pressure checked

At the clinic they could easily cut costs by not having one person hand you a form to fill out, another person type up the insurance stuff, and a third person lead you to the exam room where you sit waiting for 30 minutes and stare at glass containers full of cotton swabs, tongue depressors, band aides, etc., which makes you sicker realizing they are going to cost you around $20 each as they are used and then dumped in the trash can.

Also, whereas in Medieval Bologna, which once was located between the ancient cities of Mayonnasia and Lettucius in Italy, midwives had to swear not to use magic when helping with a birth, the new law could state that doctors must first try a magical spell to cut costs. What harm could possibly be done, other than the fact that you may be changed from a man with warts into one giant wart?

Finally, the best rule change would be that all medical facilities are required to post a notice that reads "If your treatment does not work, there is no charge." Sounds fair to me, and I'm quite confident that alone would help speed up the patient's recovery.

Hogzilla votes in South Carolina

Recently, South Carolina Republicans were up in arms after it was discovered that a 1,050-lb. Hogzilla, wearing a washtub as a football helmet, inexplicably got past poll workers and voted, not just once, but twice, in a local county election.

One poll worker, retired crawdad breeder Clarence Clodsucker, commented, "Shucks, I just thought he was a linebacker for the Gamecocks . . . and the other one was his twin."

South Carolina, as you recall, elected the late Strom Thurmond eight times to serve in the Senate. He was still a senator at the age of 100, and only decided to retire two years after he died, despite the protests of South Carolinians who offered to continue hauling his mummified remains to the capital by buggy.

In case you have forgotten, Hogzilla was created when two domestic pigs were raised on the Mississippi "Fast Track to Gastric Bypass Diet." It's the same diet followed by many obese Mississippi children (Mississippi--a Cherokee word meaning "land of broken teeter-totters").

In Mississippi, the public school system has a state test similar to the ISAT in Idaho. Only there it is called the IEAT.

Another similarity to Idaho schools is that, at one point, the Mississippi students were given laptops, but the computers kept getting lost in the students' laps and most never resurfaced, so the program was scrapped.

Due to its morbid obesity rate, Mississippi, once known as "The Hospitality State," now has the license plate slogan "The Hospitalized State."

Anyway, in response to this outrageous voter fraud event, Republicans in South Carolina, and other southern states, have enacted new voter identification laws.

Voters in South Carolina now must present a photo ID along with NRA and KKK membership cards.

The South, once a Democratic voter block, drawled into the Republican camp when the party adopted the God, Guns, and Gays platform. For one thing, it was easier to memorize.

More specifically, Mississippi ranks as the most religious state, mainly because residents pray a lot that they can move elsewhere. Secondly, Southerners need their guns to protect themselves from . . . other Southerners. And as far as gays go, just watch Deliverance again and you'll understand.

Most of the states in the Deep South rank near the worst in poverty, health, education, perspiration, etc. In fact, if it hadn't been for their ability to excel in college football, they would have been allowed to secede, no problem.

People in the South still largely cling to the myth that President Obama is not a U.S. citizen. They give reasons such as, "Dawg nabbit, we in jawja don't take to furaners who come here from wihee. Gol dern it, he might even be Eye-talian!"

Southern Baptists believe that women should submit to their husbands which is pretty difficult to do since in most Southern families the wife is gone to work while the husband is home raiding the fridge, wondering if anyone will miss the hog jowls if he eats them for a snack.

To get back to the main issue, many experts question whether voter fraud is even that much of a problem. There have only been 10 cases of verified voter fraud over the last 200 years.

The first involved one of General George Armstrong Custer's men who raised both hands when Custer asked, "Now, how many vote that we shouldn't ride into that valley?"

The remaining incidences of voter fraud occurred in the 1984 presidential election when a visibly confused guy named Reagan went into the voting booth nine times mistaking it for a Satellite toilet.

Research shows that voter fraud occurs at a rate of about 0.0004% of the time--approximately the same rate as your chances to get struck by lightning or for a Democrat to get elected in Idaho.

The true problem, it seems, is not stopping people from voting multiple times; the problem is to get them to vote once. The U.S. should really be embarrassed. During one 35-year stretch, only 48% of the electorate voted for president. Whereas in Russia, every election involving Vladimir Putin has generated at least a 139% turnout!

Even more impressive is that Saddam Hussein, former leader of Iraq, won every single vote every time he decided to have an election. Okay, there was that one guy, Abdul Insane Kabib, who voted for someone else.

As a result, Kabib became an overnight legend and his bravery was honored at Saddam's victory picnic where he was barbequed and served as the main dish—a delectable Shish Kabib.

When all is said and done, perhaps compulsory voting laws are the answer. In Bolivia, citizens who do not vote may be denied access to their salary for three months. Maybe Mississippi could enact a similar law, except non-voters would be denied dessert instead.

Huffing, puffing and howling mad about wolves

Some people you can trust, some you cannot. Charlton Heston said that they would have to pry his gun from his cold, dead hands and they did, but now they're not sure what to do with his hands. But then there's Gov. Butch Otter who long ago vowed to get rid of the wolves in Idaho. He boldly said, "I'm prepared to bid for that first ticket to shoot a wolf myself." And either he is a very bad shot or he reneged on his campaign promise because there are still wolves everywhere one looks. I mean, look out my window this very moment! There goes one now dragging my little poodle Fifi to a gruesome demise. But the wolves must go for another reason.

Now I'm not one to normally buy into conspiracy theories. For example I see no validity to the theory that Lee Harvey Oswald was Marilyn Monroe in disguise who killed JFK in a crime of passion triggered by her eventual discovery that "Jackie" Onassis was actually a woman.

It is also highly doubtful that dinosaur-like alien reptiles who must consume human blood to maintain their human appearance are ruling the world. Although I have to admit that Libya's leader "Daffy" Gaddafi does somewhat resemble a predatory velociraptor when he stands at the podium.

That being said, I must admit that I am intrigued by the widely held theory that wolves have actually formed a terrorist operation. And the craziest part of all this is that its headquarters is right here in Idaho. Some may scoff at the notion that wolves could disguise themselves as terrorists. However, didn't a wolf once give a very convincing impersonation of Grandmother? And if that is true, then surely one could mistake a wolf for 911 architect Khalid Sheikh Mohammed — I mean he could actually be a wolf in sheikh's clothing!

Of course, wolves have been connected to other terrorist-type acts. They've been known to eat cows. That is sort of like a suicide bombing since over time the wolves will get fat and blow up from high cholesterol. Then there was the wolf that literally "blew" down the little pigs' houses, but they probably would have been foreclosed on during the recession anyway. If further proof is needed, chew on this: the word "terror" spelled backwards is "rorret." If that isn't the sound of a growling wolf, I don't know what is!

Thank goodness the government stepped in to alleviate the problem, making it legal to kill a wolf under certain conditions.

For some time now one has been allowed to kill a wolf if one feels that it is causing "worry" to domesticated animals. I'm not exactly sure how you can determine what a pet or farm animal is worried about. My dog starts shaking and runs under the bed if I mention "bath." If I was a cow I'd break out into a cold sweat every time the neighbor fired up the charcoal grill.

And as far as a chicken appearing worried, isn't that their natural state? Isn't that how they got their name in the first place? And what if we had the same law involving humans? That would open up some real interesting possibilities. To defend a homicide, I could claim that I was worried that he was worrying about me, so I bumped him off first.

It does seem that the law is a bit one-sided. If leaders of countries can invade nations for no reason and kill thousands of innocent people without any punishment, why should a wolf die because it happened to be in the area when a sheep appeared worried?

Couldn't a wolf claim that it was a preemptive strike? What if there is a sissy wolf who is actually scared of sheep? Can I then shoot the bully sheep?

I think a lot of the wolves' problem is a result of bad PR. What if wolves changed their name? The very sound of "wolf" conjures up evil images. On the other hand, some animals' names sound all cuddly and innocent. Although, it's pretty obvious this strategy didn't work with the GOP to Tea Party morph.

So, for example, wolves could change their name to Forest Poodle and suddenly we have a former wolf named Tinkerbell dressed in pink, sporting sunglasses and all snuggled up against Paris Hilton's ... uh, shoulder. You see, it's all a matter of branding and good PR.

Despite all of the bad press connected to wolves, I do recall a feel-good article with wolves playing a key role. It involved a lady in Owyhee County who raised pet wolves and was feeding cats to them. Just goes to show that wolves aren't all bad.

Iceland sees economy melting away

Well, it's finally official. The nation's economy is in a recession. Personally, I have been suffering a recession for years, which I am reminded of each morning when I look at my hairline in the mirror.

And how did the experts arrive at such a startling conclusion? First off, recent figures indicate that consumer spending dropped by a record amount last month, mainly because of a drop in big ticket items such as airplanes. That comes as no surprise. I can easily imagine that, just like me, the average American consumer already has three or four airplanes lying around and figures that's enough!

In support of that claim, a press release by Santa stated that letters he has received this year have shown a 30% decrease in the number of planes requested. Secretly, he is glad because he has a heck of a time getting a Cessna down a chimney.

In another cruel economic twist, now that cars are nearly affordable and gas is half as much as it was when I woke up this morning and dropping by the minute, it just so happens that nearly everybody is unemployed so what good does it do? Where are we going to drive to? We can't drive to work since there are no jobs.

Oh, sure, we can always fill up our quad-cab premium-sucking Made-in-the-USA SUV and sit in the driveway watching a DVD on our HD LCD dual screen television built into the visors, leaving the motor running to keep us warm since gas is so darn inexpensive, and contemplate how the domestic auto industry got into such a fix. However, even that gets old after a while.

But it's not just the United States that is in the throes of an economic downturn. The world, no, make that the entire galaxy, is in a recession. Heck, things have gotten so bad that even the remote country of Iceland cannot escape verging on the edge of bankruptcy.

Iceland's gross domestic product totals around 12 billion dollars per year. That is nearly equal to what GM is currently requesting from Congress in Washington so that the auto makers' CEO's can purchase eggnog for their annual employee Christmas bash.

I used to think that "gross domestic product" referred to a country's yearly output of vomit, phlegm, and Rush Limbaugh broadcasts. But in Iceland's case it refers to the producing and exporting of fish, vodka, and steam, which are exactly what a typical "night on the town" in Iceland consists of during the cold, dark months which run from January 1 to December 31 each year.

Surprisingly, most people are not aware of the fact that Iceland is the biggest exporter of steam in the world. If you don't believe it, next time you're sitting in a sauna check closely for the "Made in Iceland" label on the steam floating around.

In contrast, the largest import to Iceland is cement. This is due to the fact that efforts at construction with bricks made of fish, vodka, and steam failed because the walls were eventually eaten.

The highway system in Iceland consists of a stretch called Pjoovegur which, when pronounced, sounds a lot like my dog when he sneezes. This road circles "almost completely around Iceland." At the end of the paved section there is a huge parking lot (constructed from frozen fish, vodka, and steam) in which travelers park their vehicles, lick their parking spot for a quick energy snack, strap on ice skates, and resume their journey.

At least in Iceland the people have a number of entertaining sports to indulge in while waiting out the money crisis which they have decided to solve by melting every county that begins with the letters "Fj" and selling them as bottled water.

One popular sport in Iceland is glima, a form of folk-wrestling in which competitors are not allowed to push their opponents down "in a forceful manner" which makes it a lot like the Notre Dame defense this past football season. In addition, Icelanders have won more Strongman competitions than any other people, probably a result of the national pastime of pushing cars which refuse to start in the frigid climate.

Even eating takes on an extreme sport feel as Icelanders feast on rotten shark, sheep heads, and ram testicles, washing it all down with a big gulp of blood pudding. Yum, yum. No wonder the bank crisis is relatively easy for Icelanders to swallow.

Looking ahead I am confident that Americans and Icelanders will stand tall once again as their economies rebound, although the people in The Land of Fire and Ice are far more likely to slip and fall on their sidewalks than we are.

In an election far, far away

A new year is coming right up, and something tells me that we're in for a long haul ahead. It's bad enough that I just got the hang of writing 2015 on checks and now somebody's changing the year on me! And something tells me that we will subjected to another 365 daily media doses of the Kardashians and the Jenners with the average person still trying to figure out which is which and how in the heck these people make a living.

But the real reason the first eleven months of the new year will be as tiresome as the old year is because of the presidential campaign. This whole thing is already getting old but, to use a Hollywood term, we've only seen the trailer.

Just as Hollywood has the slow buildup for its projected blockbusters down to an art form, that's sort of what we're getting now in the presidential campaign. This trend seems especially true on the GOP side In fact, many of the characters in this campaign have distinct parallels to those in the Star Wars movies, including the current holiday runaway hit "Star Wars: The Force Awakens."

Just as R2-D2 shows up every time a new Star Wars movie hits the screen, so too does Mike Huckabee show up whenever there is another presidential election. Huckabee's campaign rhetoric makes about as much sense as R2's "Beep boop beep boop." As one writer asked, "Is Huckabee running for pope or president?"

Ted Cruz is the C-3PO of the GOP. Droid-like, Cruz is about as dynamic as his podium in debates. Also, one of Threepio's functions is to keep things running smoothly, be a mediator. Like when the other candidates criticize Donald Trump, Cruz says, "I like Donald Trump. I think he's terrific." It appears that Cruz will say that about anyone if he thinks it will benefit him someway.

For comic relief, the GOP slate features Carli Fiorina. Just as past Star Wars movies had Jar Jar Bink, a character based on Disney's Goofy. Fiorina just seems to have a knack for telling such obvious whoppers that they are laughable, like when she confused a Planned Parenthood video with "The Texas Chainsaw Massacre." Besides, as Trump has implied, she sort of resembles Jar Jar.

Chris Christie makes a perfect Jabba the Hut in this conservative cast of characters. No, no, it's not what you think. I would not stoop that low other than mentioning that Jabba too has an insatiable appetite. No, what I have in mind is that, just as Jabba is the most powerful crime boss in Tatooine, Christie relishes projecting the Jersey tough-guy persona who, as president, will likely make offers no one can refuse. While Jabba surrounds himself with a cast of shady characters to carry out his dirty deeds, Governor Christie has been known to coerce his political cronies to, you know, close bridges and stuff.

I can't believe that I'm even saying this, but Jeb Bush so far is actually playing the part of the intelligent guy in this script, sort of like Chewbacca, the Wookiee. Unfortunately, this may explain why his voter support has nosedived. It's similar to how Hollywood knows that movies full of bluster and brashness always sell more tickets than Shakespeare.

Of course, the star of this whole cinematic political production is Donald Trump. Quite honestly, I never really pegged Trump to play the evil character Darth Vader until I read the comments that Trump has made about war. Then the light bulb went on in my head. Of course, that light bulb is no longer the bright spotlight it once was, and is now more comparable to the tiny LED on my phone which indicates my battery is dead. Well, not MY battery but the phone's.

Trump has stated "I love war" and that it would be nice if the U.S. and Russia could "knock off" an enemy together. He later added, "With nuclear, the power, the devastation is very important to me." And, as his spokesperson said, what's the sense of having all these nuclear weapons if we're not going to use them. Why, you can almost hear Darth Vader's amplified breathing through Trump's hyperventilating over the mere thought of nuclear war.

Perhaps Trump should listen to the Star Wars character Yoda who said, "A Jedi uses the Force for knowledge and defense. Never for attack."

The philosophical Yoda also offers insight concerning Trump's fearmongering comments about immigration and certain religious beliefs: "Fear is the path to the dark side. Fear leads to anger. Anger leads to hate. Hate leads to suffering."

It's just becoming more and more obvious that Donald Trump has been overtaken by the dark side of the Force. In the media we see Trump utilizing the force choke, the force crush, and, most terrifying of all, force rage when he channels his anger to increase his own speed, strength, and ferocity to silence and destroy his critics.

And we see, as Ben Obi-Wan Kenobi warned us, "The Force can have a strong influence on the weak-minded," which possibly explains Trump's persistent rise in GOP voting polls. Maybe voters should ponder Obi-Wan's rhetorical question: "Who's the more foolish, the fool or the fool who follows him?"

It's a bird, a plane, a billion dollars with wings!

A lot of political Hawks were concerned that President Obama would be soft on military policies, but with the recent deal to purchase F-35 jet fighter planes we can all rest assured that the U.S. will continue to lead the world in buying cool, outrageously expensive, high-tech weapons that are essentially useless.

Former Commander-in-Chief George W. Bush, by the way, is spending his retirement doing the honorable thing, finishing up his National Guard commitment after going AWOL back in the 70's. He will eventually receive the equivalent of a Guard GED.

Too bad Idaho failed in its bid to be the future home for the F-35, but all is not lost since the state is still in the running to supply

French fries for the Warthogs Unlimited banquet held annually in Lopjaw, Mississippi, home of the inventor of the soft toilet seat.

Even though the F-35 fighter jet sounds awesome, news reports concerning its capabilities raise some questions. For example, if it is virtually invisible due to its uncanny stealth ability, then how will we, the taxpaying citizens, not to mention the military brass, know that we have received the goods as advertised? If we can't see the F-35, then what proof do we have that we actually have it?!

In response to this question, Lockheed Martin representative Billy "Big" Diehl replied that even if we can't see the plane, we will certainly be able to hear it. Which raises another concern: couldn't the thunderous boom at takeoff cause hearing damage to humans nearby?

Diehl went on to say that he personally has heard F-35's take off hundreds of times with no ill effects on his hearing. When asked about the loudness concerns voiced by people in Boise, Diehl responded, "Noisy? I just addressed that issue!"

With the national debt doubling with each word that I type, cost for the F-35 must also be carefully scrutinized. The total cost for the F-35 project is around $300 billion which is just a tad bit less than Lebron will earn next season.

Now don't get me wrong, if the military leaders say that we need 2,500 jets that can talk, think, and text one another while traveling nearly 1500 mph without wrecking, then I say cut teachers' pay and buy the dang thing. But one has to wonder if this is what we need to best defeat our current enemies. And how does it compare to what they are spending on weapons?

Last I checked we were at war against Iraq and Afghanistan. This is not a John Wayne "Flying Tigers" type of war. This is more like crawling around in the sand picking out the good turbans from the bad turbans warfare. This is detecting explosives hidden in a false camel hump before allowing it to enter the Marine mess hall. Yet Lockheed Martin claims that the F-35 can do that – hmmmm.

And how about cost comparison? Total cost for one plane is approximately $200 million. Compare that expense to the current enemies' weapons of choice. One stick of dynamite and a roll of duct tape come to about $151.98, plus you get a discount coupon good on your next purchase, which, of course, is worthless to a suicide bomber.

The dynamite is then taped to a human; no cost there since he/she forgot to get paid in advance. Or it is placed in a car which, in Iraq, based on what I am seeing on the nightly newscast, is most likely a 1989 Ford Fiesta, retail value $490.

Of course Iraq does have an Air Force which, when it began in 2004, consisted of just 35 people. Though they had no planes at the time, one officer stated that he thought he saw a plane in the sky once ". . . but, alas, it turned out to be a large grain of sand in my eye. "

However, in a recent press release, Abdul "Top Gun" Mohammed, Iraq's Imperial Supreme Universal Commander of Fantastic Flying Machines, proudly announced plans for the future that include securing a deal which would result in the purchase of "a plane with both wings intact" from Yugoslavia, the same country which introduced the highly dependable Yugo to the auto industry last century.

Then there is the Afghanistan Air Force currently consisting of 40 planes which were purchased from a variety of international sources such as eBay, Craigslist, and also from some local outlets including garage sales in Kabul and a shifty looking door-to-door salesman named Khan who was dragging behind an extremely large suitcase.

Interestingly, at one time the Afghan Air Force's planes carried the inscription "God is Great" under a wing. However, after the U.S. invasion in 2001, when 90% of the Afghan planes were destroyed while still on the ground, the slogan was changed to "God is OK."

Kanye hip-hops over Trump

Here I was all set to vote for Donald Trump for president. After all, you can't help but admire a man who's living out the male fantasy of behaving like a seventh-grade boy again, who can call anyone who disagrees with him "stupid" and "a loser" and not only avoid punishment but be loved all the more for it!

In addition, Trump is a classic rags-to-riches American success story. Despite starting out with a measly $200 million, Trump fought and clawed his way to the top to become a real estate mogul. Add to his impoverished background the fact that he was physically able to overcome a lifetime struggle with a bone spur in one of his heels, an affliction that resulted in a military deferment during the Vietnam War, and Trump's success is truly inspirational. Sadly, he cannot recall which heel it was, no doubt a result of bone spur PTSD.

But now a political bombshell has caused me to reconsider my choice for 2016. At the Video Music Awards show this past week, Kanye West announced that he will run for president in 2020. Of course, he probably meant 2016, but when you're busy being the greatest rapper/hip-hop artist in the world, who has time to keep close tabs on politics or even occasionally check a calendar.

Kanye vs. Trump will be the most exciting presidential race in history. Never have there been two candidates with a knack for telling it like it is, or isn't, or could be somewhere in a galaxy far, far away.

When he announced his run for president, Trump humbly described himself as the "most successful person ever to run for the presidency, by far." So how does a candidate top that? Well, step aside, Donald, for Kanye believes that "For me to say I'm not a genius I'd be lying to you and to myself."

Trump emphasizes that he is the anti-politician when he says things like, "I think people of the country are tired of being ripped off by politicians . . . ." Yet Kanye got a leg up on Trump in the anti-Washington label competition when he declared, "I'm not no politician, bro." Now, that's the kind of talk that gives goose bumps to you, me, and all our . . . uh, bros who are disenchanted with Washington insiders and want leaders who refuse to be politically correct—or even grammatically correct.

When Trump boasted, "I will be the greatest jobs president that God ever created," people got pretty excited. That is until Kanye revealed, "I am the number one human being in music. That means any person that's living or breathing is number two."

Wow, Kanye's ahead of all people living or breathing, though I'm not sure that you can be doing one without doing the other. Still, that's the kind of confidence I want my president to have, and to heck with science.

Obviously, Trump can be a bully which is another reason we love him. If anyone asks him a question that he cannot answer with "I'm really rich" or "It's going to be huge," he kicks them out of the room. Billionaires can do that sort of thing.

Yet he pales in comparison to Kanye who physically shoves people aside and grabs the microphone whenever he feels slighted at an awards show, proclaiming, "You may be talented, but you're not Kanye West." Such audacity will truly make America great again.

Trump stated to a conservative crowd in Michigan that his favorite book is the Bible. Some critics doubt the truthfulness of that claim. Kanye, on the other hand, refuses to pander to his audiences and has boasted, "I am a proud nonreader of books." And I have to admit I see no reason to doubt his word.

When asked to share his favorite Biblical verse, Trump has responded that is a personal thing and "I don't want to get into specifics." Kanye is much more forthcoming about his deep knowledge of the Good Book: "The Bible had 20, 30, 40, 50 characters in it. You don't think that I would be one of the characters of today's modern Bible?" Why, the man is a veritable Biblical scholar.

Trump graciously says that his third wife, former model Melania, is a blessing. That's sweet. But Kanye, being the romantic devil that he is, put it best when discussing his wife, Kim Kardashian: "Kim doesn't understand what a blessing I am to her."

Both men have political connections. Trump has donated money to members of both parties. But Kanye has close ties to the White House as President Obama once called him "a jackass."

Yes, this will be an election campaign for the ages: Trump vs. Kanye. Trump recently said, "One of the key problems today is that politics is such a disgrace, good people don't go into government." Amen, Donald, amen.

North Korean leader looks up to. . . everyone

I do not understand why people get so excited over the Masters Golf Tournament which was just completed last weekend. Despite birdies, bogeys, and bunkers, oh my, none of those guys came close to achieving what The Great Man Who Descended from Heaven, otherwise known as Kim Jong-il, accomplished while leader of North Korea. In case you have never heard, he shot 5 holes-in-one the very first time that he played golf then retired from the sport. Now that's golfing!

Not only that, but he also scored a perfect 300 the first time he went bowling, although in the video you can clearly see little hands popping out each time to knock over the 9 or 10 pens still standing after the ball has disappeared. Oh yeah, he even invented the hamburger between bowling frames.

All this from a guy who only stood 4' 10" while standing on the backs of two prostrate members of the Socialist Comrades Under Me party, known as SCUM for short. He also had the odd habit of surrounding himself with kidnapped midgets so as to look taller. Strangest of all, Kim had expressions that he considered belittling deleted from the language: Are you getting short with me? short order cook; came up short; I'll be there shortly; a short in the wire, etc.

If you recall, as the Guiding Sun Ray grew closer to leaving this earth and entering that celestial totalitarian kingdom in the sky, his first choice as an heir to his throne, and the fur- covered portable doggy stairway he used to ascend it, was the eldest son, Kim Yo-Yo. However the young man fell out of favor when he was caught trying to sneak into Tokyo Disneyland due to an embarrassing obsession which was revealed when he publicly confessed, "I love Rickey Rouse."

Due to his complete disgrace, the eldest son then added to his besmirching of the family name through his unsuccessful attempt to commit suicide by climbing inside a blender.

After musing over his other choices short and hard, the father narrowed the pool of candidates to only men named Kim, a list approximately as long as The Great Wall of China. Eventually, The Great Sun of Life noticed someone persistently tugging on his pants' cuff and looked down to see another son, Kim Ping Pong whose mother is Ho Hee Hee, and, after getting down on his knees, patted him on the head and proclaimed him the new Supreme Leader of Munchkinland.

I recently discovered all sorts of interesting things about North Korea which, of course, has been a major news story recently due to the fact that they have a nuclear missile which, so far, has limited range, and, in a recent test, destroyed North Korea's own Ministry of Starvation headquarters. While researching North Korea, I was greatly surprised to learn that karaoke, cigarettes, and alcohol are very popular with the people there. No, wait, I accidentally Googled North Dakota.

Many North Koreans are sent to China to work, for which they receive minimum wage, no insurance, no benefits of any kind, etc. It appears that they have a Right to Work Law similar to Idaho's.

The current leader of North Korea apparently is sensitive about his height also. In fact, he and his bride made history when they posed as wedding cake top figures at their reception.

Due to his fascination with basketball, the Supreme Leader recently had Dennis Rodman visit. While preparing to play one-on-one, Rodman suggested Kim wear shorts, which he did but kept tripping over them. Afterwards, Rodman said, "Well, I have to cut my visit short," and was immediately deported.

After Kim saw media photos of how small he appeared standing next to the former NBA player, he announced that his next celebrity guest would be the actor Martin Short.

Some psychologists believe that the North Korean leader's persistent threats of military aggression are a symptom of the Napoleon Complex. If you recall, Napoleon I was the leader of early

19th century France, and a military commander so short that during battles it appeared that just a large hat was scurrying around the battlefield making him an elusive target. He was eventually removed from his office due to a lack of extra-marital affairs which the French people simply will not tolerate in their leaders.

So the theory is that men of short stature are more aggressive and belligerent to compensate for a feeling of inferiority. However, a research project revealed that, amongst male rats, 78% of fights were initiated by the smaller rat, but in 70% of those conflicts, the shorter aggressor was devoured.

To make a long story short, North Korea's leader needs to understand that it takes more than a big missile to make a country virile .

Obama declares war on amnesia—forgets why

I have read some pretty harsh, but accurate, criticism of President Obama recently. For example, "He never says really stupid things like his predecessor," or "To my knowledge his vice-president has not shot one innocent bystander." And I must admit that I agree with all of those people who are deeply disappointed in the Obama administration. But far and above such petty complaints, I have something much more substantial: Here he's been in office for 47,960,000 seconds, and he hasn't started one dad-blamed war— not one!

Remember, George W. Bush did not start just one war while in office, but two! Along with Iraq and Afghanistan, Bush was also planning to invade West Nile proclaiming that it had stockpiles of WMD's disguised as hordes of mosquitoes, but, due to a silly technicality, he could not get elected a third time. I cannot for the life of me understand why he didn't just whiteout that amendment to the Constitution like he did a few others.

And of course it was the elusive Weapons of Mass Destruction in Iraq which justified the invasion and which were never discovered despite President Bush's immortal words: "There's an old saying in Tennessee—I know it's in Texas, probably in

Tennessee—that says, fool me once, shame on—shame on you. Fool me—you can't get fooled again."

Meanwhile, right next door Iran was developing a nuclear bomb which, according to Wikipedia, definitely qualifies as a WMD, but apparently the Bush administration intelligence sources did not discover at the time because, as they later stated," It was painted tan."

We never did find the WMD's in Iraq, but at least we helped the country politically. We changed Iraq from an autocracy run by a nutcase to a "democracy" run by three nutcases: Larry, Curly, and Moe Hammed.

Then there was the invasion of Afghanistan based on the fact that al-Qaeda had training camps located there which were discovered when a highly paid double agent, after weeks of extremely complex espionage, Googled "al-Qaeda training camps."

So what wars has Obama started, huh? Name one. Oh, sure, some of his blindly devoted supporters will argue that there's the "war" on health care costs or, maybe, the "war" on the recession. How they have the nerve to even make such unpatriotically lame claims is beyond me.

It is really easy to see why so many people are upset with President Obama. Whereas Bush had two wars, corporate corruption, and water boarding to his credit, Obama has a "stimulus plan." Ooooo, how exciting! The closest thing to torture he can come up with is forcing us to watch news video of his family romping with the First Dog!

And how daringly original was the Cash for Clunkers bill? Why, my whole life I've been putting out cash for countless good old American-made clunkers and proud of it.

When asked why, after three years in office he hasn't started one war, the President replied, with a straight face and no grammatical errors, "There is no reason to." Now what kind of answer is that?

You would never have heard George W. Bush give the American public such a wimpy excuse. If he didn't have a logical reason to start a war, then, by gosh he could make up one right on the spot. And if you didn't quite understand what he said, so much the better. However, there was no ambiguity when he declared, "We'll let our friends be the peacekeepers and the great country called America will be the pacemakers."

Many of the current President's critics are demanding that he "do something" about the recent atrocities in Syria or that he "do something" about North Korea's nuclear threat. Well we all know what George Bush would have done—two more wars for a total of four! And that is why he could proudly claim, "You know . . . I said, I want to be a war president. No president wants to be a war president, but I am one."

Now that's the kind of presidential leadership we long for and the type that gets a president re-elected. It worked for George W. Bush, and a similar strategy can get Barack Obama a second term, despite the fact that Sarah Palin remains adamant that the President was not born in the United States but in Hawaii.

No one doubts that William Tecumseh Sherman was right when he stated, "War is hell." Or, as Republican candidate Mitt Romney recently proclaimed, "War is heck." Nonetheless, President Obama has surely learned from history and his own experience that it much more politically astute to start a war, or even wars, and guarantee re-election than to get stuck with fashioning a graceful exit from one.

Okay, class, take out your Ouija boards

Alleluia! In the current session of the Idaho state legislature, senator Sheryl Nuxoll (R) has introduced a bill to make the language more "explicit" in the existing bill which allows the Bible to be used in the classroom because, as she said, "A lot of teachers are scared to use the Bible." This is no doubt true. I know that when I was teaching I avoided referencing the Bible because I could never spell "Ecclesiastes" right. Plus I always got mixed up in my pronunciations of "Book of Job" and "Steve Jobs."

This is not the first time that Senator Nuxoll has used her position as an elected official to help her constituents in a relevant manner. In the past she has voted in favor of a bill that prohibits texting while driving and in favor of a bill that prohibits the establishment of local knife regulations. So, thanks to the senator, you can't text but you can play with really big knives while driving in Idaho.

Nuxoll defended her latest bill by expounding that the Bible is "embedded" in American culture. Certainly the Bible is one of the top selling books of all time, along with Quotations from Chairman Mao Tse-tung. However, in a recent year, the top three selling books in the U.S. were Fifty Shades of Grey, Fifty Shades Darker, and Fifty Shades Freed. Now there's some literature that would certainly liven up class discussions!

One theory supporting Senator Nuxoll's bill is that knowledge of the Bible will enhance one's understanding of people of faith generally, including those of other religions. Of course, we see ample evidence of this religious empathy towards various faiths from such Biblical connoisseurs as Donald Trump.

Nuxoll herself has demonstrated an educated understanding of people of faith by once stating that Hinduism is "a false faith with false gods." Possibly she feels this way because Hindus hold cows in high regard. Ironic, when one considers that we Idahoans also like our cows, generally rare to medium rare.

Another argument proposed in her favor is that it is hard to imagine that a person could be an educated individual unless one at least has a working knowledge of the Bible. Maybe so, but Idaho students' SAT scores indicate that their working knowledge of math could use some divine intervention.

The Republican senator pointed out that several states have already passed laws supporting the Bible as literature in their schools, including Florida, Georgia, S. Carolina, Alabama, Tennessee, and Arkansas. For some inexplicable reason, it seems that GOP leaders in this state look to the Deep South as a role model to follow when it comes to education. Possibly, their goal is to make all the children in Idaho resemble the kid sitting on the porch playing the banjo in the film "Deliverance."

I'm just a little nervous that if we start pushing the Old Testament too much, say, for example, the "eye for an eye" passage, it could result in class pictures resembling the cast of the film "Pirates of the Caribbean."

Along that same line, one unfortunate result of Southern schools' use of the Bible as literature is pretty obvious to all of us. You do not need to look at very many pictures of Arkansas graduates' smiling faces to see the harmful consequence of instilling the "tooth for a tooth" scripture in their young minds.

Nuxoll's Bible bill states that the book can be used as a reference for astronomy, biology, history and geography to name a few. For example, one could cite Ecclesiastes 1:6-7, "The wind goeth toward the south, and turneth about unto the north; it whirleth about continually, and the wind returneth again according to his circuits" in a unit on meteorology, since it makes about as much sense as the weatherman on television.

I think that using the Bible in class would be a huge boon to world history teachers as far as conserving valuable class time is concerned: "God created the earth, Adam, and Eve. Then came the Renaissance."

For some reason, the bill does not mention using the Bible in driver's education classes. What could be more practical than teaching high school students 1 Timothy 2:12, "I do not permit a woman to teach or to exercise authority over a man; rather, she is to remain quiet"? Good-bye backseat drivers!

Certain Bible passages could be incorporated in the physical education curriculum and apparently already has been in some states. One can easily imagine that Ronda Rousey's high school PE teacher frequently quoted from Judges 9:52-53, "And a certain woman threw an upper millstone on Abimelech's head and crushed his skull."

The only catch that I see to all this is that the Supreme Court ruled that teachers can discuss the Bible or religion if "it is presented objectively." So it could work as long as teachers do not use the Republican presidential candidates as role models.

Peek-a-boo, everyone sees you

The headline-hogging incident involving Edward Snowden is just the most recent chapter in the great American tradition of spying. For example, it has long been common practice for baseball players to spy on the opposing catcher and steal his signs to the pitcher. In football, there are coaches who disguise themselves as cheerleaders and spy on the opponents' practices, as if anything a football team does could be so complicated you couldn't figure it out five minutes after kick off.

However, the Snowden saga is more like the Spy vs. Spy comic in Mad Magazine where the two agents quite often get caught looking at each other simultaneously through periscopes—just a bungling farce of espionage escapades.

First of all, just what did Snowden do for a job? He labels his position with the NSA as "infrastructure analyst" which sort of sounds like he's really good with Legos. He is also a self-described "computer wizard." Boy, we've all heard that one before, like the guy in the next cubicle at work who claims he can delete that graphic for you, and the next thing you know your entire report has been permanently replaced by a Super Mario game and ads for poker!

Recently, Snowden has been holed up in a Russian airport for nearly as long as it takes to fly from Chicago to Atlanta over Thanksgiving. He claims that the hospitality has been outstanding as his Russian hosts have helped keep him up to date on the world scene, supplying him with daily newspapers covering the Nixon Watergate scandal and providing him generous discounts at the airport concession stand which features vodka and cow-tongue salad, vodka and pig's head meatloaf, all topped off with vodka and your choice of cabbage or rutabaga pie.

But what will Snowden do for work if he eventually is able to collect enough frequent flyer miles to afford a flight to Latin America, his next goal? Fortunately, Bolivia has graciously offered to let him referee soccer matches. Seems they have an extreme shortage of refs since the last two in South America were chopped into four pieces, decapitated, and then thrown into prison for life.

In another generous move, Julian Assange, founder of WikiLeaks, a company which makes adult diapers, has offered to share his British embassy broom closet apartment with Snowden if Ecuador should offer him asylum.

Speaking of our neighbors to the south, it is a mystery why we are spying on so many Latin American countries. Is it really worth the time and expense to discover that farmers in Costa Rica are secretly developing a self-peeling banana? Sure, but only if the process also removes those gross stringy things that cling to the peeled banana and get all tangled up in my Cheerios. And it's already general knowledge that in Paraguay, instead of elections, they hold regularly scheduled coup d'états which are a lot less expensive and they avoid all of that mind-numbing campaign baloney.

Understandably, the Latin American countries are outraged that their legitimate cocaine, marijuana, heroin, and opium operations are being illegally spied upon. But wouldn't it be even more upsetting if you were one of the two or three countries in the world not being spied upon? Isn't this sort of a blow to their national pride—realizing that their country has no information or activity important enough to be sought after by other countries?

For example, you don't see Tuvalu on the list, possibly because Micronesians are so small that their activities cannot be monitored by any current satellite spy device. And what about the tiny South Pacific country Nauru which is still occupied by forgotten Japanese WWII soldiers Larry-san, Curly-san, and Moe-san who have vowed never to surrender?

Even Canada did not make the spied-upon list which one can understand since US agents can simply disguise their voices and shout across the border, "What are you aboot to do, eh?" To which an alert Canadian will typically respond, "Are you a real Canuck or a hoser Yankee, eh?" And so on.

Let's face it: we live in a society in which one day we are upset because classified government "secrets" have been leaked; the next day we are livid about "lack of transparency." It is sort of like when Bieber and Gomez snap a cuddly photo of themselves with a cell phone, put it on Facebook, Twitter, Flickr, LinkedIn, YouTube, etc. then are outraged that their privacy has been violated when the photo appears in newspapers' gossip columns.

Personally, my government can spy on me all it wants because I have nothing to hide. Okay, there was that one website that I accidentally went to which had a somewhat grainy video of hamsters wearing skimpy ballerina skirts twirling to "Call Me Maybe," but other than that, I'm clean.

Praise the Lord and pass the hummus

I don't normally like to talk about religion because sure as I do some weirdo starts hyperventilating while swinging a decapitated chicken in a figure-eight over his head and chanting "booga-booga." Or a deranged dude will ramble on about "so and so beget so and so who beget so and so," as he coaxes a rattle snake to bite his face, until I cut him off by saying "Well, I got to be gettin' to work." The worst is the crackpot who offers me a free first-class flight, with Wi-Fi, on an alien spaceship soon to be sucked up into a comet by an enormous Super Vac.

But, by golly, something has to be done about this Israeli-Palestinian conflict which I can't understand, although religion appears to be somewhat of a factor. And it needs to be done soon because even a casual observer can sense that it's about time for the bimonthly outbreak of violence and accusations, followed by more fruitless negotiations, sort of like the current modus operandi of our own members of Congress.

The origin of this conflict is quite complicated. One theory is that the Palestinians rebelled when the Jews established a tax on sand. Adding fuel to the fire is a long on-going debate over whose prophet had the best looking beard. Compared to the longevity of this friction, The Hundred Years War looks like a half-hour sitcom. Or, to put it in an even more shocking perspective, it has lasted longer than it takes to listen to In-A-Gadda-Da-Vida.

The Palestinians are so desperate for someone to lead them out of this quagmire, that, back in November, they exhumed the remains of the man with the black and white checkered NASCAR flag do- rag, the legendary Yasser Arafat, aka Ringo Starr, to lead them to victory. The Arabs are confident that, with a little sprucing up, Arafat, who died in 2004, will look "as good as new" which, if you recall his appearance the first time around, is not saying much.

It seems that whenever the Palestinians get bored playing the national sport Rubble Collecting, they start shooting rockets across the border at Israel, or throw the rockets by hand which they can due to the fact that their country is so narrow that all the flat-screen TVs must, by law, be placed north to south lengthwise. But there is evidence that some citizens have brazenly dared to turn their sets the other way to share a program with their Israeli neighbors.

Shooting rockets is basically a waste of time, since Israel is protected by huge slingshots which catch the missiles and fire them back at Gaza. In addition, there is the cutting edge Iron Dome over Israel, a giant chastity belt which enemy rockets bounce off of, thus missing military targets, and, instead luckily landing in the midst of people's backyard barbecues resulting in very well done kosher shish-ka-bobs.

The constant threat of violence has forced changes in the Israeli culture. Instead of a lovely young lady broadcasting weather advisories, as we view here, the Israeli TV stations feature an announcer dressed in camouflage and a gas mask pointing out on a large map where the next wave of bombs is expected to hit.

To ensure Israel's security, and since the U.S. is part owner of Israel due to a gazillion dollars in foreign aid, why don't we just trade Texas for Israel since Texans want to secede anyway. The only loss to the U.S. would be the state's oil production from Rick Perry's hair.

The dominant political party in Palestine is Hummus which is also the name of an extremely popular food in the Middle East. In fact the largest dish of hummus in the world was made by 300 cooks in Lebanon and weighed 23,000 pounds which broke the previous record set by a team of Arab and Jewish cooks—thus proving they can work together peacefully!

Actually, the party's name is Hamas. Hamas, a terrorist organization, has pushed for a Palestinian culture in which women's sexual behavior is controlled by a male dominated government, all citizens are armed, and public education is unfunded. Hmmm, for some reason this sounds vaguely familiar, but I can't quite place it.

Secretary of State Hillary Clinton recently brokered a cease fire when she threatened the two sides that they had to sit at the negotiation table and "stare at my mug" until a settlement is reached which promptly led to an agreement. But it's pretty obvious that every time the two sides shake hands, they have their fingers crossed on the other hands.

As a final thought, I do appreciate the fact that an Israeli created the Mighty Morphin Power Rangers, but I cannot find it in my heart to ever forgive the Israeli company that first developed the cell phone.

GOP supports EITs with a little TLC

Reaction was swift and sharply divided over the recent release of the CIA torture report. Comments on the use of enhanced interrogation techniques (EITs) ranged from "abhorrent" to "this little piggy cried wee wee wee." Some critics argued that the condensed version of the report was too negative and "left out all the good things about torture." One Republican congressman even proposed that it all depended on your definition of torture: "Why, what's torture to you could be flat-out titillating to me."

Senator Marc Rubio (R-Fla) applauded the U.S. interrogators for bravely serving their country then immediately turned around and condemned "human-rights violators" in Venezuela, a seemingly complete 180 which left readers' eyeballs spinning around in confusion.

The Senate Intelligence Committee indicated in the report that the interrogation techniques did not result in any useful information, an implication refuted by committee member Senator

Saxby Chambliss (R-Georgia) who stated that important intelligence was obtained from one prisoner "after he went through the EIT program" which makes torture sound more like a Microsoft internship .

Strangely enough, Republicans, who tend to decry President Obama for violating the Constitution if he so much as wears a tan suit, have completely steered clear of mentioning the unconstitutional aspects of torture, possibly, of course, because they see nothing "cruel and unusual" about it. Personally, I prefer that my physician does not include rectal hydration on my physical exam checklist.

The history of torture goes clear back to the Bible which stated "He that spareth his rod hateth his son; but he that loveth him chasteneth him betimes." Book of Adrian Peterson.

Torture took various forms in Ancient Greece including when Socrates tormented his students with deep philosophical questions such as "Is there life after death; and, if so, will they accept Visa?"

Warring African tribes in the 19th century would bury a captive up to his neck then release a horde of lawyers to descend upon him and vie with one another to represent the victim in personal injury litigation.

Torture has a long history in this country too, going all the way back to 2001, the year Republicans George W. Bush and Dick Cheney were sort of elected into office. They tortured the American people for eight long years by entering unwinnable wars and crashing the economy.

But even worse, President Bush, who probably thought water boarding was something The Beach Boys sang about, consistently tortured the English language, a skill that he no doubt could have used to help the CIA interrogators:

Suspected terrorist: "I have nothing to say."

George Bush: "Amigo! Amigo! Don't misunderestimate me. I know that you never stop thinking about new ways to harm our country and our people, and neither do we. There's an enemy who would like to attack America who has no disregard for human life, and I wish him all the very best. I just want you to know that, when we talk about war, we're really talking about peace. Families is where our nation finds hope, where wings take dream. I met the mother of a child who was abducted by North Koreans right here in the Oval Office. So I ask you, is our children learning?"

Suspected terrorist: "Stop! Stop! I'll tell you anything you want to know!"

If that strategy did not work, the interrogators could have ushered in then vice-president Dick Cheney, wearing camouflage, an orange vest, and carrying a shotgun, who would growl to the prisoner, "Let's you and me go do a little quail hunting." That would surely do the trick.

When it was pointed out to Cheney this past week that "nearly 25 percent of the detainees in the CIA program turned out to be innocent of their supposed crimes," his response was along the lines of "Win a few, lose a few."

I can sort of see his point since, even at that rate, odds were better for CIA prisoners than for men and women held in Texas prisons where nearly half of all executions in the U.S. take place— and that in a state which also leads the nation in wrongful convictions!

Cheney said that during his time as vice-president, "We were very careful to stop short of torture." So it's a good thing they used water boarding, or "controlled drowning," only 183 times on one particular suspect—184 would have possibly qualified as torture. Never one to miss out on an opportunity to subject humans to pain and suffering from a safe distance, Cheney concluded with, "I'd do it again in a minute."

Call me crazy, but it sure seems fruitless to torture people who are willing to blow themselves up for a cause. I would guess that most of their information cannot be trusted because, just like atoms, they would make up everything.

Chapter 5   Travel

All roads lead to . . . an exit

It must be very different trying to sell used vehicles in the Middle East what with all of the car bombings taking place. Here in the U.S., customers ask questions about mileage, warranty, air, stereo, etc. Whereas, an Afghan car transaction goes something like this: "Does it have doors?" "No." "I'll take it." Such an option makes the vehicle perfect for a quick exit before detonation.

Selling real estate there also faces some unique challenges. Property lines probably keep shifting in the sand. In fact, how do you tell when one Middle East country ends and another begins? Like is part of Syria actually in Libya or Algeria but the media just switches names so it sounds like a new country is undergoing upheaval? Couldn't Pakistan and Afghanistan at least spray paint their sand different colors—that would be a step in the right direction to help television audiences.

The general public, both here and there, is not able to tell the difference because the people, landscape, teargas, rubble all look identical. Likewise, it must be simply impossible for Middle Easterners to tell when a traveler has crossed the border from one country to another which explains why hikers out for a Sunday picnic in Pakistan suddenly find themselves locked up in an Iranian prison and on the ABC nightly news.

It's not anything like that here in the U.S. For example it is easy to tell the moment I cross from Wyoming into Idaho or Utah because suddenly there are two guys on bikes wearing ties peddling like crazy to stay next to my driver's window on Interstate 15 so they can share their faith with me.

However, all the traffic whizzing by makes it so that I can hardly hear them as they shout something about dumping out the sinful contents of my coffee mug, to which I shout back, "But on the eighth day God created Starbucks!"

Then just as suddenly they disappear due to a semi truck nearly side swiping me as it passes. Thank goodness they were wearing their helmets.

It is also possible to tell that you have crossed into the Beehive State because Utah drivers tend to go a lot faster than residents of other states which is probably a result of the fact that they get terribly confused by those double-digit numbers on the highway speed signs.

Generally, it is not too difficult to be aware that you have crossed into Nevada since immediately you will come upon a drove of pudgy tourists wearing Bermuda shorts, flowery shirts, and hearing aids, casually lined up for the all-you-can-eat buffet at Circus Circus in Las Vegas. I've always wondered if, by all-you-can-eat, do they mean in one's lifetime or just during this one visit? There is a big difference, you know. After all, there is no time limit printed on the menu.

And why do the buffets charge the same price for everyone? I mean you can tell that a guy who resembles Elvis from his grease-backed hair, hip-gyrating svelte era when he recorded Hound Dog isn't going to consume nearly as much as an impersonator of the later Elvis in his Pillsbury Dough Boy white spangled jumpsuit period, the one who broke out into a sweat by simply squeezing mustard onto his third bratwurst.

Once you get past the gambling geezer parade, the next sure sign you're in Nevada that you will encounter is a convoy of gargantuan buses full of Japanese tourists dangling cameras the size of bazookas around their necks hoping to get a shot of Siegfried and Roy's white lion regurgitating Roy's neck.

In addition, entering Nevada is unique in that, whereas at a Middle East country checkpoint you are taken into custody if you have guns in your car, those crossing into The Silver State are arrested if they do NOT have guns, preferably at least three, visibly attached to their body. Folks brandishing knives, swords, grenades, personal-sized rocket launchers get a big "Howdy, Partner" welcome also.

If instead you head east, it is clearly obvious when you cross into The Cowboy State of Wyoming because the year on your atomic watch switches from 2013 to 1873. Sure, women had the right to vote by then, but it was pretty difficult to get to the polls when the men were using all of the horses to "ride the range", forcing the wives to saddle up Old Bessie the milk cow to ride into town. Yet, statistically, women have outnumbered men at the polls in this country just about ever since.

Of course, Wyoming has always been a leader in individual freedom. Just this week the state legislators voted to repeal the law that made sodomy illegal. Previously, a man could be sent to prison for up to ten years for sodomy, which certain fellows might think sounds like paradise rather than punishment. In addition, making sodomy legal resulted in all the Wyoming sheep breathing a big sigh of relief.

Finally, a backseat driver you can mute

There's nothing like a long road trip to bring family members closer together. My wife and I recently returned from just such a trip and, after ten straight hours in the car, at times we were closer than ever. In fact, during one stressful moment she had me in an elevated double chicken wing hold that would do WrestleMania proud. Plus our black Lab was sitting on my lap, panting in my face causing me near asphyxiation. And all of this is happening while I'm trying to manipulate the car through big city freeway traffic with some lady on the GPS barking out orders to "Turn left. Turn right. Stand up, sit down, fight, fight, fight!"

While dodging thousands of vehicles on the Interstate, all driven by individuals who inexplicably appear determined to kill me, I can understand why Oregon law allows people to end their own lives with dignity. In fact, it would not have surprised me in the least to see some fellow ease his vehicle onto the shoulder, exit his auto, and pull out a Samurai sword to end it all right there. Self-immolation at state rest areas in the manner of Tibetan monks could become so common as to attract no more interest than a quick Smart phone snapshot by passing tourists.

Surely the rest of the motorists could see by our plates that we're from Pocatello, Idaho, where the closest experience to a perilous traffic jam is when a naïve citizen carelessly drives by Holt Arena immediately following the conclusion of the Big Foot Monster Truck Show and thousands of guys exiting the parking lot in giant pickups are trying to imitate the demolition they just witnessed in the Dome.

Admittedly, much of my stress is self-imposed. First of all, I have a tendency to get lost while driving in unfamiliar territory. I'm not talking about navigating the Malay Archipelago either—downtown Rexburg will do.

And for logical reasons I get real nervous in freeway traffic. There's just something about being surrounded by bumper-to-bumper vehicles going 80 mph, their Buttkicker-Sonic Shaker bass stereo speakers booming, all driven by guys who are texting, eating Whoppers, and guzzling cans of Mega Monster Energy Drink while attempting to steer 4,000 lbs. of steel that makes it difficult for me to coolly and calmly look for my exit sign.

Once I make the exit, I can feel my blood pressure drop as rapidly as the temperature from a polar vortex, which is a large pocket of very cold air that the Canadians occasionally send south to get even with Americans for making fun of the way they talk, "You know what I mean, eh?"

Of course getting off the freeway is only the beginning of my stress. Next I have to find the motel that we carefully chose beforehand after viewing hundreds of queen bed and swimming pool photos online. In the old days getting a room was easier since there were only a few mom-and-pop motels, none of this luxury suite, piece of chocolate on the pillow stuff. Back then a guy could just pull into a gas station to ask directions, and the clerk would tell you how to get there without insisting that you buy a $1.98 candy bar first.

To find the motel in this age of technology we need to ask the GPS lady who apparently is a speed reader with access to every

Atlas and city map ever printed. You just say into the device "Timbuktu," loudly and clearly, wait a moment for her to stifle a giggle then state in a garbled response, "Turn right in 6,120 miles" never to be heard from again until Hailey's Comet next passes earth.

During long, quiet stretches of highway I often forget that the GPS is even on. Just as I nod off in the passenger seat, counting semis in my sleep, this robotic voice will suddenly blast out, shattering my slumber, and I will jerk around to see if my wife has picked up a hitch hiker.

Following her directions, at one point I got stuck in a huge roundabout resembling St. Peter's Square for a quarter hour because I kept losing count of the exits and had to keep starting over. Luckily the GPS lady loads up on valium before coming to work so she stays very cool and never raises her voice in contrast to my wife and me.

But my biggest beef is that I cannot even understand what this lady says half the time. Directions like "Turn left on Diarrhe Street" or "Enter the traffic circle and take the ellefti exit." To which I scream back "Diarrhea Street?!" "The eleventh exit?!"

But, then, of course, once I realize that she's speaking Icelandic, I relax and calmly begin searching for my Samurai sword.

Hi ho, a camping we will go

Well, we are deep into the summer camping season which has been a particularly challenging one. First of all, the price of gas has forced many campers to downsize their great outdoors adventures. For example, I know a guy who had grandiose plans to camp near a waterfall, soak in a hot springs, and see elk. Instead, he set up the camper in the driveway, hooked the garden hose to the roof, filled up the bathtub with steaming hot water, and attached plastics antlers to Fido's head.

Another obstacle this summer has been the abundance of wildfires. One effect that they have on the camping experience is that they diminish the quality of the normally fresh forest air--I mean it is simply not the same wearing a surgeon's mask while singing "Kumbaya" around an imaginary campfire. I don't mind the imaginary campfire nearly as much as I do the imaginary toasted marshmallows which I find rather unsatisfying. Of course, the fire is imaginary because most of the state has banned real fires which is quite sensible since many campers try to extinguish their fires through the bizarre technique called "throw a real big log on it." That is why in the spring you will sometimes pull into a campsite abandoned at the tail end of the previous summer which still has a smoldering tree section in the fire ring, along with beer bottles, smashed pop cans (as if smashing them will aide the burning process), and mysterious chunks of wire and tinfoil. Didn't these people learn the definition of flammable in high school science class?

But let's let our imaginations run wild and, for the sake of discussion, pretend that one could afford gas to go camping this summer. That leads us to the variety of interpretations of the term "camping."

It seems quite obvious to even the most casual observer that there is a big difference between "camping" and "moving one's house to a campground." A true camper would never consider using any type of habitat other than a tent or simply a ground cloth and sleeping bag. Any abode more elaborate simply eliminates the inhabitant from the category of camping. Instead one enters into the murky realm of mobile condo dwellers or a rolling luxury KOA timeshare. Let's face it, it is simply not manly to cruise the highway in a motorized mansion that has more options than a wishbone quarterback.

Okay, back to the great outdoors. In my opinion, the only way to truly connect with nature is to simply sleep in a bag on a ground cloth. Only then will you experience the little chipmunks scurrying over your body during the midnight hour. Imagine, Chip and Dale playing King of the Mountain on your upside hip and you get the picture.

Of course, there can be drawbacks to this most basic of camping styles. Such as when my buddy and I were thumbing our way across Montana and threw our bags down on a ledge near the Yellowstone River. All was peaceful for a short time then our faces became the main landing strips for a fleet of blood-seeking mosquitoes. Thank goodness this all took place prior to West Nile which, if you haven't heard, President Bush recently added to the list of countries in his "axis of evil."

My friend and I, to avoid being devoured, pulled our mummy bag hoods tight around our faces. This did ward off the aerial invasion, but created a new source of discomfort. Just as we were about to drift off to dreamland, we noticed that we were roasting and sweating profusely. I attempted a quick escape but was thwarted as my zipper stuck. While wrestling with it, my face got completely twisted around so now I was gasping for air up against the musty canvas surface. My gyrations next led to the bag slowly rolling down the embankment towards the river. At that moment I was certain that my mummified remains would someday wash ashore somewhere near Bismarck, North Dakota. Luckily my traveling buddy was able to get free and rescued me in the nick of time. It became obvious that we would get no sleep that night, so we dragged ourselves to the nearby truck stop and sat nursing a cup of coffee until dawn.

I think a logical question is why are there so many titanic RV's on the road today? On a recent trip, I saw an extremely large man driving a $70,000 camper van. His midsection was so big that he had heavy duty custom air shocks, not on the van but on his belt! I mean this guy was so large that he would need a trailer hitch on his van, and not for a boat or an ATV (as if either would hold him) but for the rest of his family!

So is that why the campers have grown in size? Is such a transportation evolution connected to the recent statistic that by 2015, 75% of Americans will be overweight? By the way, if 75% are overweight, then that creates the question of over what weight? Wouldn't we have to adjust the definition of "average"?

Of course there are some midsize options when it comes to camping, but I will need to discuss them at another time since Fido appears to have his antlers stuck in the fence.

If you get a call of the wild, don't answer

Camping season is upon us, so time to chase the spiders out of your sleeping bags where they've been holed up nice and cozy all winter. While you're at it, probably a good idea to set up your tent in the yard to make sure you replaced that bent pole. You know, the one you rammed your head into after tripping over a rock last July while stumbling back to your tent after sitting around the fire drinking beer until 2 AM.

This uncontrollable urge that humans get each summer to venture into the impenetrable forest primeval and grovel amongst the weeds, wildflowers, and dust, setting off an allergy sneezing attack that could trigger an avalanche, is the result of eons of evolution.

I heed the call to head for the hills and spend several sleepless nights camping out about that time in the spring when the first hummingbird shows up tapping on my bedroom window demanding its sugar water fix.

Honestly, I can't understand how they came up with the name "sleeping bag" when sleep is about the last thing that you're going to experience in one. Every time I roll over, the bag rolls with me and I end up upside down, inhaling mouthfuls of flannel lining. Then if it happens to be a very warm night and the zipper gets stuck you'll experience what it's like to be a baked Idaho russet wrapped in foil.

Anyway, since I'm an old hand at this whole camping thing, I felt that the least I could do is share some of my expertise with all you greenhorns out there by providing a FAQ column dealing with bears and other camping hazards.

Q: What is the most difficult part of camping?

A: For me, just getting to the campsite is the hardest part since I apparently have a bladder the size of a pencil eraser and get the urge to go approximately every Interstate mile marker.

Q: Is it safer to stay in an actual campground or seek dispersed camping?

A: Dispersed camping is safe as long as you aren't awakened on a moonlit night by the sounds of the Manson Family beating on drums and chanting "Helter Skelter." Of course, in an established campground you can always get help from the camp host, unless he's from Georgia and has an eerie resemblance to the kid playing the banjo in Deliverance all grown up now, in which case you should run to the Mansons for refuge.

Q: Should I obey the rule to not feed the wildlife?

A: Yes, but if you should happen to come face to face with a grizzly sow and her cub while hiking you may not have much choice since you will be the main entree.

Q: Experts say to be on the alert for "bear signs." What do they mean?

A: One sign is bear scat. If you see poop on the trail and upon closer examination notice it contains a set of dentures, chances are they did not belong to the bear.

Q: Is bear pepper spray a good investment?

A: Yes, but use caution. If attacked by a bear make sure the sprayer is pointed away from you. Otherwise, Yogi will get a good chuckle watching you blindly running into trees before he enjoys a well-seasoned feast.

Q: How about attaching a bear bell to my dog's collar?

A: Good idea, but don't get confused and attach a bar bell instead or your dog will get tired real fast.

Q: Is it safe to sleep in a tent?

A: Yes, but if your campsite has a bear proof food storage locker I recommend just sleeping in it.

Q: How do I distinguish a black bear from a grizzly bear?

A: Easy, a black bear will simply eat you; whereas, a grizzly will first eat the black bear then you for dessert.

Q: Are fishing regulations very complicated?

A: You bet. For some fish you can only use flies or lures, for some only barbless hooks, and for very rare fish only hookless hooks.

Q: Is it safe to peer down a geyser hole?

A: Ask Freddy Krueger.

Q: Is it legal for a guy to urinate in the National Forest?

A: Yes, as long as you keep it on a leash.

Q: Should the kids and I be afraid of getting West Nile?

A: If you're going camping with the kids, West Nile is the least of your worries. Statistically, you are much more likely to require medical attention for injuries suffered from your kids flinging red-hot marshmallows around the campfire than from mosquitoes.

Speaking of kids, always double check your campsite before you pull out to go home. I can't tell you how many children I've lost by being negligent in that.

I'll take my chances on bears over bugs any day

Not sure why some people are dead set on removing grizzly bears from federal protection just so they can hire a guide, set out a carcass for bait, sit and wait until the bear is trained to regularly dine in that exact spot before shooting it—then call it "hunting." May as well just sneak a rifle into the Bear Country U.S.A. tourist trap.

No, I think that the effort of such "sportsmen" is misguided. Bears are not a real big problem when folks seek the nirvana of the great outdoors. The odds of even seeing a bear in the wild are about as good as seeing your doctor on a Friday afternoon once golf season rolls around.

Many incidents involving bear attacks on humans are the result of hikers not obeying the bear safety rules like travel in a group, talk real loud, wear bear bells, etc. Of course, if you follow all the rules your mellow nature experience turns into something resembling a New Orleans Mardi Gras parade.

I say leave the bears alone. On the other hand, you can bag all the bugs you want. It's estimated that the world holds 300 pounds of insects for every pound of humans, and, based on national obesity statistics, that's a lot of bugs.

This whole problem with bugs goes back to Adam and Eve. They ate the forbidden fruit and suddenly were shocked to discover that they were walking around naked. I've experienced this myself some mornings when I step outside to pick up the newspaper without having my coffee first.

To punish them, the Lord declared that man would have to endure hard labor, death, and, even worse, Donald Trump. But He never mentioned mosquitoes. And the way Adam and Eve were dressed out there in the garden I'll bet they wished they'd had a gallon of Off!

Malaria, West Nile, now Zika. Mosquitoes have a long rap sheet. There are about 3,500 species of mosquitoes and only three species are known to transmit disease. Of course, it's the tiny minority of bad ones that dominate the headlines. When's the last time you read an uplifting story about any of the other 3,497 mosquito species—never.

Interestingly, it's only the pregnant female mosquitoes that bite people. Now I'm not sure if that's because they need the blood or it's the result of some sort of nasty mood swing. All I know is that I've taken camping trips when it was just my luck to pitch a tent smack dab in the middle of a huge mosquito maternity ward!

And mosquitoes are so stealthy. You're just standing there grooving in the forest primeval when, out of nowhere, one of those blood-suckers nails you on the arm. That would never happen with a 600-lb. bear.

You also have to watch out for those creepy, sneaky ticks too. Even if you make it through the whole camping trip without a single bug bite and think you're home free, you may discover later in the shower that there are five ticks silently strolling around on your body in various locations looking to set up housekeeping, sort of like eight-legged U-Haul moving vans.

When you do locate ticks before they have time to bond with you, they are difficult to kill. You can punch, pinch, and poke them with little effect. However, one source provided this encouraging advice: ". . . stepping on an engorged tick, filled with blood, kills it easily, though messily." So your idyllic camping trip may end up looking like a Quentin Tarantino flick after all.

We've found ticks whose one-year lease living on our dog has about expired that are so bloated with blood they resemble tiny hot-air balloons ready to take off in flight.

The other reason bugs are a bigger problem than bears is that even when you're not out in the wilderness camping or hiking you still have to deal with them. Whereas, it's very rare that you'll have to fight off a grizz with a large spatula while grilling in the backyard, bugs seem to think that "Welcome" mat on the front porch is meant for them.

On the first warm day each spring it seems as if someone fires a starting pistol and out of nowhere bugs are swarming all over the yard. I already have wasps just daring me to try to enter the shed to retrieve a rake. Bees are defending their territory in the flower garden. And it won't be long before June bugs wallop me in the head while I'm sitting out watching the sunset.

And where have these flies been hiding out all winter? They just seem to pop to life on a warm windowsill with the sole intent of driving me crazy by staying just out of swatter reach behind the blinds.

Finally, it really bugs me when people make such a big deal out of killing bears. It would have been a much bigger deal if, as someone suggested, Noah had swatted those two mosquitoes.

Instant karma's gonna get you

I just got back from California. And you know it wouldn't be a bad drive at all if someone would just move that dang Nevada out of the way. Northern Nevada is basically three towns connected by several hundred miles of dirt with an occasional bush one can view from a scenic turnout. There is also a string of brothels which, apparently, Nevada has in place of rest areas.

After spending a night at Harrah's in Reno, I decided that a gambling addiction is surely the worst addiction of all. At least with alcohol, cigarettes, or drugs, a person feels good for a brief time so your money isn't completely wasted. Sexual addiction obviously has its upside and is curable since most of us guys went through it starting about the time we were 14 years old and here we are fifty years later completely clean. But gamblers do not appear to be having any fun at all, except, of course, for those smoking, drinking, gambling, and having sex— all at the same time.

The hotel room was relatively cheap except for some annoying extra charges. For example, they charged $1.50 for in-room coffee which I had never seen before and stubbornly refused to pay. So I out- smarted them and, early next morning, hustled down 19 floors and bought Starbuck's for $2.50. Ha!

Leaving Nevada, we first had to pass through a California border protection station where they check for a variety of pests like bugs, weeds, diseases, Nevadans, etc. I almost did not get in due to the fact I was an Idahoan with a head cold which Californians consider an invasive species.

After you cross into California, first thing you notice is all the beautiful scenery that you're missing out on because you are surrounded by huge semis, SUVs, limos, etc., all traveling so fast that no one apparently can see the speed limit signs which are a blur. Unaccustomed to such traffic, I stared straight ahead, clinching the wheel with both hands and my teeth trying to recall some of the prayers I had learned in kindergarten religion class.

Californians own something like 40 million vehicles, and how they all ended up on this same stretch of road on this particular early spring morning, seemingly competing in Death Race 2014, is beyond me.

First city I came to I pulled into a convenience store to use the bathroom which was located in a separate detached building. Everywhere in California you have to get the key to unlock the bathroom because, for some reason, everyone in the state thinks he's a gifted artist and there is graffiti all over. I was told it is gang graffiti, but I thought gangs are crime syndicates, not some sort of arts and crafts club. Someone said that the gang members are "marking their territory," sort of like my dog when I take her for a walk in the park.

As I approached the store, the young Pakistani clerk ran out the door towards the restroom carrying the key and shouted, "I go bathroom. You wait. You're welcome!"

I have to admit that I was exposed to some new and very hip businesses while visiting California. Top on my list is the drive-through Colon Hydrotherapy Center, sort of like fast food for the other end. And my timing could not have been better as they were offering a "Spring Cleansing Special."

Next to the colon center is Karma Psychic Boutique where you can "Connect with your loved ones on the other side." This service could be handy since you can ask them how the weather is, do I need to bring my big coat, do they accept VISA, etc.?

I was also intrigued by a profession referred to as Animal Intuitive or Pet Medium. This individual claims that she can carry on a conversation with your pet and "understand his or her needs." She even offers to do this long distance, say, for example, if your pet iguana has a Twitter account.

Just to check it out, I had her ask my dog why she always sniffs other dogs' butts instead of their heads when they meet. The psychic told me that my dog exclaimed, "They have heads?!" So I guess now I'm a believer.

Even the local farmers market offers some different features. Along with locally grown turnips and mushrooms, you can get a Botox treatment while they bag your carrots or even liposuction to make room for a delicious homemade cinnamon roll.

Other unique services I discovered in California include tools for transformation, energy awareness exercises, my body wisdom, angel therapy, love's art, etc. Come to think of it, aren't these the same services offered by the ladies working at the Moonlite Bunny Ranch and other Nevada brothels?

It's Yellowstone, not Jurassic National Park

Score: Bison 2, Tourists 0. Yep, it's early in the summer vacation season, but things have gotten off to a rocky start for the tourists. It looks as though the strenuous off-season training of the wildlife is really going to pay dividends this year as already tourists have suffered some serious beat downs.

Over the last few weeks in Yellowstone National Park alone there have been two knock-down, drag-out confrontations, with the animals doing all the knocking down and dragging. Both incidents involved tourists getting too close to the park bison for photo ops. Of course one would never suspect that bison could be so touchy about something as innocuous as a selfie. Adding insult to injury, the tourists have discovered that pictures tend to come out a little blurry when snapped as the photographer sails ten feet through the air, plus landing is hard on the phone.

There are around 5,000 bison in Yellowstone and they do tend to hang out together in small groups so as to chat amongst themselves and make snide remarks about the goofy tourists, so there is a strong possibility for a mano a mano clash when people cannot resist the temptation for a close up shot to impress their friends back home in Tallahassee or wherever.

Of course you can always try running away from an angry buffalo, but unless your name happens to be Usain Bolt, world's fastest human, you probably are not going to reach the car before getting an uplifting experience compliments of a bull's horns since bison can sprint three times faster than the average human. Then once they toss you through the air with the greatest of ease and pin you to the ground, it's just real hard to dislodge 2,000 pounds of Omaha Steaks on the hoof.

Luckily, bison are vegetarians so at least after they have finished tenderizing a tourist with their hoofs and horns and calmed down, they will simply saunter off and leave what's left intact. Not so with bears which generally crawl out of hibernation in the spring in a foul mood, sort of like me when I've overslept and missed the complimentary all-you-can-eat breakfast bar at the motel.

Along with the basic grumpy from too long of a nap syndrome, the female bears also may still be watching over their cubs, and just like human moms have taught their young to be wary of strangers and not to accept candy from them unless they take the hand along with it, or at least to bawl real loud so Mom can come running to open a can of whoop ass on some careless photographer.

Another trait that makes bears particularly dangerous is that they rely on their strong sense of smell, and, if you are anything like me, you do not need to be out in the wilderness for very long before you have developed an intense Pepe Le Pew aura that even a bear suffering from allergies will pick up on from a mile away.

As a safety precaution, whenever I go hiking in the woods I attach a bear bell to my dog's collar and send her ahead on the trail. That way if I should happen to hear a tremendous racket up around the next bend including a bell ringing nonstop, then find only the collar when I get to that spot, I'll do an abrupt 180-degree turn and run like the dickens.

You would think that the mere fact that most bears step out from the den yawning and sporting an XXX-L bib would provide a pretty clear- cut warning for campers to be on the alert in bear country. And make no mistake about it, once you crawl into your sleeping bag the reality is that, to a hungry grizzly bear, you are simply a giant enchilada.

So why are tourists so casual about approaching wildlife that they often risk their last tweet? I suppose it's possible that an entire generation confuses Yellowstone National Park with Jurassic Park. In fact, it's easy to understand why young people who have grown up playing video games have a hard time distinguishing virtual reality from the real McCoy. Countless times they have been pursued by wild beasts or alien creatures, and with a mere push of a button safely blasted them to smithereens with a few well placed pixels.

Add to that the millions of kids who are currently viewing action movies like the recent blockbuster Jurassic World and it's no wonder that when approaching a real bison for a close-up, they may confuse it with a computer-generated Indominus rex and assume that a Steven Spielberg inspired T-rex will come to the rescue.

Folks my age, on the other hand, who grew up spending time reading stories about Davy Crockett and Daniel Boone, aren't so easily buffaloed by a seemingly tranquil bison.

Life's no picnic, thank goodness

Ah yes, the 4th of July certainly brings back fond childhood memories of near disasters involving sparkler sword fights and firecrackers blowing tin cans sky high just as I bent over them to check the fuse. Of course, this time of the year there is also the obligatory summer picnic that one had to attend as a kid, the one where Uncle Marv thought it was a barrel of laughs to throw lit firecrackers at the children and dogs creating a cacophony of screams and howling mutts. Thankfully, Grandma would put a sudden end to the insanity by bopping Marv over the head with her umbrella. Gosh, those were the good old days.

The allure of picnics has always escaped me. I'm just not sure why people happily look forward to bellying up to a sweltering hot picnic table where you spend half of your time trying to hang onto napkins, paper plates, and potato chips to keep them from zipping away on the torrid breeze and the rest of the time swatting flies, bees, and combating an army of ants which magically emerged just at the moment someone sliced open the watermelon.

Got to have a watermelon otherwise you wouldn't end up with twenty people sitting around with juice stains soaking the front of their shirts and a few of those black watermelon seeds stuck to their chins. I was always leery of the seeds, wondering if I accidentally swallowed one would an ugly creature form inside me and pop out of my stomach like in the film "Alien."

Then there's the omnipresent giant mutant fly that's hardly distinguishable from a drone that attempts to fly into your mouth with each bite of corn. Just isn't a picnic without corn-on-the-cob, the only vegetable which, when you're done eating, half of it is still lodged in between your teeth so that when you smile you look like you just stepped off the set of "Hee-Haw."

While waiting as the food is prepared, the kids play with a Frisbee which no one can throw correctly and no one can catch so they just run around aimlessly for ten minutes until the Frisbee mercifully gets stuck high up in a tree. Then they kill more time throwing rocks, sticks, and empty bottles at it with every guy apparently thinking he is the reincarnation of Peyton Manning. That lasts for another ten minutes until ending abruptly when Uncle Marv throws a large firecracker in a futile attempt to blow the Frisbee out of the tree.

This is followed by a friendly volleyball game amongst all the folks which goes well for a time until some young stud teenager imagines he's playing in the Olympic gold medal game and rockets a spike directly into the face of cousin Matilda who was just an innocent bystander sipping on some iced tea and playing Angry Birds on her phone which is now lying on the ground in two pieces right beside cousin Matilda who is out cold.

Of course, there is always the possibility of food poisoning as a result of Great Grandmother bringing the bowl of potato salad that she forgot to bring last 4th of July!

I will say that my dislike for picnics does not carry over to summer campfire cookouts. In fact there is nothing I like better than to gather a pile of dry kindling the size of a funeral pyre, squirt the pile with a half can of lighter fluid, then light and throw a match, creating a fireball visible from the International Space Station.

Once the flames settle down and I've grown accustomed to no longer having any eyelashes, the real fun begins as I cook my own meal over an open fire just like the pioneers. When roasting a hot dog, be sure the wiener is stuck tightly on the stick because it could fly off when you gesture while singing "Kumbaya" and smack a fellow camper in the forehead before landing on the ground. If this happens you may as well just start roasting another one because Fido will immediately gobble it up.

Usually my success with cooking over an open fire depends on how much beer is consumed before and during the process. For example I've been known to mistakenly cover a roasted marshmallow with globs of catsup, mustard, and relish. My mom always said "Food taste better outdoors," but then she never went camping with me.

Another problem with drinking beer around the campfire is that it increases the possibility of tripping over the tent guy-lines while trying to find the cooler in the dark and landing on top of the tent, crashing the entire works to the ground. If that happens I suggest you just go ahead and sleep right there. I can tell you from experience it's a heck of a lot better than falling in the fire.

Man shoots GPS during road rage

When I go shopping for an automobile, I only have two options in mind: the car starts and it stops. I guess this goes back to when I was a kid and that's essentially all cars were expected to do back then. Of course, if a car failed to perform the first feat, the second requirement was moot because, as my best buddy would often say, "We're not goin' nowhere." My buddy was a devoted student of the sage philosopher Emanuel Can't who coined the famous line, "I don't think, therefore I ain't." To my friend, the cup was neither half empty nor half full; it was dry as a bone.

Looking back, it's no wonder my buddy had such a negative attitude as he was undoubtedly the epitome of a three-time loser: he was an altar boy, a Boy Scout, and was recruited to play defense at Penn State.

Sometimes my car refused to start despite the fact that the two of us applied all of the mechanical wizardry we had available such as applying a mixture of baking soda and water to the battery posts (then running to avoid electrocution), pouring gas down the carburetor (then running to avoid the explosion), or pushing the car while it's in neutral (then running to avoid a collision with the neighbor's shed). More often than not none of these efforts resulted in the car starting, but we were in great physical condition.

Today, shopping for some new wheels is about as complicated as designing a sandwich at Subway. Naturally you have to decide how many speakers you want, how many air bags you need, how many payments you can miss before the repo man shows up, etc. But I think the option decision that divides the bland from the grand is the automotive navigation system.

The earliest navigation devices that were used by sailors on ships were the stars and a weird guy named Ahab who just kept mumbling, "Follow the white whale." These obviously proved inefficient as Columbus mistook the West Indies for India despite the absence of call centers.

Later in history, cowboys would have found themselves stumbling around forever near god-awful places like Rawlins, Wyoming, lost in the cacti and sage, if it wasn't for their trusty stallion that had an innate knack for heading towards the nearest water hole and the nearest mare.

In contrast can you imagine the Lone Ranger turning to Tonto and asking, "Well, by jingo, this place is as hot as a whorehouse on nickel night! Where in tarnation are we?" To which Tonto responds, "Just check the GPS on Silver's saddle, Kemosabe"? No way! But that is exactly what we commonly do today because we have lost all sense of adventure.

Recently I had to rent a car to get me around after flying to a strange city and chose one with a navigation device because on a previous trip I opted for the budget rental that, in place of a fancy-schmancy dashboard device, included a Somali taxi driver who rode along in the backseat and provided directions. But I alertly became suspicious as he said things like, "Arrrrr, turn to the starboard here, ye scurvy pox-faced swine." At that moment I realized that my life was in the hands of a Somali pirate.

But then again the last thing most men need is another woman telling them what to do while they are trying to drive. That female voice use to come from Mom, sister, girlfriend, etc.; now it is a screeching sound from an annoying screen on the dashboard, a voice as persistent and nagging as the alarm that's always reminding me to fasten my seatbelt, take the key from the ignition, and remove the cat from the trunk.

I had not driven far before I had about as much as I could stand so a big argument broke out, and, of course, she won't listen to a word I say because she's a woman and a computer chip to boot, as she droned over and over, "Turn right, you idiot." To which I, with a large blood vessel in my forehead about to pop, screamed back, "I can't turn right because if I do I will t-bone Ricky's El Ranchito food truck which currently has tacos on sale 3 for $1.00!"

Personally, I've always preferred more manly ways to find my way around in unfamiliar territory, like stopping at a convenience store to ask a clerk for directions who most likely is in the process of being robbed by two guys wearing ski masks and while they pause to pose for the video camera I can grab a bag of pork rinds, some energy drinks, and a city map and find my way without the help of any navigation device.

Please feed the bears so they won't eat me

On a recent camping trip to Yellowstone my wife and I were sitting around the pretend campfire discussing Idaho license plate numbers. We were not clear on the prefix 2B. She asked, "Is Bonneville County 2B or not 2B?" I responded, "That is the question."

Of course, this summer the fire is imaginary because many campgrounds in this part of the country have banned real fires. It's probably just as well. That way you can avoid being asphyxiated by your neighbor's smoldering attempts at a fire which consists of dirty diapers, beer bottles, Styrofoam, etc. At least that is what I often find in an abandoned fire ring. You would think that those people could at least buy those bundles of three logs for $5.00 that the camp hosts often have for sale.

And for crying out loud, how many times do people have to be told to close the lid on the campground toilet? I know, I hate touching the thing too, but if we don't follow the sign's directions, who knows what alien creatures will escape and come crawling out of that black hole during the night and abduct everyone in the campground? There now, that should straighten out you slackers.

At one campsite the flies were so big that you needed a license to kill them. At another site, mosquitoes kept up a steady attack. Fortunately, the disease carrying mosquitoes from West Nile are easy to recognize since they wear tiny turbans.

Basically, I see camping as a rather masochistic experience. Besides the bugs, there are the other issues such as sleeping in a bag which resembles a strait jacket with a zipper. Ever try to escape one quickly in the pitch dark when Mother Nature calls? Even if you do manage to get the zipper unstuck in time you are still faced with going outside and facing the spooky forest primeval. Is that a bear or Uncle Harold passed out in the lawn chair?

Speaking of bears, we saw two in the park that were real and about a thousand others which actually turned out to be rocks or stumps. We also saw an elk, lots of chipmunks, but, disappointingly, no Bigfoot. However, I do believe Bigfoot exists because at a recent garage sale I saw a size 18 shoe for sale and there's no way the little old lady asleep behind the cash box wore those, so . . . .

Every campground has a sign that says "This is Bear Country." Well, duh, mountains, thick forest, no fast food joints, other than the campers themselves of course. No brainer, if I was a bear, this is where I would hang out. To avoid a bear encounter while hiking, my wife bought a bear bell which keeps ringing while we walk, but it sounds like a dinner bell to me announcing loud and clear: "Come and get it!"

It is now very confusing as to what you should do if you encounter a bear in the forest. Years ago the Forest Service taught us to curl up into a bite-size ball and cover our head. Now they say to Stand Your Ground. I say there is a big difference between standing up to some whacked out meth head trying to mug you with a clothes hanger and an 800-pound grizzly bear wearing a jumbo-size bib!

They also advise you not to run because the bear is faster than you. But isn't it possible that I could get a bear that has been on a human diet so long that it is as severely obese as the average American and I could kick its fat bear butt in Usain Bolt fashion, running backwards and taunting it with a "USA" chant?

Often after a bear attack you read about the park rangers trying to track down the guilty bear. How is this possible? Can they match paw prints? Do they round up every bear in the vicinity and march them in for a police lineup? "Yes, I am sure it is bear number three, the one wearing my husband's Red Sox cap."

Overall, I concluded that Yellowstone is a really dangerous place. People fall hundreds of feet into canyons. Some trip and fall into scalding hot pools. Others get gored by buffalo.

It is even possible to turn around suddenly and be knocked unconscious by a five-foot long camera held by a four-foot tall Asian.

I find these tourists quite intimidating. It got to the point that I was actually embarrassed to pull out my little disposable Kodak camera. Whenever I did some guy from Korea would point, giggle and say . . . okay, I can't write Korean, but I believe it meant, "Ha, ha! Look at the American's tiny thing," or something like that.

See the world this summer—buy an atlas

Well it's finally starting to look like summer. Never too soon to start making some summer activity plans. You could always check out the Hollywood summer block busters. Leading the way is sixty-five-year-old Harrison Ford's new action flick "Indiana Jones and the Nursing Home of Doom." You may have seen the trailer in which Indy is careening down the hallway in his wheelchair in a desperate attempt to warn the residents against eating the squash puree. Then there is the latest Stallone effort "Rocky XLIV" in which the boxing legend trains relentlessly and is even tempted to try steroids to reclaim the checkers crown at the manor. Another potential blockbuster is "Iron Man Meets Magnet Woman." The titillating ads proclaim "... an immediate attachment" and "Sparks will fly!"

Feeling adventurous? Then consider a trip to some exotic locale, say some place like Afghanistan. Reports indicate that nearly 10 square miles out of about 250,000 have been secured by the allied forces. That's the U.S. Army, Navy, Marines, Air Force, Coast Guard, and Boy Scouts. Oh, and the two ambulance drivers from

Botswana, but they aren't allowed to use guns unless they are on the brink of being skewered by some tribal warlord. Once there, you could participate in the national sport Buzkashi, which literally translated means "goat grabbing." Ironically you could be arrested for the same activity in certain parts of Utah.

On the other hand, Iraq is probably a place that you want to avoid. If you recall, around five years ago the US Commander-in-Chief accidentally invaded Iraq due to faulty intelligence, both his and the military leaders. The President carelessly typed a q in place of an n, an understandable error. When informed of the situation, President Bush replied, "Oops, I did it again!" He later went on to say that as long as we're there we may as well stay—considering the price of gas and all.

How about just a simple family trip? Due to high fuel costs it's possible that you may have to greatly downsize your summer vacation plans. For example, I know a guy who had grandiose plans to camp near a waterfall, soak in a hot springs, and see elk. Instead, he set up the camper in the driveway, hooked the garden hose to the roof, filled up the bathtub with steaming hot water, and attached plastic antlers to Fido's head.

And how did we get into this energy fix in the first place? Well, I believe the problem started in 2000 soon after then Governor Jeb Bush was allowed to vote 1400 times which gave Florida's electoral votes to the Bush/Cheney ticket. Vice President Dick Cheney called a summit and met with top oil executives behind closed doors to form our nation's energy policy for the future. The public now has access to a tape recording of those meetings. Here is a transcript:

Cheney: "Ok, guys, what should be our new energy policy?"

Oil executives: "Sell more SUV's and quadruple the price of gas."

Cheney: "Done. Hey, let's go shoot something."

Now if you didn't spend all of your tax rebate check on gas for the drive down to the post office to pick it up, and you're considering a vacation to, say, Yellowstone National Park, Grand Canyon, Mt. Rushmore, etc., you know, a major tourist attraction, then prepare to make a slight modification to what you have done in the past. For example, plan on walking. And plan on leaving real soon, like tonight, so you can get there before the snow flies next fall. Of course, you could buy one of those high-mileage scooters you see around town, load up the family, and head out. Maybe you could balance some 20 foot long poles on the motorbike for the kids to sit on, sort of like the Flying Wallendas.

The reason I say this is, once again, due to the price of gas. Oh, I know it is high here locally. It has gotten so bad that at one pump station I had to choose a button for Debit, Credit, or Drive Off. But wait until you pull up to the pump in some ritzy tourist trap resort. In fact, I am willing to wager that for the first time in history half of the people who drive somewhere on vacation will not be able to afford the return trip. Some families will need to work the winter season washing dishes, bussing tables, handing out flyers on the Vegas Strip, etc., so as to collect enough money to buy gas for the drive home next summer.

Of course there are countless other possibilities for summer fun, but I will need to discuss them at another time since Fido has his antlers stuck in the fence.

Time to gear up for another sleepless camping season

The other day I saw a saying about camping, the primitive kind, not the condo-on-wheels variety. It said "All we left behind is what we ate yesterday." I'm not sure if this saying is by the campers themselves or by the bears speaking about the campers, but it did make me aware that now that the monsoon season appears to be nearing an end, it's time to start seriously preparing for camping season.

For me such preparation is quite simple. First I need to hunt down my twenty-five-year-old, black, two-man tent. It was green when I bought it, but it's black now, the result of pitching it too close to smoldering campfires. In fact, the same is true of all my camping clothes. They're easy to locate by simply following the smell, a sort of combination deet, burnt marshmallow, hoppy scent.

By "camping clothes" I don't mean LL Bean high-tech gear, I simply mean jeans and a flannel shirt that cannot be worn anywhere else in public due to EPA regulations. It gets to the point that near the end of a normal camping season, I don't even bother to start a campfire to experience that intoxicating scent, I simply take a whiff of my shirtsleeve every little bit.

Today, as I hold my nose and unfold my crusty . . . uh, trusty old tent, I grow dizzy from the flood of memories it unleashes, or possibly I am just swooning from the smoky stench. There is the once straight aluminum pole now crescent shaped from the time I was jolted upright from a sound sleep by a crack of thunder and rammed my head into it. And here, captured between the tent sides and the rain fly is the colony of insects collected over the years, some of which have mutated into previously unclassified species. They greet me with an excited buzz, happy to be back in the warm sunlight after hibernating all winter in the shed.

In addition, I recall from last summer that none of the zippers on my tent work quite right anymore. Oh sure, back in its younger days I could zip that baby up air tight to ward off the elements, then wake up in pitch dark, sweat pouring down my face, gasping for air and grappling blindly for a way out.

Or I would wake up on a moonless night in a mad rush to answer nature's call and, after wrestling my way out of a mummy sleeping bag designed to hold Gitmo detainees secure during interrogation, grab all three tent zippers simultaneously in a race to freedom. A few minutes later, after stumbling around in the woods and in the course of blindly finding my way back, I would trip over a tent stake and crash head first into the tent.

Sadly, after years of such abuse the old tent is leakier than a cow wearing Depends. That's because now, after climbing inside the tent and finally getting all of the zippers shut to protect me from the dangers of the forest like rabid chipmunks, if I even sneeze, they all instantly pop open. So I just pile some logs along the bottom of the "door" hoping this will discourage little critters from Storming the Bastille and entering the tent for a late-night visit.

Next in line is the sleeping bag. I've always felt that camping would be lots of fun if you could eliminate two things: going to the bathroom and sleeping in a bag. And it's particularly maddening when you accidentally combine the two!

Sometimes as I roll out the sleeping bag at bed time, I get the eerie feeling that it is sneering at me and whispering, "Do you actually think that I'm going to let you get any sleep? Ha, ha, ha . . . ."

There's another thing about sleeping bags that drives me crazy. Have you ever noticed when you buy a new bag how it is perfectly packed into a stuff sack? I am always reluctant to take it out the first time because I know that it will never fit in that little sack again.

The people at the sleeping bag stuffing factory must be on some heavy doses of Prozac to have such patience. I would not last one day on that job. Sometimes I get in such a hysterical rage after a dozen fruitless attempts to cram the bag in its wallet-sized container that I actually end up with more of me inside the sack than the sleeping bag!

But I figured out how to eliminate the frustration. I simply wrap the sleeping bag up with my tent so the bugs have something warm to cozy up to during the long, cold winter.

Tortoise crossing—expect long delays

I'm not a very religious person, but I must admit that I did a lot of praying on a recent car trip to Southern California. Getting past Las Vegas was particularly taxing. Average daily auto traffic for Vegas is over 100,000 vehicles and, I swear, on both our trips past the city all 100,000 waited for our car to enter the city limits before zooming up the on ramp! Or maybe it just happened to be rush hour which in Vegas runs from midnight to midnight.

My wife's strategy on urban freeways is to stay in the middle lane and not budge for anything. This can occasionally result in some long intervals stuck behind a cattle truck which just spent all day crossing the blazing hot desert hauling a ton of cow poop which, by now, through a magical chemical process, has morphed into a deadly brown cloud of methane gas which is streaming from the truck straight into our car's air vent.

We did manage to navigate the traffic successfully though I never witnessed how that happened since I was hiding in the back seat cuddled up with the dog, both of us with our heads under a pillow until the car was no longer surrounded by speeding deranged gamblers all feeling just a tad bit grumpy after staying up all night throwing away money on watered down drinks and rigged slot machines.

It's no wonder that the Interstate leading into Vegas is lined with billboards advertising lawyers since a lot of tourists will end up filing for bankruptcy once they return home from "Sin City." That is, the people will make it home—while all their money "stays in Vegas."

On this latest trip I noticed that large metro areas like Salt Lake City have an Express Lane which you can use under certain criteria which I assume includes experience as a former NASCAR driver. It seems many Utahans interpret "Express Lane" as synonymous with "Bat out of hell Lane."

If you ask me, it only seems fair that, with so many retired baby boomers now traveling year around, a logical option would be to add a "Senior Lane." It would have no minimum speed, no passing, and rest areas every mile offering free coffee and bingo games.

When it's my turn to drive in Nevada, I prefer long, desolate stretches of two-lane where I just have to deal with an occasional crazed, sun-stroked jack rabbit bounding across the road to get to the other side for reasons that escape me because the desolate landscape on the left looks just as God-forsaken as that on the right.

But at night, even driving endless two-lane stretches of deserted desert can be troublesome for me when every bug that pops up out of the blackness and into the headlight glare becomes an imagined deer, coyote, or even an Islamic terrorist who somehow got his deserts mixed up and is now a Mojave Jihadi.

An interesting trait of the highways in Southern California is the presence of call boxes, roadside telephones apparently available for emergency situations, some 4,000 in Los Angeles County alone. This seems like a waste since the average middle school student now has a phone that can do just about everything except warm up the kid's enchilada he just picked up at the convenient mart on the way home from school.

Instead of call boxes, how about an occasional rest area to use for the most important call of all—nature's call!? I realize that the drought has gotten pretty severe in the state but surely Californians can squeeze out and drink an occasional drop of water from a sliced-up cactus, causing a man to eventually need to "drain his lizard" (appropriate desert slang, don't you think?).

Of course, there are truck pull-off areas, but I'm a little reluctant to park between two monstrous semi-trucks with their hoods raised to cool their roaring engines which are bigger than my entire car. Or slide past a couple of truckers who resemble 1950s professional wrestler Haystacks Calhoun, who weighed 600 lb. and wore an actual horseshoe on a neck chain, like some sort of hillbilly bling bling, so I can mosey over behind the nearest yucca plant to take a whiz!

We topped off our trip with some relaxing time exploring the desert. We actually stumbled upon a rare desert tortoise. That's one species with every justification to be bisexual due to the slim chance of encountering any other turtles in the middle of nowhere, let alone one of the opposite sex. I mean, after waiting patiently in the shade of a bush for a year, even a cross-dressing lizard, say a Gila monster with a discarded Pizza Hut box attached to its back, would look darn good.

Yeah, I could see that happening. After all, it is California.

Yo ho ho and a tanker of oil

This morning, as the thick fog finally lifted, I discovered that Fluffy, our tiny white poodle, had disappeared. My first thought, naturally, was that some roguish German Shepherd had taken advantage of the poor visibility and scooped up poor Fluffy in his filthy paws and absconded with her.

Or, possibly, my pampered pooch's fate was much more dire. What if Fluffy was the latest kidnap victim of Somali Pirates! They would hold her hostage and demand a huge ransom. What could I do? Rent a helicopter and fly over this East African nation to drop off the ransom money in a parachute? Carefully hoist up my terrified little Fluffy in a basket attached to a long rope? I shudder at the thought.

Apparently, Somalia did not always have such a bad image. Early Egyptians thought the area so fragrant they referred to it as the Land of Punt, the same nickname given to the Detroit Lions football stadium this past season. But the Somali pirates are anything but aromatic.

Keep in mind these pirates are not your masqueraded strolling balladeers at a seafood restaurant who switch their eye patch between shows. Furthermore, we are definitely not dealing with classic, romanticized Johnny Depp types here who slur mild threats then retreat full speed when faced with an actual danger. And quite clearly they are nothing like Errol Flynn swinging from deck to deck on a rope, fighting off an entire crew with a penknife, and whisking away a fainting damsel in distress with nary one of his hairs out of place afterwards.

No, these are Somali pirates. They don't sport Jolly Roger tattoos or have peg legs. They don't sit around a roaring fire with their compadres singing colorful rum drinking songs. Nor do they have exotic names like Black Dog or Long John Silver. Instead, they have names similar to a seemingly endless stream of people in the news nowadays, even U.S. presidents, like Ibn Abu Mulaika, Hadith Abu Dawud, or Kareem Abdul-Jabbar. No wait. He isn't a pirate; he's a pilot in the movie Airplane.

179

If you should ever be a passenger aboard a hijacked cruise ship along the coast of East Africa someday, it could come in handy to be familiar with some common social taboos of the culture and frequently used Somali expressions. For example, amongst Somalis the "thumbs up" gesture is considered obscene and could result in a "thumbs off" response by a Somali pirate brandishing a sword.

In addition, the country of Somalia has an extremely high divorce rate. That's because if a man in Somalia wants a divorce he simply repeats three times to his wife, "I divorce you," and the couple is considered legally split. That is one reason why most Somali lawyers have moved elsewhere. The trick is that the husband has to say it real fast or else, before he can complete the sequence, he might get a frying pan crashing through his little black sideways pirate hat resulting in his utterance of that popular pirate expression "Arrrrrrrr!!"

Somali men greet one another with the expression "Soo maal," which is a polite invitation to milk an animal and help yourself to a drink. Now compare such pedestrian talk to classic pirate sayings such as "Avast, ye scurvy dogs!" "Shiver me timbers!" or "Chips, Ahoy!" and stuff like that.

Notice that real pirate talk always ends with an exclamation point! Pirates always shout at each other since most are nearly deaf from over exposure to cannon fire.

I think that we would all agree that real pirate talk is much more colorful than, say, the Somali expression "Wayaan doonayaa in aan gurigo tago" which means "Milk the goat, not me, you idiot!"

Other ways in which the Somali pirates are different is that they use rocket launchers instead of swords to subdue their victims. However, you have to be mighty careful when firing a rocket at an oil tanker full to the brim with crude. That is sort of like striking a match to check if there is any gas left in the can.

Another challenge that the Somali pirates face in dealing with their booty (as in treasure, not like in a hip-hop video) is that, unlike a wooden chest full of gold doubloons, how does one bury a super tanker filled with 2 million barrels of oil? Of course, once they do manage to cover the ship with sand they do not use crudely designed maps drawn on parchment to locate it later. No, modern day pirates use GPS devices.

However, one has to wonder whether a pirate has consumed too much Captain Morgan and is wearing two eye patches when he can't locate a sandy hump the size of AT&T Stadium without help!

We are surrounded by nuts

We all do our share of dumb things. For example, I'm one of those guys at the concert who accidentally applauds during the brief break between movements of Beethoven's Symphony No. 9 in D minor, causing the rest of the audience to turn around and try to spot the uncouth lout who apparently got mixed up and thought he was at The Corner Bar's karaoke night.

And I have to admit it's pretty embarrassing during the one time a year that I go shopping to purchase that real crunchy kind of potato chip that I love and customers are lined up behind me at the check-out stand because I'm the only guy in the city who still writes checks. But since I forgot my reading glasses I'm not sure if I just wrote one for $3.87 or $3,087, so I decide to use some plastic. However, I need assistance from the checker because I can never remember if my card is debit or credit and which direction to swipe it.

But I feel fairly stable compared to some people that I encountered on a recent trip to Oregon. Like the guy in the motel breakfast room who's blocking the path to the food so that no one else can get to it, one of those guys who should have a "Wide Load" sign pinned to his back.

While I'm waiting for my chance to fill my Styrofoam bowl with off-brand Raisin Bran, this guy is preparing a mixture to make a third waffle that is so big it resembles a catcher's mitt. Plus, he's filling up the pockets of his bib overalls with apples, sweet rolls, little jelly packets, etc., apparently stocking up to avoid starvation during the long trek back to his motel room.

Or how about those people who, no matter how fast you drive on the Interstate, they have to pass you. You know, the type of guy who tries to pass you on the right because he feels that you're taking too long getting by that semi-truck loaded with cattle. I always speed up when they try that so I can keep them boxed in until I feel they have suffered long enough or until the methane gas forces him to back off.

When I finally pull into a town on the Oregon coast, I suspect that the strange guy in the car next to me at the red light, the one who's bobbing his head back and forth within an inch of the dashboard and listening to "Scream Bloody Gore" by Leprosy, then suddenly glances my way with blazing red eyes, is surely Mephistopheles come to collect my soul. So that when the light turns green I turn off the ignition and pretend to have car trouble, letting him go on ahead until clear out of sight.

During a lunch stop at a Chubby Dog food truck (slogan: "The more you weigh, the harder you are to kidnap!"), I feel pressured to tip generously the guy working the counter due to the fact I slipped up and told him what motel we're staying at right before noticing how he closely resembled Norman Bates in "Psycho."

At the next town, I stop to exercise the dog when a man shows up who looks like he just stepped out of a scene from Road Warrior, with his purple Mohawk and chains dangling from every orifice. A guy who obviously did not (or could not) read the sign which states "Friendly dogs only allowed" before entering the fenced-in dog park as he's got one of those really mean looking dogs with scars all over it and missing part of an ear. The dog is wearing a collar that appears to be some sort of medieval torture device made out of barbed wire and with sharp prongs jabbing the dog in the neck, apparently intended to work it into a fighting frenzy. So when your poodle attempts a "Howdy" sniff, Rambo's dog does its best impersonation of Cujo, flipping your little Fifi around like a Frisbee.

Of course, one does not even need to leave the house to encounter wacky characters, not with access to the Internet. Certainly the Internet is handy for certain things, say, for example, before I step outside, I can check the forecast to see how much hair spray I need to apply to prevent my three hairs from whipping around like one of those inflatable air dancers advertising mufflers on sale,

But the real insidious result of using the Internet is that one begins to strongly suspect that we are surrounded by nuts twenty-four seven. To the point that I find myself nervously glancing back over my shoulder while even performing the most innocuous computer task, such as seeing what the stars of the 1968 television show "Laugh-in" look like today. Hint: not good.

Chapter 6   You Name It

Bond . . . Bobby Joe Billy Bond

The holiday stress is approaching its peak. What with researching innovative ways to create a palatable left-over turkey dish (By the way, the frozen turkeysicle is to die for--or from), trying to recall if I bought the boys new underwear for Christmas last year, and trying to determine if the receiver's foot was inbounds or not, a guy could go crazy.

Thank goodness for the annual great escape from reality provided by the James Bond Movie Marathon which I, once again, boldly sat through this past Thanksgiving weekend. I always find it a bit confusing that Bond's appearance morphs from film to film which I assume is just part of the stealthy business of being a secret agent.

I find it interesting that James Bond operates out of England. Naturally, this adds an instant touch-of-class to his entire persona. There is no doubt that our modern U.S.A culture still feels inferior to the British in some regards. We assume that someone who speaks with a British accent reeks of intelligence and sophistication. And, I guess, compared to someone from New Jersey or Yahoo, Arkansas, it's true.

But what if Bond operated out of a far different culture, say a place like Timbuktu (formerly spelled Timbuctoo, Timbuktoo, and, in Texas, Tim Bucks Too?)? Located in West Africa, Timbuktu suffers from desertification which has nothing to do with a third trip to the buffet dessert bar. It means that every morning you will crawl out from under a foot of sand, take a warm sand shower, and dig into a hearty breakfast of scrambled sand.

Just how cool do you think our dapper secret agent would be as he crawls out of his tent and uses a step ladder to climb aboard his "even-toed ungulate within the genus Camelus, bearing distinctive fatty deposits known as humps on its back" instead of the sleek, silver Aston Martin? Then after rescuing a rather "full-figured" belly dancer from a marauding band of sweat thieves, our hero introduces himself as "Bond . . . Sheik Mustapha Salami Aswan Bond." Just not the same, wouldn't you say?

Possibly the Bond character could operate out of a location much closer to home, say Utah. Can you just imagine James in hot pursuit of an evil antagonist who failed to feed the parking meter the correct amount? While tearing up the pavement in his all-electric vehicle, smaller than some of James' guns, and just as he closes in to nab the culprit, the car's batteries run out of juice and it dies. So James attempts to hop aboard the TRAX which is capable of hitting a top speed of 35 mph on the Bonneville Salt Flats, but he is stymied since he is a nickel shy of the $2.35 fare, so he lies and says he is 65 years old and now has money to spare.

The pursuit leads to the Salt Lake International Airport where James is delayed again due to Advanced Imaging Technology which reveals his personal arsenal. However, the TSA security lady falls head over heels for James, so he suggests that they meet back in the unclaimed baggage room, but since this is Utah she says that they must get married first.

Even after finally tracking down the villain, James has a difficult time celebrating with his favorite beverage. In Utah, you can be served a drink as long as nobody can see it, so you have to ask everyone in the place to close their eyes briefly while you shout, "Ah, what a yummy glass of lemonade!" Most bizarre, in restaurants you can order a drink as long as you also order food, after which an employee will sit on your lap and verify that you take one mouthful of lasagna after each sip of your chosen elixir.

A final interesting twist in the Bond saga could involve the fact that James has a long-forgotten brother named Bobby Joe Bond who lives in a backwoods cabin in Mississippi and fits right in among the proud ranks of the most obese state in the most obese developed nation. Bobby Joe and his wife Ruby Sue suffer from a serious inferiority complex because neither one of them could even fit into the seat of one of those "fancy, girly-men cars that James drives" let alone their eleven children.

Bobby Joe concludes by lamenting, "Oh, James will send us an occasional postcard from Istanbul or some other 'bull' showing him all duded up with a martini in one hand and some harlot under each arm. I pray for him at the Baptist church each week during the rattlesnake handling when the minister lets a snake bite him. By the way, do you know any ministers looking for a job?"

Confessions of a shopaphobic

Now I avoid shopping like the plague, especially groceries. About the only time I go to a grocery store is when my wife forgets to buy my favorite chips. Then, and only then, will I jump in the car and make a special trip to the store because that is an essential part of my diet.

For one thing, I get flustered every time I try to purchase something with a credit card. It seems that they just change the system overnight without any warning. One day I hand the checker my credit card and sign an actual paper receipt with an actual pen. But then, my next trip to the store, a short year and a half later, I'm asked "Debit or credit?" I have no clue. I panic and feel sweat dripping down my face.

So why wasn't I warned about this basic change in the shopping system? Like the warnings every five minutes that we all received over the last two years about the switch from analog to digital television broadcasts. I mean, everywhere you turned there were flashing red lights, blaring sirens, ominous black birds rapping on your chamber door. Frantic strangers would just run up and grab you as you walked down the street screaming, "It's coming!" like it's the invasion of the body snatchers. But when the day finally arrives, half of the country is whining, "Why didn't you tell us?"

But the real kicker is when it comes time to sign the little screen. Of course, by now there is a restless line of customers behind me and the pressure is building. So I grab the "pen" which is dangling on a chain, as if anyone would run off with it. After all what good is it since you can't see the writing, which I couldn't see even if I could see it because I forgot my dang reading glasses! So I just sort of guess where the line is and when I'm all finished my name appears on the screen and looks like something a pet chimpanzee would scratch out right before it playfully ripped off its owner's face.

Overall, though, filling up at the gas pump tops all stressful situations. The first problem is remembering which side the gas tank fill spout is on. I've developed a clever trick to help me in this regard which involves hanging half way out the car window while driving down the Interstate at 75 mph in a raging blizzard and looking back

Once at the station, the frustration builds as you swing your car around to the pump in a nifty little maneuver, hop out, grab the pump, then realize that it's the wrong side after all. First you try to stay cool and calmly stretch the hose well beyond its limit around the rear of the car. Next you foolishly look under and over the car to see if it will reach. You even consider opening doors on both sides and running the hose across the baby's lap in its car seat to reach the gas tank. Finally you cancel the transaction and stealthily exit.

And how about the endless series of questions you have to answer before you actually get the privilege of filling up your tank? I always say "No" to the receipt question because I fret that I will forget to grab it then some crook will get it and my bank account will be even emptier than it already is due to a slight miscalculation by every financial institution in the universe which apparently took place in a five minute span sometime last summer.

Also, I always worry what will happen if I accidentally push "Yes" for the carwash, yet I actually don't want a carwash at 6:30 AM as I fill up on an icy cold January morning. I have this fear that the station attendants will force me into the carwash bay since I said "Yes" and five minutes after I exit, my car will be encased in a block of ice and I'll be stranded in the middle of the freeway like a giant Popsicle.

It gets worse-- if there is a malfunction with the pump you are really in for an adventure. Because then you actually have to enter the truck stop/restaurant/tobacco shop/video store/motorcyclist boutique. You suddenly feel like a real wimp when you compare your $28.00 fuel charge to the guy in front of you who looks like half of ZZ Top with his $348.00 diesel bill. To add insult to injury you're sucking on a kiwi Slurpee while he has a carton of Camels, a pound of Red Hot Beef Jerky, a new skull-and-crossbones bandana, and is chugging a liter of some high energy drink named after a Norse mythological god!

Doomsdayers postpone making Christmas layaway payments

Whew! Gotta' take a break from digging an underground shelter in the backyard. I am sure that you too have been making final preparations for the end of the world which coincides with the end of the Mayan calendar and the end of the college football season.

It is not clear to me why we, a highly civilized society that has developed a telephone which is used for everything other than making a phone call, would put much stock in a prediction made by ancient people who ritually drew blood from parts of the body which, today, cannot be displayed in public outside of tattoo parlors.

And why should the end of the Mayan calendar have any more significance than the calendar on my wall given to me last Christmas by Harold's Auto Shop which features a pinup of Miss Ratchet Set 2012, sprawled across the hood of a 1979 pickup, wearing only a pair of greasy coveralls and seductively fondling a crowbar?

When you look at the artifacts depicting images of Mayans lined up for blood-letting or to be sacrificed, don't they remind you of today's long lines of customers waiting to purchase the latest cell phone innovation? I would propose that there's little difference other than, whereas the Mayans worshipped the maize or cacao god, we worship the Apple or Blackberry god.

One source notes that the Mayans "were far less prolific in sacrificing people than their neighbors" which is sort of like saying,

"Yeah, sure, I'm a crackhead, but, hey, the guy next door gets food stamps and listens to Guns N' Roses."

To cash in on the doomsday prophecy, Russian entrepreneurs are selling an "Apocalypse kit" that includes a bottle of Russian vodka and a CD of classic Russian Christmas songs sung by Vladimir Putin, including "I'll Be Home from Siberia for Christmas" and "Rudolf the Red-Nosed Commie." Not sure if the kit is to help one survive the end or provide a slow, painful way to end it all.

One cannot totally discount the Mayan knack for making correct predictions. For example, they predicted the future existence of a black hole in the center of our Galaxy called "Hunab Ku" which is Mayan for Republican Party, and that prediction has come true. In addition, they predicted hotter air in the future, but since that prophecy originated in the present-day Mexican state of Tabasco, experts are skeptical.

Some other Mayan states were Xunantunich, Uxmal, and Uaxctun. Apparently, names containing the letter x were popular back then. Sort of like names ending in te today, such as Lavonte, D'sante, and Jimmy Durante.

When I was younger, my mother predicted that Elvis marked the end of the world due to his hip gyrations, but the only things that he personally wiped out were all the hog jowls, ham hocks, and liver mush in Tennessee. Later, she said the Beatles signaled doom because of their hairdos. Thank goodness she was not around for Lady Gaga.

Of course, there have always been religious quacks who have tried to sell salvation to the naïve with the end of days' arrival. They usually end their spiel with, "But, wait, call in the next ten minutes and receive two doomsdays for the price of one!" And people call.

However, there is no denying that, recently, American culture is full of signs that the end actually is near. For example, it has been at least a week since Lindsey Lohan has been arrested. And, obviously, the plot to castrate Justin Bieber is another sure sign, although I assumed he already had been.

Then there are the political doomsday markings such as the Fiscal Cliff, which could dump us all in an economic chasm. The Cliff follows on the heels of the presidential election landslide which was preceded by a campaign waste heap of lies.

On the other hand, history is full of predictions that failed to come true. A few months ago, Mitt Romney vowed that he would win the presidential election. He came close, but was nipped by 126 electoral votes which is comparable to losing the Super Bowl by 21 touchdowns. However, he did get three votes in Puerto Rico and carried the Cayman Islands.

Just to be on the safe side, I am preparing for the end by fessing up to some of my youthful misdeeds. To my fifth grade teacher, Sister Mary Christopher Theresa Bernadette Felicity, yes, I threw Andrea's earmuffs out the classroom window. And, yes, Sister, you did have a left hook that would have made Smokin' Joe Frazier proud.

Finally, I am predicting that, if there is a Holocaust on December 21, afterwards the only living creatures remaining on Earth will be the cockroaches, banks that are too big to fail, and The Rolling Stones.

FYI 2B or not 2B is the FAQ

While reading up on the recent commemorations of Shakespeare's life, the thought came to mind that it's a good thing he lived when he did. If Shakespeare was around today, his writing career would be quite different.

First of all, he would have a lot more difficulty even writing down his classic lines. Oh sure, you probably think that it would be much easier today due to developments in technology. But think about all the times that you have picked up a ballpoint pen in your home to write down one of those fleeting, precious ideas—one that you know darn well you're going to forget the moment you move on to a simple task like rinsing out your coffee cup—and the pen won't work! Along with five others that you manage to dig up during a mad scramble.

You try using any scratch paper you can find to scribble around and around with the pen, thinking that scratching out a blank circle bigger and bigger and faster and faster will somehow magically produce ink in a dried up Bic pen that you last used clear back when your wireless, portable phone had an antenna the size of a '59 Chevy's that would allow you to talk while out in the backyard just as long as you did not absentmindedly stroll behind the tall lilac bush.

Along that same line, one would think that having access to the computer would be a huge boon to Shakespeare if he were writing today. Yet, perhaps you've experienced that no matter how dead set you are to stay on task and not get distracted when working on a computer, how easy it is to naively wander off into the Internet hinterland resulting in the hours melting away until you're startled by the sound of the rooster's crowing and the only information you've garnered is that Caitlyn Jenner is nervous about dating men.

Can't you just see the Bard googling "Cleopatra" for some biographical information and up pops photos of pole dancers at the notorious Berlin nightclub?

I'm sure we all agree that it would have been a literary disaster if Will, led astray by an endless stream of Kardashian articles and pictures, had run short on time while working on his tragic romance drama so settled for a bit shorter play titled "Romeo."

And I'm not convinced that having access to the online dictionaries and thesauri would really be all that beneficial for Shakespeare. It's so easy to revise and rewrite with the computer that I just can't help but feel that a perfect word like "methinks" would end up on the cutting room floor and be replaced with an annoying expression like "Just sayin'." That would not be cool, methinks.

On the other hand, it's a pretty safe bet that Shakespeare's tweets would be in iambic pentameter.

In today's culture, Shakespeare would have more entertainment offerings to compete against than bear-baiting and toad-tossing. Exciting choices like Beyoncé's visual album "Lemonade" in which she screams "You ain't loving hard enough!" Yikes, I get a charley horse just thinking about that.

It's a well known fact that financing for plays was hard to come by back in 17th century England. If Shakespeare was seeking investors for his theatrical endeavors today, he would have quite a few more options.

He could even post something like this on the personal online fundraising website GoFundMe to seek financial backers: "I've got an idea for a comedy play in which all the female parts are played by men and the men playing the females disguise themselves as males so they can get the real men to fall in love with them."

Now it's possible that some people might think that this sounds more like a reality TV series set in San Francisco. But it's also possible that Shakespeare would have money rolling in from every state. Well, maybe not North Carolina.

Speaking of TV, it's hard to imagine that Shakespeare today would not be heavily influenced by the current popularity of zombies in shows like "The Walking Dead" and "Fear the Walking Dead." Instead of the ghost of Hamlet's father, it would not be that much of a stretch to have Hamlet's father return as a zombie, seeking an eye (leg, arm, etc.) for an eye in revenge for his murder.

There is little doubt that Shakespeare would find a wealth of dramatic ideas in "The Tempest" otherwise known as the 2016 presidential campaign. Why, the entire slate of GOP candidates could step right in as the cast for a production of his play "Comedy of Errors."

Once the frontrunners from both parties go head to head, the poet's pen would hardly be able to keep up with the drama. Will Donald Trump triumph in "The Taming of the Shrew"? Or, during a midsummer night's debate, will Hillary Clinton expose Trump as an ass, like Nick Bottom?

Whatever the outcome, it's a safe bet that Shakespeare would be glad when it's all over, and the media has ceased making "Much Ado about Nothing."

Graduation—time to party because the party's over

It must be graduation time since the stores are displaying colorful inflated Mylar balloons with cheerful sayings like "Congrats Grad" and "See, You Aren't So Dumb After All!"

It seems like you can get a balloon for almost any occasion nowadays although I don't recall seeing a hearse crawling down the street with black balloons attached, not yet anyway. Once I purchased eighty inflated balloons for a school fund-raiser and tried to load them in my car during a wind storm, which nearly sent me floating over Pocatello like Mary Poppins sans the umbrella.

Most countries only have formal graduation ceremonies at the university level. But not here in the United States since we tend to turn every minor achievement of our children into a BIG DEAL. In this country we have preschool graduation—giving the youngsters an opportunity to show off their newly acquired skills such as the ability to use crayons for something other than a snack— kindergarten graduation, middle-school graduation, junior-high graduation, and on and on.

Of course, I understand that high school graduation is a time-honored tradition which allows parents to justify the recent purchase of their new $9,000 high-tech waterproof HD video camera. Plus, it gives graduate families, friends, and relatives an apparently socially-acceptable excuse to whoop and holler in public like a troop of monkeys that just won the Publishers Clearing House 5,000-bananas-per-month-for-life prize!

During my years as a student, teacher, and parent, I attended so many of these ceremonies that I developed the unique ability to play a nearly recognizable rendition of "Pomp and Circumstance" on the kazoo and have personally witnessed the modern evolution of this enhanced interrogation technique otherwise known as high school graduation.

Traditionally, it is believed that the long graduation gowns were first worn because early universities were not well heated back in the 12th century. Plus, the large size of the gowns allowed a medieval student to secretly fiddle with his abacus beneath the gown, which isn't as bad as it sounds. Whereas, today's graduates are simply texting one another that Mr. Snodgrass, the school counselor, is asleep and about to fall off the stage.

The graduation mortarboard caps appeared around the 14th century and were originally popular with artists since, I suppose, they could double as a palette. Today's students' ability to successfully move the cap tassel from the right side to the left is the final graduation requirement, and I have to tell you that I lost count over the years as to how many seniors were retained another semester due to failing this last standardized test. Hopefully, the Common Core will correct this sad situation.

The robes and caps were still being worn when I graduated in the 1960s despite the fact that where I lived it was ninety degrees with ninety percent humidity in mid-June and the auditorium did not have air conditioning. Either that, or the teachers and administration were simply trying to get even with my senior class and forgot to turn it on.

All I remember about my graduation is sweating like a pig and praying that it would end before I died from dehydration since those ubiquitous plastic water bottles that people today can't seem to leave the house for five minutes without apparently had not been invented yet.

No one from my family attended—Dad was at work and I told Mom to stay home because it was too hot. Same was true of most of my friends' parents. Back then graduating from high school was just something that my friends and I assumed we had to do, not really something to celebrate. Basically, I wanted to get it over with so I could get back to work at the grocery store.

Today it seems that everything about graduation other than the garb has changed. Now graduation is a major production: bands, videos, beach balls, posters, cow bells, thirty-two valedictorians, etc. Graduates' clans scream, whistle, and applaud when they hear their kid's name like he or she just won the Power Ball. When I hear such a reaction my thought is "Wow, is he the only limb in your family tree to reach this scholarly height?"

Some keynote speakers today simply cut and paste a string of quotations from the Internet, which wouldn't be so bad if they quoted people like Woody Allen ("Sex without love is a meaningless experience, but as far as meaningless experiences go, it's pretty damn good") instead of folks like Sigmund Freud ("Time spent with cats is never wasted"). And, I swear, speakers who read entire books by Dr. Seuss should be tarred and feathered so they can share the audience's pain.

Finally, today's parents go to a lot of trouble selecting graduation gifts, everything from laptops to dorm furniture. But I'm pretty sure that another aspect of graduation which hasn't changed is that just receiving plain old-fashioned cash is still greatly appreciated.

Have you hugged your gun today?

You have no doubt noticed that guns are in the news a lot lately. For example, around the country, people recently celebrated Gun/Teacher Appreciation Day on which kids brought their teachers shiny, new guns instead of apples.

But by far, the main cause of this massive interest in guns is the report describing a Louisiana woman's recent marriage to an AK-47 which, of course, triggers the debate: Gun marriage—should it be legalized? Is it morally right? Although gun marriage is not currently legal in any states, it is legal to purchase a permit to own a gun. But what if the relationship develops into something more than just casual target shooting?

This particular woman's story may be more common than we think. "My first love was a Taser. It was a relationship full of electricity, though it ended in a shocking manner. I got home early from work one evening and caught him in the act of cheating: he was plugged into the wall socket!

"It took a long time for me to get recharged emotionally, but then I met Colt, a snub-nosed revolver. He was a perfect fit in some ways, but his barrel was so short I just couldn't get no satisfaction, to paraphrase the Stones. I should have done a background check on him and I would have found that he formerly was a starter pistol for track meets, so, shoot, this guy was obviously firing blanks.

"Next, there was Harry, a .44 Magnum. Wow, what a stud. But it did not take long to discover why his nickname was "Dirty." He kept forgetting to turn on his safety, so, of course, he would fire prematurely which really took its toll on our relationship. He was careless. He wanted to go out without his holster, and I would plead with him, 'Look, we need protection. At least wear a silencer.' But to no avail.

"Even worse, Harry would go out by himself at night. He would sneak in late, but I could smell gun powder. I never knew whose holster he had been in. It eventually deteriorated into one of those bang, bang, thank you, ma'am relationships.

"After a couple of years, Harry was running out of ammunition, so a friend introduced me to her cousin, Winchester, a .30-06 hunting rifle. After cuddling his stock and feeling his long, sleek barrel—I knew this was the one for me. He was good looking, but, what a temper, certain things he would just go ballistic. So now I am single again, cruising the shooting range circuit, still aiming for Mr. Right Caliber."

It is obvious from her story that there may be a place for legalized marriage between a woman and her gun. What about men? Is it possible for a man's relationship with his gun to go this far? Man's obsession with guns goes clear back to the prehistoric caveman period when Fred Flintstone came home a day early from his Tyrannosaurus hunt and caught Barney clubbing Wilma and dragging her away by the hair. Fred shot him dead. The obsession continues today.

Here is one man's story. "I have always loved guns. I've watched the entire six-volume DVD set "Guns Gone Wild" countless times. My favorite video is "Nuzzle My Muzzle." I have a copy of the Ammo to Go 2013 Swimsuit Calendar with various handguns, rifles, bazookas seductively posing, wearing nothing but skimpy holsters and see-through gun cases. A bit shocking, I know. Eventually, I realized that my gun and I were not just attached at the hip--it went much deeper.

"A short time back I registered with the on-line match making site "eArmory" and it wasn't long until I discovered a 9mm pistol in a little pink holster with the frills hanging down. I tell you, I immediately got an itchy trigger finger. I knew her handle would be a perfect fit, and I told my friends to scope her out. Now, we just like to hang out and listen to .38 Special and the Sex Pistols."

Another male gun lover had a similar experience. "It was sudden impact when I saw her hanging in the back window of that pickup truck, and, boy, she had a nice rack. When I'm with her, it doesn't take me long to reload. I'm crazy about her. I guess you could say I am pistol whipped. Oh, we've misfired a few times, like I got in trouble one night, hanging out at one of those gun shows. My wife gets jealous real easy, and, you know, at those gun shows, you get to fondle a lot of different guns."

Listening to these gun lovers, it is obvious that gun marriage, in the long range, is a much safer choice than having multiple gun partners.

I believe in love, children, and allergies

Recently I was listening to my favorite show starring Ann Coulter, who is sort of an anorexic Lady Gaga, in which she was stating her list of personal beliefs, and it inspired me to put together my list of basic beliefs. Any of which you are welcomed to turn into an inspirational poster.

I believe in Rush Limbaugh, Glenn Beck, and Jesus, but not necessarily in that order because Glen Beck could be first.

I believe that the Common Core Standards are a government conspiracy and that teaching our children critical thinking skills will result in the death of the Republican Party for sure.

I believe Glen Beck when he says that the Common Core Standards, when read backwards, contain a subliminal message about socialist gay zombies eating our kids' brains. And I believe that he will have more to say on this issue once he can find someone who will actually read them to him.

I believe that along with Kahn Academy for math skills, Idaho schools should also utilize Con Academy on the Internet because it will prepare our young people to be politicians and used car salespeople.

I believe that we should provide every student with a laptop and a gun, so when their computer freezes up they can shoot it.

I believe that our schools should teach our children personal health tips, such as the hand sanitizer dispenser is not meant to be used for a complete shower and that they should cover their mouths with someone else's hand when sneezing.

I believe also that children should say a prayer AFTER they eat the school lunch.

I believe that federal guidelines for school lunches will result in our students only being allowed to eat boiled cabbage drippings.

I believe that science teachers should not use the term vagina in the classroom, but should use something less offensive, such as Foofy Bird.

I believe that condoms should not be available in our schools but some deodorant and floss dispensers couldn't hurt.

I believe that all Americans should be required to speak Standard English, including senators from the Deep South so they won't say things like, "Ida claire, the great state of Jawjuh shore don't need no Yankee gubmint sayn we hafta get edgy-cation."

I believe that wolves are responsible for so few Idaho students going on to college, and I believe that the Idaho Education Association is secretly breeding all those wolves and releasing them at night.

I believe that soon the feds will be turning over wolf protection to the states, so you can kiss those puppies goodbye. Won't be long they'll go the same route as the dodo frog and the Edsel.

I believe that with map apps, MapQuest, Google Maps, the GPS, etc., being so popular, there sure must be a lot of people getting lost out there.

I believe in Rand Paul, or maybe it's Ron Paul, no, wait a minute, it's Paul Ryan, or possibly Peter, Paul, and Mary.

I believe that, instead of invading Syria, we should invade Cuba next. It's close, it's communist, and its climate is nice, so soldiers could wear camouflaged Bermuda shorts instead of that totally uncool desert attire. We wouldn't even have to use drones for bombs, we could just stand on Miami Beach and fly heavily armed kites. We could use Ski-Doos to land instead of ships. However, once there, troops would have to be careful of IEDs such as exploding cigars.

I believe that we should not worry about Iran since it's in the past tense.

I believe the Southern states should secede and become The United States of Diabetics.

I believe that men should have access to the "Morning Before Pill" which causes them over the next twenty-four hours to be limp as a wet noodle.

I believe that using cell phones in public places is much more hazardous to our culture than smoking pot in public.

I believe that Miley Cyrus and Justin Bieber are actually the same person although he looks better in a tank top.

I believe, as someone once said, that in basketball a good center and a good point guard should go hand-in-hand, but not into the shower.

I believe that Reagan, Nixon, and George W. Bush should have busts carved into a giant haystack in an even more popular tourist state than South Dakota, say Kansas.

I believe in Big Foot as well as in Big Bird, Big Bad Wolf and Big Head Todd and the Monsters.

Finally, I believe that the Fosbury Flop, originated by Ketchum's own Dick Fosbury and which has resulted in continual new highs in the high jump, is nothing compared to the Luna Limbo which is constantly striving for new lows in state support of education.

I'd rather be at work than a workshop

Summer time is full of opportunities for professionals of various types to sharpen up their skills. Whether it is in the field of education, Information Technology, or circus clown, there is a summer workshop for a person to attend. I have experienced many summer workshops for my profession and have noticed certain characteristics common to most of them.

First rule is to never, I mean never, arrive early for a workshop. If you should seriously slip up and think you will "beat the crowd" and arrive a half-hour early to register, it will not take you long to realize your error because the front door of the workshop facility will be locked. If you're lucky, the night janitor just finishing up his shift may hear your angry pounding or spot you jumping up and down, pointing at the door, and let you in.

After you do manage to enter the building, those involved in the registration process will be frantically setting up a table and looking for pencils and forms to sign you up while sounding a bit miffed, exclaiming, "Well, aren't you the early bird!" as if you just violated a principal garage sale rule.

Inside the conference room, the fun really begins. First, you must take a nametag and place it around your neck. Now this is something that I have never understood although I have actually seen individuals during the obligatory "Let's introduce ourselves" segment of the workshop look down at their tag when giving their names. So maybe there is a practical reason for them.

Next, they shove a goodies bag at you which generally contains some stuff that the workshop sponsors haven't been able to get rid of over the last few years. Stuff like a water bottle to add to the dozen you already have and a cute squeeze toy whose eyes pop out when you attempt to relieve the stress that is going to start building up over the next few hours.

And of course we can't make it through the morning without a muffin so big it could double as a life raft.

Once the actual presentations begin you endure the groups of late comers who go by 'Idaho time' which usually means that most of them will have trickled in by the first morning break. Groups of late comers always strive to put on a big show by standing in the aisle discussing where to sit, eventually selecting seats near the center of a row so as to make everyone stand up, and then pausing half way to their seats to check their cell phones.

Of course first we have to suffer through this spiel: "Good morning! Before we get started, some housekeeping—the ladies' restroom is located down the hall a quarter mile, turn right, take the third left, ride the elevator to the 14th floor, hustle across the parking lot, where you will find a large bush. Since ladies need more time we will dismiss you now and expect to see you back here right after lunch. Men, on the other hand, usually go to the bathroom anywhere including where they are currently sitting, so . . . ."

My biggest pet peeve are the people who call in with questionable excuses to skip a workshop: "We just got a call from Mary Jones whose beloved poodle Puffy was abducted by aliens early this morning and her husband has mysteriously come down with both the East and West Nile viruses."

While sweatshops are defined as work places which are "unacceptably dangerous," certainly this description applies to workshops too. How many times have you seen an attendee fall asleep during a lecture and have his head come crashing down onto a laptop keyboard that he was pretending to take notes on but was actually making a desperate attempt to remove Tebow from his Fantasy Football roster?

And I intentionally used the masculine pronouns in the previous example since it does appear that men find workshops about as interesting as operas and have a much more difficult time staying focused at them which explains why you will see large groups of male attendees seated near all of the possible exits.

In fact, I have developed a theory that females actually look forward to summer workshops since they normally make up about 90% of those in attendance. What is even more inexplicable is they always seem so happy and excited to be there! Their nametags look like a work of art while mine looks like a baboon scribbled on it with his own feces. And the goodies bag! My gosh, you would think they were children opening presents on Christmas morning!

Finally, have you ever been to a technology conference where the technology used actually worked? Neither have I.

I'll take the Wily Coyote stir-fry, please

Why did the chicken cross the road? To escape the coyote that was heading to the Chinese restaurant! That's right. Bet you did not realize that if you enter a Chinese restaurant and order food to go, they will bring your dinner out on a leash. Another way of looking at it is "Chinese takeout" now means that you're taking your dinner out for a walk—that, or they need to make those funny white takeout boxes a whole lot bigger!

Really this coyote in the restaurant freezer story should come as no surprise. Look, these are the same people who offer such items as caterpillar fungus duck, crab and fish stomachs, fried tofu curd balls (oh, those poor curds!), fish ball soup (fish have them?), and dongpoo (don't ask), etc.

Plus, when you consider the Chinese zodiac, things could get a lot worse. Personally, I'm sticking with McBurger when I eat out during the Year of the Rat. On the other hand, it might be kind of fun to pick up a monkey to go.

In my way of thinking, is eating coyote any worse than eating a cow that's been lying on a dunghill for a month in the mid-July heat? Or a pig that would not hesitate to eat its brother pig which had just finished digesting Farmer Jones, as in the Oregon incident where all that investigators found in the pig pen were the decease's "dentures, hat, and a package of cigarettes"?

Investigators did not suspect foul play—well, of course not, these are pigs, not chickens. Also, to the pigs' credit, they apparently do not smoke.

Despite a few interesting eating habits, the Chinese are obviously producing some top-notch athletes. Take for instance tennis star Li Na, aka, Na Li. Just depends on whether she's coming or going, I guess. Li recently made it to the finals of the Australian

Open. This surprised me since I was only aware of the Chinese dominance in table tennis—a sport that got its more popular name from China's legendary athletic twins Ping and Pong.

In China, table tennis is formally called ping pang in which, I believe, after scoring a point the player shouts, "Walla walla bing bang!" Children start playing ping pong when they are infants. For a ball, they use a grain of rice which they get to eat if they win. And let's face it, anyone who can eat with chop sticks has to have excellent hand-eye coordination. When I try to use chop sticks, it usually results in hand-eye contusion. I personally feel that most Chinese food would be easier to eat with a giant straw.

Surprisingly, the contrast in the physiques between the Chinese tennis players and the Americans is stark. I mean it looks like Venus Williams could hide two of those little fellers inside her tennis outfit.

Li's opponent in the Open title match, Victoria Azarenka from Belarus, was a surprise to me as well. First of all, I thought Belarus was a type of whale. So I did a little research and found that Belarus is a country near Smolensk—big help that is! Next, I learned that at one time people migrated from Belarus to Siberia which should tell us something about the quality of life in her home country!

Just to be fair, Belarus does host some exciting cultural events. For example, just this past year the city of Kolozhsky hosted the 12th International Festival of Orthodox Chants, an event that annually sets new world records for caffeine consumption during a 48-hour period. Another don't-miss happening is the Belarusian Grooming Forum and Championship which could probably benefit me personally.

To circle back to the food topic, in Belarus the favorite dishes are potato dumplings, thick potato pancakes, and baked grated potato pie—ummm, nothing like a well balanced diet. This may explain why men there die, on average, 12 years younger than women: females play tennis while the men sit in the bleachers and eat potatoes.

Whatever she has been eating, it doesn't appear to have hindered Azarenka in her athletic exploits. She is 6-feet tall and so tough that she prefers to play tennis in her bare feet since, from the time they are children, bare-foot Belarusians stomp on turnips to make the nation's traditional turnip wine. She is also well adjusted to Western culture, having moved from Minsk to Arizona and dating a member of LMFAO which cranks out some pretty good turnip-stomping tunes.

Belarusian and Chinese tennis stars—next thing you know there will be a dominant black golfer. Oh, yeah, there was one, but since he stepped out on his wife, his putter just hasn't been the same.

It's time to vacuum the old sod house

Before I forget, could someone please teach June bugs how to read a calendar.

Spring cleaning time is always a hassle, but imagine what the early settlers of the West had to deal with. In a good year they were dirt farmers, but when the weather was hot and dry, they had to switch to dust farming, then came along a monsoon and they were mud farmers out of necessity. And can you imagine the frustration when the man came home after a hard day of harvesting clods only to discover that his wife had accidently sucked up the entire sod house with a Super-Vac?

Yes, it's springtime in the Rockies. Graduates are popping up like dandelions and have just about as good a chance of finding a decent job—decent job meaning a job not in Idaho, the minimum-wage capital of America only outdone in cheapness by The Republic of Vanuatu, a South Pacific island where the current exchange rate is two giant cockroaches for one mummified marmot—what a rip-off!

One can't help but wonder about the basic common sense of graduates, sitting for hours, suffocating in long hot robes, wearing goofy hats they normally would not be caught dead in, and suffering through boring speeches by obscure professors who only emerge from their offices one day out of the school year. Wouldn't it be much more logical for the students to simply pick up their diplomas at the unemployment office while waiting in line?

Another thought that I have as we approach the end of the school year is some concern that I feel for homeschooled students. First of all, prom must be really low-key. Furthermore, if I am homeschooled, how depressing would it be if there was a parent-teacher conference, and my parents didn't show up? In a discipline matter, if I am being homeschooled and receive out-of-school suspension, do I get sent to an actual school to serve my punishment? Lastly, if I am homeschooled, wouldn't it be a bummer to celebrate the last day of school before summer vacation, only to wake up the next morning and discover that I am still in school?! These are some real concerns.

We all know that springtime is the season for romance. A time when young men's minds turn to thoughts of hooking up on Craigslist, and young women completely ignore whatever guy they are with by constantly checking their cell phone. Nothing more romantic than couples holding hands, strolling through fields of wildflowers, sneezing and eyes watering as their nostrils suck in ragweed pollen by the bucket.

Mother Nature is showing other signs of spring in the air. Early in the morning I can hear the robins tweeting each other which made me think that Tweety Bird was actually way ahead of his (her? its?) time and was a pioneer in social media.

On a more serious note, there is ample evidence of global warming this spring what with the early spate of wild fires around the country. Closer to home, due to the early heat I have noticed a hummingbird in my own backyard wearing a tiny dew rag, or do-rag, or doo rag, or scooby dooby doo rag. Birds have historically been harbingers of climate change, so when one sees geese migrating south only as far as Bismarck, North Dakota, one can't help but wonder.

Recently I saw a picture in a nature magazine that clearly showed penguins which had exchanged their tuxedos for black tank tops and white Bermuda shorts. Even more alarming is a report that, due to an ice shortage, Eskimos must now construct their igloos out of large white Legos.

Bears that hibernated in hammocks this past winter due to warmer temperatures are now trying to wake up after sleeping for months, so don't go hiking with steaming cups of Starbucks in your hand. And don't be surprised to see sluggish bears gulping down five-gallon jugs of 5-Hour Energy Drink. Speaking of which, I was wondering if I just take a little sip can I get five minutes of energy. Say, for example, I want to run a mile instead of all the way to Salt Lake City.

I have heard rumors that some of the bears are in a particularly bad mood this spring because they have been informed that, due to sequestration, the number of campers they can eat this summer has been reduced.

As the hot summer progresses, don't be surprised to hear about folks who live in Las Vegas booking vacations in Saudi Arabia so they can cool off.

Finally, speaking of Las Vegas, you would think that Senator Mike Crapo would know that what's invested in Vegas, stays in Vegas.

Just like gold, the golden years are costly

Well this is a moment that I have been dreading for quite a while: time to update my picture. I knew the time had arrived after several people, when they heard my name, asked, "Oh, is that your son who writes for the newspaper?"

As you can see, there have been some changes over the last ten years, for example, the size of my forehead. My wife says that is caused by a receding hairline, but I argue that my brain has increased in size, thus my forehead has grown to accommodate it.

But who needs hair anyway? Besides, for every hair that falls out of my head, a new one pops up on my nose. When I was young and mentioned "my hair", I referred to a thick, Robert Plant-like mop, but now "my hair" refers to a single extremely long strand of hair which I spend hours strategically winding around my head.

Whereas, I used to need a big heavy brush to style my hair, now I can easily comb it with a toothpick. Another advantage is no need to wrestle with a cumbersome, hot blow dryer to dry it anymore. One well placed sneeze by my black lab does the trick. In addition, I get a senior discount on haircuts, but with only three, oops, make that two hairs left I still feel like I'm getting ripped off.

Another change in the photo is that the expression seems more strained, as if I am thinking, "Hurry up, would you, I have to go to the bathroom" which, as a matter of fact, I do at this very moment. To be honest, one reason I retired from teaching is the custodian balked at installing a commode in my classroom's book closet.

Besides being about as afraid to look in the mirror as I am to open a text from Anthony Weiner, there are other alarming signs of change—my mail for instance. Use to be I would get notices to subscribe to Playboy and offers on romantic cruises. Now the mail consists of weekly deals on hearing aids. Then there are the offers on funeral home tours, ads that I can only read with the help of reading glasses which magnify the words "Nearly Dearly Departed."

And why is it a funeral "home"? It's not like I would want to reside there permanently and listen to that creepy organ music 24/7. Plus, how did they find out that I was starting to fall apart? Who told them?

Reading glasses are great, but sometimes I forget to remove them before driving off in the car which makes everything blurry. Recently I saw a highway sign that said "Trash pickup ahead" and I thought it said "Trashy pickup ahead." My son looked puzzled when I turned to him and said, "If we see her, we are not stopping!"

Another change is that I get songs stuck in my brain that I sing over and over. And not cool songs but stuff by Abba or Engelbert Humperdinck.

For my most recent birthday, my wife prepared me a special dinner: pureed steak, pureed baked potato, and to top it off, a delicious pureed birthday cake which held so many flaming candles that midway through blowing them out, I had to pause to take a short nap. Plus, when it came time to sing, I forgot the rest of the words after "Happy."

One of the few pleasures in my life now is when the doorman at a local bar checks my ID when I walk in, so I always give him a nice tip. People tell me, "Mike, he's only using you." But I say that's okay.

A lot of people have told me that they would like to retire also but are afraid that they will not be able to keep busy and will get bored. My advice to them is don't worry—you will have plenty to do. Along with a busy social calendar packed with peers' funerals to attend, you will have a cornucopia of activities to choose from: picking up prescriptions, checking your blood pressure, trimming nose and ear hair, reading inspirational books like "Creative Ways to Serve Prune Juice", teaching your dog in the car to bark and wake you up when he notices that the light has turned green, attending a seminar on "Fifty Foolproof Ways to Cheat at Bingo", contacting Social Security, insurance, and pension folks to get your money, searching the dump for a large cardboard box to move into when you can no longer make your house payment, etc.

My final tip is to never fall asleep in the senior discount buffet line or, guaranteed, some old codger will cut in front and grab the last bowl of Jell-O.

Man electrocuted while smoking in bathtub

Here the new year 2014 is only a few days old and there are already early signs that it will be as boring as 2013. People are still getting sick trying to cope with the health care website, a photo of Mitt Romney's 153 grandchildren makes headlines, Miley stuck her tongue out on New Year's Eve but with little enthusiasm, and folks in Colorado can't get excited about anything since half of them are stoned.

One thing that is pretty clear about the future is that cigarette smoking will continue to undergo some exciting changes. When I first heard about the development of electric cigarettes I envisioned smokers dragging around miles of extension cord. I imagined James

Bond lying in bed with his latest female conquest, the two of them smoking e-cigarettes, their partially covered bodies entwined with a bright orange cord—a truly electrifying scene!

I remember back in high school when a bunch of guys in the restroom would "hotbox" a cigarette between classes—one cigarette, five guys, four minutes. By the fifth guy's turn, the ash was glowing as red hot as the Fukushima nuclear plant after meltdown. If a teacher happened to enter, one guy would actually curl up the cigarette and hold it inside his mouth. Luckily smoke doesn't exit through the ears. And thank goodness the smoke detector had not been invented yet or I'd still be serving detention!

Of course back then cigarettes were 50 cents a pack and gas was 25 cents a gallon, so if a guy had a dollar he was all set to have a great Friday night.

Remember when half the fun of smoking was having that cigarette pack snuggled securely in your shirt pocket where you could coolly grab it, thump it upside down a few times to pop one out, then firmly replace the pack like a real man. Since that was apparently the only purpose of even having a shirt pocket, why do shirts still have them? Especially since the e-cigarette requires so much equipment you would rip your shirt to shreds attempting to lug all that around in a puny shirt pocket. After all, you got your cartridge, batteries, vapor liquid, charging device, along with your "personal vaporizer" which sounds like a weapon used by Storm Troopers in Star Wars.

In America, tobacco smoking obviously started a long time ago as archeologists in this country have dug up a 5,000 year old BIC Lighter—and it still works! There is evidence that the country's earliest inhabitants experimented with an e-peace pipe, but it kept shorting out the e-smoke signal. History shows that the first colonists did not start smoking regularly until the newly arrived Puritans told them that they couldn't because it was a sin.

The first verified report of a smoking Englishman was when a smitten Pocahontas proclaimed that John Smith was "smokin' hot!" and rushed to save him from being snuffed out like a butt.

A pioneer in the electronic cigarette industry is the Chinese corporation Golden Dragon Holdings. Golden Dragon is a company which also manufactures Chinese fireworks. In fact, the company's first overseas shipment of e-cigarettes intended for Little Rock, Arkansas, accidently got switched with a load of fireworks headed for the 2006 Akron, Ohio, 4th of July celebration. This mix up resulted in a real snoozer at the Akron fairgrounds "Greatest Show in Ohio" with kids trying to figure out how to light electronic cigarettes using punks. In contrast, Independence Day parties in Little Rock were thrilling as celebrants attempting to smoke sky rockets abruptly kicked the nicotine habit when they blew their heads off.

Smoking opponents commonly list the harmful ingredients in old-fashioned cigarettes, such as tar. However, the anti-freeze chemical in some e-cigarettes does not sound real healthy either, but at least you won't freeze to death when forced to smoke outside in the winter.

Laws concerning the use of e-cigarettes vary around the world. Florida wants to ban all smoking where children are present which is weird since that's probably when adults need a cigarette the most. Any kind of cigarette is legal in China; in fact the China National Tobacco Corporation has proclaimed that all Chinese must smoke or face execution. In Mexico, the Federal Commission for the Protection Against Sanitary Risks has forbidden the selling of non-tobacco objects that include tobacco products—but dumping decapitated bodies in the local drinking water supply is apparently okay.

The emergence of e-cigarettes will affect American culture. Instead of that macho image of the Marlboro Man, young men in the future will emulate the Electronic Nicotine Delivery System Man. In films, when Lauren Bacall tells Bogie to give her a light, he will hand her a battery.

What's next? E-chewing tobacco? Not a bad idea since, instead of spitting toxic black globs, chewers will simply spit harmless colorful sparks.

My hair is fifty shades of grey

I can tell from recent television commercials that it's time for Valentine's Day again. They're hawking all sorts of pink and red goodies. Of course, you could just resort to a card. The French take credit for the first Valentine's Day card back in 1415 when Charles, Duke of Orleans, sent love letters to his wife while imprisoned in the Tower of London ("Wish you were here . . . instead of me.")

In modern-day Saudi Arabia, Valentine's Day is banned because such a holiday is sinful and "encourages immoral relations between unmarried men and women." On the other hand, it's perfectly acceptable for Saudi princes to maintain harems of fifty or more women. Apparently, under Sharia law, what's good for the gander is a lot of geese.

At my elementary school kids loved Valentine's Day when we could exchange cards during recess. Most popular with boys back then were the Cracked Valentines with sarcastic sayings such as "You look like a million bucks—all green and wrinkled." Boy, were we clever or what?

As a young man, my Valentine's Day consisted of wine, women, and song. All right, more often than not it was just wine while my single buddies and I hit various nightclubs. Of course, marriage narrows a guy's focus quite a bit and the Valentine's card with flowers routine usually will suffice.

Nowadays, the only February holiday I get excited about is Groundhog Day, while trying to guess whether Punxsutawney Phil will bite the mayor or not. Maybe that's because, at my age, I'm starting to resemble Phil more than Cupid.

People used to tell me that I looked a lot like Clint Eastwood as Dirty Harry back in 1971; now they tell me that I just look like Clint Eastwood. It's like when we were younger, my wife would say "Look but don't touch." Now it's gotten to the point that she says "Touch but don't look."

This year for Valentine's Day, young men could skip boring boxes of chocolates and take their sweethearts to see "Fifty Shades of Grey," the movie based on the best-selling novel of the same title which is the fastest selling paperback ever in England, beating "Harry Potter," while flashing magic wands of a different sort.

The movie is rated R due to some "unusual behavior" which is sort of like saying that Pete Carroll made an "unusual call" on the goal line play that most likely cost Seattle the Super Bowl.

In the film, a man and woman perform acts that the media refers to as BDSM, a new acronym for me. Now AM I'm familiar with, along with FM and a good ol' healthy BM, but BDSM? Why, with my memory as weak as it is now, even if someone told me what it stood for I'd forget everything after "B" by the time I jumped into bed.

Based on a trailer available on the Internet I know it has something to do with wearing a blindfold while handcuffed to a bed. If the blindfold is so you cannot see what's going on, well I'm way ahead of these folks because my eyes are so bad that I have to use my reading glasses just to avoid putting my underwear on backwards.

I do see an advantage to being handcuffed to the bed since I have fallen to the floor during nightmares in which I'm being chased by a doctor brandishing a colonoscope.

Due to the novel's popularity, sales of blindfolds, whips, and chains have soared, and not just to the CIA. Why, if I showed up in the bedroom wrapped in chains, my wife would dive under the covers thinking that Jacob Marley's ghost has crawled out of his grave again!

In addition, when I read that online erotic adult toy sales of something called "jiggle balls" have risen by 200%, I immediately logged on and bought some . . . shares of jiggle ball stocks!

Very surprising is the fact that women by far outnumber men as the purchasers of the book. Why would that be? When I was younger, only men bought Playboy magazine. In fact I just recently cancelled my Playboy subscription and now subscribe to the AARP Magazine which has some pretty arousing ads for new hearing aids.

Maybe it's because women are concerned over the fact that in England, France, and the U.S. sex frequency has decreased from five to three times a month. Three times a month! Gosh, I'm exhausted just thinking about that.

I doubt if I will spend any money on either the "Fifty Shades of Grey" book or movie. Although I wouldn't mind having a trapeze that hangs from the bedroom ceiling that I saw for sale in an online adult store—I could use it to help pull myself out of bed in the morning.

Pump up the jam for the sounds of summer

Is there anything funnier than when your neighbor has his windows open and sneezes real loud? No, I don't think so either. It is certainly one of the perks of warm summer weather, something you can never experience in the winter.

You notice how it's nearly always a man? Women with their dainty "achoo" you hardly ever hear. But men sound like a dang horse that sucked an entire box of pepper up its nose.

Reminds me of back when my parents rented a house from a landlord named Frank Murphy who use to come out on his porch next door on summer evenings just wearing bib overalls with no shirt. Frank would walk to the edge of the porch, lean over, and blow his nose using a finger to plug one nostril at a time.

That nightly ritual was a highlight for us kids and established Frank as one of our childhood heroes. Thinking back, I wonder where he blew his nose in the winter.

Summer sounds for me this year started off with a dirge as I received another one of those ominous funeral home promotions in the mail. Is there anything more depressing? I didn't even open it, but I'm sure it was some sort of Memorial Day sale. Maybe something like "Buy one, get one half price." Gee, who should I give the other one to? Perhaps it would make a nice graduation gift.

Or possibly the offer was for the music of my choice to be played at my viewing. Like, what good is that going to do me?!

It's amazing how summertime changes the soundtrack of life. When you step outside in the winter, it's all calm and peaceful, especially in the evening. But that changes on the first warm day of

213

spring, as if someone threw a big switch and turned on a cacophony of annoying sounds.

For example, I didn't even realize that our new neighbor had kids. In fact, I didn't even know that we had a new neighbor. But soon as it warmed up, those kids were hanging from a tree teasing the neighbor's dog which threw it into a tizzy setting off a chain-reaction of every dog in the vicinity barking its fool-head off.

I admit all those barking dogs throughout the summer do serve some useful purpose. They never fail to alert me to the imminent arrival of the mailman. Even more importantly, they provide me a last-minute warning on Fridays that I better get the garbage can down to the curb.

Mornings are entirely different in the summer. Whereas, I had no trouble sleeping until 7:00 when it was twenty degrees and pitch dark outside, now I am awakened around 4:30 by the sound of hummingbird wings whirring outside the screen window as the little fellas line up at the feeder, jostling for position.

They're sort of like those people who show up in your driveway at 6:00 AM for a garage sale when your ad specifically stated 9:00 and no early birds! I guess their philosophy is "The early bird gets the George Foreman Grill."

It's right about now that our neighborhood crows start to get real belligerent what with little ones to protect. You can hear the hovering helicopter parents jabbering all day long with what an encyclopedia calls a mixture of "grating coos, caws, rattles, and clicks."

I don't know about the other birds, but I find these birds in the hood sort of intimidating. In fact, I get a bit uneasy when a flock of crows start congregating around me in the backyard, giving me that badass look, making me feel like I'm about to star in a reenactment of a scene from Alfred Hitchcock's "The Birds."

With the grass growing like crazy this spring, lawn mowers provide a constant summer soundtrack. Never had to deal with that noise when I was a kid since we just had one of those old-fashioned push mowers with no motor. Which worked out fine since we also had no grass. Luckily, we did have the occasional dandelion to spruce up the yard a bit.

Of course, now I own a noisy motorized lawn mower like everyone else. Well, not exactly like everyone else's since I purchased mine used ten years ago for $25. You're probably thinking, Mike, that thing must be a pile of junk. But, hey, it does the job, and I'll bet if you wanted to buy a new one like it today, you'd pay. . . oh, gosh, at least $50.

I admit that I'm probably due to give in and buy a new mower soon, but I've grown fond of its coughing and sputtering along with the choking cloud of smoke it puffs out occasionally. Besides, we've sort of grown older together.

Like me, the old mower still runs pretty good once it gets warmed up, but, again, just like me, it needs a few more pulls on its rope to get started.

Retirees have little money, but lots of teeth

There have been a rash of stories in the media recently decrying the fact that most Americans simply do not have much money saved up for retirement. In fact, when asked how much they do have, a large percentage of respondents had to grab their piggy-bank and run down to a coin-cashing machine before answering—not a good sign.

To help us all figure out how much money we need for retirement, some personal finance websites provide a Retirement Calculator which you can use to calculate your financial goal for the golden years. This simple chart has two columns for your current and future financial status labeled "You have. . ." and "You will need. . . ." I got pretty stressed out trying to use the chart and ended up filling in the blanks with "headache" and "Ibuprofen."

Experts say that by age 66 you should have eight times your annual salary saved to be financially secure. Since I currently have zero salary, it looks like I'm right on track. Based on my calculation, 8 x $0 = $0.

One poll indicates that 27% of Americans have no personal savings at all which, coincidentally, is about the same percentage of people who regularly camp out for a week waiting to purchase the latest Air Jordan shoes. And those who do save, on average, only put away a paltry 5% of their disposable income. Compare that to the Chinese who save 25% while spending the other 75% bribing public officials.

Two obvious reasons it is difficult for Americans to save money are the rising costs of health care and education. But it's likely that feeling compelled to monthly upgrade their iPhone, iPod, and iPad is keeping a lot of young people iPoor.

An alarming number of folks in this country plan to rely solely on Social Security for their retirement income. That should work out just fine if your idea of traveling to acquire more world knowledge is taking the metro bus to the library once a month.

Just when I was feeling down about the fact that I may have to purchase my next MacDonald's Happy Meal on layaway, I came across some really good news for retirees: baby boomers are the first generation in which the majority will reach retirement age still in possession of most of their natural teeth.

I suppose it's possible that "in possession" could just as likely apply to a retired moonshiner living in the backwoods of Tennessee who has kept all his teeth in a Mason jar after losing them one-by-one biting off beer bottle caps.

Still, I have to admit that this is great news. As one writer gushed, "Boomers may be the first generation to anticipate dying with their teeth." Now there's something to look forward to a few years down the road!

After chewing on this amazing announcement for a moment, I skedaddled to the bathroom for verification. And sure as heck, in the mirror I saw a full set of pearly white teeth. Well, okay, not exactly pearly white, maybe more like oyster grey with a few gold caps scattered about.

One obvious reason that my generation has kept our teeth is the improvement in the quality of dental care over the years. Today's dental profession is much more specialized than it was in the Middle Ages when a customer at the village barber shop could walk out minus an infected molar, a gallstone, and a pint of blood, in addition to a shaved head and a trimmed beard.

One notable advancement in dentistry took place when the 16th century Japanese carved dentures completely out of wood. One advantage to this was that having wooden dentures allowed the patient to choose a redwood or cedar stain. A drawback of course is that, along with sweets, now termites could create some serious cavities.

Closer to home, George Washington was well known for his dental problems throughout his life. Prior to getting dentures made out of ivory, Washington only had one tooth left in his mouth by the time he became president. This probably explains why he is not smiling on the dollar bill.

The discover of floss also contributed to better dental health. In some early cultures people would floss using the hair of a horse's tail. After a number of people nearly died from getting kicked in the head, it dawned on them they should probably remove the hair from the tail first.

An early form of dental anesthesia was nitrous oxide or "laughing gas." Patients who used this at the dentist would "get the giggles" and sometimes erupt in laughter which could be hazardous while the doctor is drilling.

Maybe dentists should still use such anesthesia today. It would certainly be less painful while checking out at the front desk to tell the secretary, "Ha, ha, I'll pay you, hee, hee, just as soon as I, hardy har har, remortgage the house."

Sexting your twitter will get you five to ten

How did we ever get along without the cell phone? It is such a time saving device that. . . . Wait. Hold on. I've got a call.

Like I was saying, the cell phone has made our lives so much easi. . . . Just a minute, it's the dog's psychoanalyst calling.

Now, where was I? Oh, yeah. The cell phone has greatly reduced our stress lev. . . . Oops, sorry, got a text message from my Zen master. Let's see ... here it is 'om, om.'

With cell phones we can talk to anyone from anywhere, unless, of course, there is a large pile of dirt blocking the signal or you happen to be in an isolated area, say outside of Los Angeles or New York City.

Not only can we converse with family, friends, and other people we're trying to avoid, but the cell phone can also take and send pictures. Like the guy who recently got a close up of a tornado just before a 2 x 4 impaled his forehead transforming him into the real "Mr. T." The lucky stiff became an overnight sensation on YouTube.

Another way in which the cell phone has contributed to the improvement of the world is at large, crowded events many people play "Can you see me?" Let's say it's a college basketball game and a fan arrives "a little late" which in Idaho means midway through the second overtime, and he wants to hookup with his brother-in-law whom he sees on the average of four times a day since he rents the trailer parked in his driveway. But this is different because it's out in public in front of a large crowd so it's "a big deal."

So he walks blindly up and down the aisles tripping over popcorn boxes, stopping frequently to gaze intently across the gym like Christopher Columbus attempting to see through the haze of smoke signals which were much more efficient than texting announcing his arrival, staring at what he thought was India where he was hoping to establish the original telemarketing franchise.

Meanwhile our sports fan, while blocking the view of those who had the audacity to arrive on time for the game, is holding the cell phone to his ear and shouting above the din, "Can you see me? I'm in front of the big guy in the red sweater who's choking me for blocking his view!"

Then when they finally see each other he's ecstatic—waving, jumping, tears gushing down his cheeks as if he just was given a vacuum on 'The Oprah Winfrey Show.' Of course, by then the game is over and he has no idea who won. The guy in the red sweater is furious because he couldn't see the winning three-pointer and is digging in his backpack for the loaded revolver he can now take to college ball games.

As far as driving while talking on the phone is concerned, most people can't do either one separately very well let alone trying to combine the two. Nothing like dealing with rush hour traffic after a stressful day at work while some guy on the phone is telling you that your home's water, electricity, and cable TV have been shut off due to a slight financial oversight on your part.

One interesting quirk of the cell phone is that both people can talk simultaneously. This quite often creates an echoing effect, sort of like your head is inside a large empty tin can. It also results in both parties repeating the phrase "go ahead" so many times that the conversation begins to take on a NASA to astronauts-in-outer-space feel.

In addition, some awkward situations can arise involving cell phones. Such as in a conference room when a phone blasts out "My Green Tambourine" by The Lemon Pipers, and the guilty party is reluctant to answer it to avoid people snickering at them, so everyone is looking around at everyone else with an accusatory expression on their faces.

I guess along with everything else phones do nowadays you can also "twitter someone." I'm not really sure what that means, but it sounds like something you could get arrested for back in the old days.

Then there's sending nude photos of yourself called "sexting" which I tried once on my cell phone, but all I got in return was a bunch of pop-ups advertising various funeral homes.

One thing about the cell phone which I personally hate is when I'm in the middle of a raging blizzard on an icy, foggy stretch of the Interstate passing a semi and the phone starts blasting AC/DC's "Hells Bells" and I have this irresistible urge to answer it. That's when I find myself longing for the old days with a big black phone on a table in the hallway at home—and with peace and quiet everywhere else.

Shorten your life, have an affair

Okay, how many other guys who just turned 66 can boast that they recently got busted for trying to sneak a beer into a summer music festival? I had the bottle hidden in my backpack and when the security guy approached me I considered running through the crowd shouting, "Grey lives matter!"

I think I've arrived at the age when a man realizes that this may be his last chance to stir things up a bit. However, I'm sure glad I wasn't one of the over 30 million men who had an account with Ashley Madison, the infidelity dating site.

Talk about the hackers getting hacked! Ashley Madison, an online service to help married people hack into other couples' marriages, was hacked itself recently. Ashley Madison's slogan is "Life is short. Have an affair." Well, life could get a whole lot shorter for husbands greeted at the front door by wives brandishing a large frying pan!

A small number of women also had accounts with the site. It really comes as no surprise that there were about nine men for every woman registered on the site. That's about the same odds as you witness in most bars on weekend nights.

First of all, why would women want to have affairs with guys so naïve as to take the risk of revealing fifty shades of their sexual fantasies on such a website? Don't men know that just about every federal government department including the FBI and CIA has been hacked despite being protected by the best security systems that taxpayers' money can buy?

Men are reportedly nervous that their wives will discover their email listed in the exposed information and file for divorce— or worse for some men, not file for divorce! I'd say that if a wife is even checking, she already has some solid reasons for being suspicious.

The median age of Ashley Madison users is 46, so you can see how it fits in with the traditional midlife crisis period when both men and women are questioning whether they "still have it." Of course many are completely overlooking the fact that they never had "it" in the first place. All they need to do is to dig out their high school yearbook picture to verify that.

Based on the revealed data, users can be grouped according to states and other criteria. The fact that Idaho ranks 47 in per capita spending on the site may not necessarily be cause for righteous celebration. In fact, any statistic which ranks Idaho neck and neck with Mississippi is nothing to brag about. I'd say the low ranking is probably more likely connected to the fact that Idaho ranks 48 in per capita income. Idahoans simply can't afford to have an affair!

Despite my current midlife crisis—midlife in the sense that scientists predict someday humans will live to be 120—I've never considered registering on the extramarital affair website. In fact, prior to the well-publicized security breech, whenever I saw the name Ashley Madison I thought it was just another cookie company like Little Debby or Dolly Madison.

If I did create an account with Ashley Madison, it would look something like this:

Married male desires love affair with married female.

I'm looking for a woman who will watch football on TV and pretend to enjoy it despite not knowing the difference between a nose guard and a nose job.

She must have an interest in antiques. I'm not referring to me personally but to my 1994 Subaru with 204,000 miles. Just to let you know, the warranty has run out on both the car and me.

Sexual fantasy: I have a recurring dream that I'm chasing Kim Kardashian wearing a sexy nurse costume—only I'm the one in the nurse outfit which probably explains why Kim is running. Not sure what I'd do if I actually caught her, but doesn't matter since I always get winded and give up.

Some medical knowledge on your part would be helpful since I've been accused of being a hypochondriac and . . . hold on, the entire right side of my body just went numb and I'm seeing double but not normal double, like side-by-side, but vertical double, like . . . . Wait, I'm okay now.

Anyway, I forgot what I was talking about which leads to another requirement. You need to be willing to spend half your day helping me search for lost car keys, shoes, reading glasses, etc. Naturally, I'll help you too, but you'll have to keep reminding me what we're looking for.

Hey, you know what, on second thought, cancel my application. I just realized I've had a thirty-seven year love affair with a woman fitting this description, and I think I'll just keep her. Besides, I'm not sure that I have enough time left to train a new one.

Smart phones plus dumb people equals terror in the friendly skies

Can you think of any punishment worse than sitting next to a teenage girl during a two-hour flight while she has an intense conversation on a cell phone over why Latisha unfriended Clarissa after Jamal asked Hermione to the Winter Fantasy Dance? Well, it just so happens that you could soon be paying $648 plus baggage fee, seat selection fee, debit/credit card surcharge, non-farting section fee, etc., for just such a privilege.

When I read about a proposal to allow passengers to use their cell phones during flights, the first image that came to mind was the scene from Airplane! In which Ted bores an elderly lady with his life story until she hangs herself.

However, this imaginary episode pales in comparison to the reality of a Spanish Inquisition world of in-flight cell phone use. If airlines allow this, they should provide each passenger with a parachute and easy access to an escape hatch—plus a refund for the number of miles that the escaped customer will have to walk to arrive at his destination which will be physically strenuous but better than sitting next to someone with a Chim Chim Cher-ee ringtone.

If they are going to allow the use of cell phones on planes, another option is to allow the rest of us to carry handguns. If not, then at least a Taser would be nice.

Even without this additional opportunity for the millions of insecure people in the world to constantly maintain long-distance assurance that someone out there loves them, the cell phone plague has obviously reached epidemic proportions.

When I was a teenager, females loved to talk on the phone while males avoided it if at all possible. In fact, the only time I used the phone was when I received a call at home from a girlfriend bugging me or from my boss checking up to see why I had not shown up for work. I personally never called anyone because it was considered unmanly.

But now that phones have evolved from frumpy black blobs setting on a hallway table at home to sleek, snazzy toys that don't just ring but make oodles of cute sounds, have teeny built-in typewriters, and humans can carry them everywhere as a constant distraction from the everyday boredom of their real lives plus talk with the whole world watching as if to shout out "Look at me! I am somebody! I have friends!" boys are suddenly as nuts about phones as girls.

My wife just recently acquired a Smartphone. Someone gave it to her because that person moved up to a Brilliantphone. Where does this all end? The Einsteinphone? The Hawkingphone?

She has attempted to teach me how to use it, but it's like Diane Fossey trying to teach a gorilla to sign its name using calligraphy. Truth is, I was just getting fairly competent at using a Jitterbug which is a cell phone with numbers so big that it doubles as a Bingo card and when it rings you simply press "Answer" or "Get lost." That's it.

With the latest Smartphone, men do not even push buttons anymore, they swipe icons. Just a gentle, ladylike swipe with the pinkie will do. So men have regressed from "aggressively grabbing" a large heavy black receiver to answer the phone and then "slamming it down" to hang up when really upset, to daintily swiping a cute icon for both results—like guys have suddenly morphed from the Stones to One Direction. I mean, with these new phones, how do you "hang up" on someone to show anger? It's just not the same to send a frowny face.

223

It's similar to the television remote. It use to be that if my favorite football team was losing, I could stomp across the room to the set, grab the dial, and violently twist it to turn the game off, possibly breaking off the dial in the process and throwing it at Percy the family cat before picking up my bowl of popcorn and dumping it on the dog's head, resulting in at least the dog being happy.

Then the television remote comes along and all I have to do, and can do, is push a little red button in disgust before tossing the remote onto the couch resulting in a remote that is deeply entombed in a dark, spooky Mirkwood Forest-like area between the cushions which I'm afraid to even reach down into, lost forever, which means another temper tantrum when I look for it to watch the next scheduled game.

Now the latest innovation of a Smart TV with voice control when my favorite team plays like the Milli Vanilli of football, I simply say to the TV "Coach so-and-so sucks" and . . . nothing happens, but I feel a whole lot better, and that's what really matters.

Snakes on a pulpit!

Amen, I say to you brothers and sisters, we are going through a sinful time. What with Miley kissing Katy, Bill Nye shooting down the creation myth using, of all things, a bunch of facts, Girl Scouts selling cookies outside of stores with names like Wacky Tabacky, Hungry Hungry Hippie, etc. Let us all attempt to restore some logic and moral reason to our depraved society and put our hands together around the neck of a slithery rattler, cobra, or black mamba and pray together for salvation. Personally, I prefer my pet garter snake on steroids named Bubba.

Now let's all plant a big, slobbery kiss on our snake's snout in memory of our dear friend Pastor Jamie Coots over in Middlesboro who died recently after being bitten by a rattle snake because God had chosen that it was time for him to join that giant reptile farm in the sky.

Reverend Coots first refused to seek medical care then changed his mind after looking in the mirror and noticing that he was swelling up like the Pillsbury Dough Boy. However, after spending hours attempting to register for Obamacare on the government website, he finally threw his Popeye-like arms up into the air and proclaimed, "Obamacare is Satan's work!" and succumbed.

As all the members of the faithful flock worshipping here today know, Pastor Coots used venomous snakes in his services because of the Bible verse, "They shall take up serpents." Of course when Mark said "take up" did he mean take upstairs, take up town, take up in a plane and make a scary movie? We just don't know.

So we here at the Lord's Christian Church of Serpent Smoochers in Toad Suck, Arkansas, assume he meant take snakes up in our hands and let them get all cuddly with our nose, eyes, ears, etc. which, occasionally, due to the good Lord taking a brief nap or possibly being momentarily distracted by the announcement of the Powerball winning numbers, he lets down his guard and the evil serpents go all crazy and by the time they are finished the snake handler resembles Mr. Potato Head after he's been assembled by Ray Charles

Jamie Coots himself said that taking up serpents clearly shows God's power over things that He created that can injure or kill you. I suppose we could prove that same point just as well by "taking up" a psychotic Siamese cat that hasn't been declawed or by "taking up" one of Miss Trixiebelle Lee's blue-ribbon winning 5-pound zucchinis and trying to swallow it whole. But are people going to pay their tithe to witness that? I don't think so.

Snakes are the logical choice since they have always represented evil or even demons incarnated, so handling snakes shows power over evil. One may ask why not just use a Justin Bieber bobblehead doll. However, despite the fact that 666 is the number of times that he has been arrested so far this year, he is not specifically mentioned in the Bible. Besides, we believers do not wish to be confused with Beliebers.

Along with handling snakes, over a hundred churches in The Deep South also follow Mark's passage, "if they drink any deadly thing, it shall not hurt them." So we drink strychnine, gasoline, raw sewage, etc. But, of course, as good Christians we will not touch the evils of alcohol.

Also we believe that, as the Bible states, "If a man lies with a man" it is a sin. But what they do standing up is their business.

Just like our friends over at the Church of Holy Tongue Yodelers, we too believe in a baptism of total immersion rather than a light sprinkle on the head. After the adult candidate slips on a pair of Sacred Speedos, we give him a complete scrub down. For some, it's their first bath in years. Then we all take Super Soaker water guns and rinse him off. Baptism by fire is an option, but you don't want that.

No women can be preachers or pastors. However, since I am a Christian man who believes in acts of charity and mercy, I do allow my wife to feed the snakes, clean their cages, search for escaped snakes down in the pitch-dark cellar, capture replacement snakes by hand in the backyard swamp, etc. For this, of course, she receives my special blessing. And, yes, I have been a widower more times than I can count which is any number higher than five.

Now, hopefully we can get Brother Purvis to collect your donations without pulling any tricks like he did last week when he hid a snake in the wicker collection basket and it jumped out and bit Brother Cletus. By the way, Brother Cletus' funeral will be held this Wednesday.

Talkin' about my generation

I was looking at some old photos recently and two thoughts came to mind: How much I've changed since the 1960s-70s, The Age of Aquarius, and how lucky I was to survive, considering some of the guys I hung out with and some of the things we did.

Funny how a guy my age can remember experiences fifty years ago much more vividly than recent events, such as right now

I'm wondering if I turned off the sprinkler that I turned on last Wednesday.

Of course, one can't always be absolutely sure that things happened the way we think they happened when we were younger. Unfortunately—or fortunately as far as violating the law is concerned—we did not have Smartphones to take pictures of every single moment of our lives and every single expression on our faces. No, we had dumb phones that we used to actually speak to people, the black ones so big that if we wanted to take one with us we had to rent a U-Haul trailer.

Plus, back then, if I had $299 I sure as heck would not spend it on a phone. I'd go out and buy me a better car than the Nash Rambler station wagon I bought for $150!

I really feel sorry for anyone who missed out on the 1960s. What an exciting time, with cultural movements such as anti-war and free love. You remember "free love" which was any lovin' that a guy got before he was married and charge cards were invented.

Back in the 60s, hippies were taking LSD so they thought green and pink paisley shirts were actually cool. They wore bell bottoms so wide that they could store an entire tepee up one pants leg while hitch-hiking to the next music festival.

Well, those days are long gone. For many of us, the New-Age has given way to old age. And just as my generation back when we were young tried to trick itself into believing "All you need is love," we appear now to be pushing for a campaign to create the illusion that growing old can be "fun."

When I recently turned 65, my son said that "65 is the new 45." Some days, to me, 65 feels more like the new 85.

Sure, some celebrities spotlighted in magazines can defy Old Man Time, stars like Joan Collins and Michael Caine, but such articles overlook the fact that these people have millions of dollars to spend on personal trainers, cosmetic surgeons, doppelgangers, etc.

I tend to agree more with the fellow who wrote the song "Old Man Time Ain't No Friend of Mine." Heck, I've had the dermatologist fry so many age spots on my face at $35 a pop that I asked for a frequent-fryer discount.

The Internet is full of suggestions to help seniors enjoy life more. Some experts feel that we should accept new innovations such as Smartwatches and iPads. Oh, I accept them all right; I just can't read the darn things without using a giant magnifying glass straight out of Sherlock Holmes.

Others suggest that at this stage of life we can finally relax and accept the fact that occasionally we could be wrong about things. Which, of course, means that we could be wrong about the possibility of ever being wrong—right?

Another suggestion is that boomers should get out and meet other people. After all, you never know who you'll run into on a daily walk to the end of your driveway and back. They even believe that naps increase life expectancy, so, hold on, I'll be back in about an hour.

Finally, it's okay to think about death but we should have no fear of it; in contrast to Woody Allen who said, "I'm not afraid of death; I just don't want to be there when it happens."

In regard to physical fitness, the late Joe Weider, "the father of modern bodybuilding," has a website with senior exercise tips. Myself, I've noticed that recently when I do pushups, I have no trouble with the "down" part, but that "up" maneuver is a struggle. In a note of caution, Weider warns, "A break in form can result in injury." I would add that form is not the only thing one might break.

There are even sites with tips for what some call Senior Sex. One therapist suggests that older men may require more foreplay. Possibly, but remember what I said earlier about "A break in form can result in injury!"

Even though my wife doesn't need to worry anymore about my not coming home "till a quarter to three," overall, I'm just glad that the answer to the Beatles' questions, "Will you still need me, will you still feed me, When I'm sixty-four," at least according to her, is yes.

Things are looking up in Massachusetts

So, let me see if I've got this straight. In Massachusetts it is perfectly legal to slyly sneak my cell phone up a woman's skirt to snap a photo without first texting her and asking for permission. On the other hand, in Idaho if I film dairy workers cruelly beating the hell out of cows, I can get a year in jail and a $5,000 fine. What on earth is going on?

First of all, how could one not notice a guy sticking his cell phone up her or his (let's be fair) dress? And wouldn't you be the least suspicious as to why he or she (same reason) is doing that. I mean it's not as if he'll get better reception ("Can you hear me now?")

Second, if I'm a cow I'm moooving to Massachusetts on the first cattle truck out of Idaho because it's obviously a lot safer to live there as long as I don't go out grazing while wearing my tutu. Plus, I'll be covered by that state's Romneycare which the Republican Party apparently supported until it was renamed Obamacare.

Truth is, none of this high-tech voyeurism—voyeurism: the uncontrollable urge to place the letter u before the letter e—would even be possible if cameras had not shrunk so much over the decades. Perhaps the solution to these modern-day Peeping Toms is to go back to those 19th-century cameras the size of a breadbox on a tripod and the photographer's head placed under his own skirt where it belongs.

This whole problem started with Polaroid's development of the instant Land Camera. You know, the large camera that contained an entire cadre of tiny Asian workers inside who could develop a picture in under one minute and spit out a grainy print.

By the way, I recently read that, in 2012, Polaroid partnered with Google and Lady Gaga to produce a phone camera called the Google-Gaga phone.

Camera evolution's next milestone was the Kodak Instamatic, so simple that even I could operate it. And, due to the film cartridge innovation, I no longer had to fear strangling myself with film while attempting to install a roll into the camera. But, again, film quality was questionable. In fact, if you go through your photo albums today you can pretty much take out all of the Polaroid and Kodak prints to stoke the backyard fire pit with tonight.

The first camera phone was sold in 2000 in Japan. I'm not sure who got the bright idea to combine the two functions. Now we not only have to hear from people that we're working hard to avoid, we have to see them! Or at least I think it's them, or, possibly, it's a coconut having a bad-hair day. The pictures are so tiny that I cannot tell what I'm looking at: "Hmmm, this is either the face or the rear end of Uncle Harold's black Lab. Or it just might be Harold himself."

Another problem that I have with the camera phone is that I keep using it backwards when taking others' photos. As a result, I have the world's largest collection of nostril selfies.

Unfortunately, I do not believe that Anthony Weiner can use that excuse. You know Weiner, the New York representative who started to write an erotic story to send to his girlfriend but decided to make a long story short so instead just sent a photo of his penis.

I recently read that, due to people secretly taking pictures under innocent victims' clothes, "Your crotch could be on the Internet and you may never know about it." I say, if my crotch is on the Internet I don't want to know about it! What am I going to do, text my grandparents and tell them to check out reddit? Besides, if my friends somehow connect that photo to me then we obviously have a relationship problem.

A few countries have devised solutions to such sneaky snapshots. South Korea and Japan require that all cell phones make an audible sound when a picture is being taken. Maybe this country should implement such a law, so that if you're a female passenger on a bus and hear the "Looney-Tunes" theme song coming from the weird looking dude sitting next to you, look down quick!

If the camera voyeurism problem continues to grow, perhaps we should consider requiring background checks for camera phone purchasers.

Better yet, maybe we should have periods of abstinence from using our cell phones altogether like they do in North Korea—no Peeping Kims there. In fact, in 2011 when then President Kim Jung-il died, the government banned cell phone use for 100 days. If you had been caught violating that rule, I imagine you would have taken your last selfie right before the firing squad leader yelled, "Fire!"

We rent to squirrels

Kids throwing cats into the river! What's this world coming to? But the cat throwers better start looking back over their shoulders. Cats are spooky. Those kids are liable to wake up some morning to discover a freshly severed mouse head lying in bed next to them.

No doubt, cats have a mean streak. It is true that if you play fetch with a dog, yes, the ball will be delivered slimy as a bowl of jelly fish soup, but at least it can usually be retrieved by you from the dog safely. And, granted, Fido the dog has a nasty habit of eating string and then re- dumping it in the yard completely intact. On the other hand, if you attempt to take a tiny piece of yarn from your kitty-cat while she's rolling around, tearing into it as if it is her archenemy Doctor Doom, you'll be lucky to come out of it with just minor face realignment.

This cat tossing is simply another in a long list of animal abuse stories that pop up in the news. I predict that animals will someday soon get their revenge. Because of the common core standards' emphasis on building critical thinking skills, many animals, which humans have traditionally controlled by merely waving a chicken bone within sniffing range, are increasing their knowledge to higher levels and demanding equal rights.

In fact everyone is suddenly demanding equal rights. The LGBTs, the GLBTs, the BLTs with extra mayonnaise, etc. all want equal treatment and rightfully so.

Recently the Boy Scouts of America decided to allow gays to join. Next thing you know, girls will want to join, then zombies, or, even worse, liberal socialist Democrats. I don't really care, but sharing a pup tent with a zombie? A Democrat? As a former Scout,

I shudder at the thought of watching a zombie gobbling down s'mores while I try to deal with the fact that a dead person earned his Eagle Scout badge before I did!

I don't understand why the Boy Scout gay policy is such a big deal. Are they implying that gay children have not been admitted into the organization up to this point? If so, then how do you explain your own Scout experience as a child—you know, the time there was that boy sitting next to you by the campfire who was daintily dining on chocolate zucchini fondue while you were gnawing away on a hunk of raw beaver tail?

Or, possibly, you recall the particularly fragile little fellow in your troop who always smoked you in knot tying competition by adding a bit of flourish to his adjustable hitch knot, topping it with a large red bow. When all is said and done, it simply appears that the Scouts' membership policy is finally catching up with its uniform design.

It appears that there is some misunderstanding concerning the whole Scouting affair. For example, a sheriff in northern Idaho is considering dissolving a Scout troop sponsored by the local sheriff's office. He said that it would be inappropriate to be involved with a group that "violates Idaho's sodomy law." Is he possibly suggesting that the Scouts will add a Sodomy Merit Badge?

His comment struck some people as weird since the law had been struck down in 2003, a change which affected Idaho along with the "Deliverance" Belt states, states not normally placed on a high intellectual pedestal: Alabama, Louisiana, Mississippi, Texas— you get the picture.

Dealing with the sodomy issue in this country goes way back to 1778 when Thomas Jefferson tried to cut some slack (no pun intended) for those convicted of such an "unnatural act" by changing the punishment for sodomy from execution to simply castration, but the legislature at that time rejected his proposal— not sure who was doing anyone a favor on that one.

It's interesting that, worldwide, a lot more countries outlaw male-male sex than female-female. I guess the various religious groups do not want to appear too narrow minded, or maybe something else is going on here, something that Playboy cashed in on a long time ago.

In 1075 BC, Assyrian law stated that if a man had intercourse with another man while in the military, he would be turned into a eunuch. I suggest that the US military today consider the same punishment for men who prey on their sisters-in-arms.

Locally, the big debate has to do with housing equality for all types which I am for since my son lives next door to a house inhabited by marmots and they are good neighbors. Of course they are a little messy, but no loud parties and they always pay their rent on time although the landlord isn't quite sure what to do with a pile of chewed up worms, spiders, and grass.

Welcome to Voodoo High

There is little doubt that charter schools are all the rage in Idaho in recent years. At last count there are 40 in the state. Now State Superintendent of Schools Tom Luna has convinced the state legislature to speed up the establishment of charter schools by removing the current cap of six per year.

If that happens, by the year 2049 there will be so many schools that each student in the state will have a school all to himself or herself which will result in some really quiet pep rallies! This will also result in tremendous school budget savings since the hundreds of gas-guzzling school buses can then be replaced with a fleet of rickshaws.

There seems to be a variety of reasons for parents to start a new charter school. Some parents have children who can't spell, so they start a school that focuses on math. Parents who love the performing arts and who feel that their child will be the next American Idol can organize a school with a drama-based curriculum in which the kids run around wearing Stanley Kowalski sleeveless sweat-stained tee shirts shouting "Hey, Stella!" and who order "Fillet of a fenny snake, in the caldron boil and bake" for lunch in the cafeteria.

Other schools have been organized by parents who love the outdoors so the kids show up wearing little L.L. Bean-type outfits including tiny safari hats, carrying nets and magnifying glasses, and spend the day catching and torturing butterflies. Or maybe little Cedric is a whiz at the Socratic Method, so his parents create a school where the kids sit around for hours debating the question: "I think therefore I am, so what's your story?"

If some parents had started a school back when I was a kid to give my buddies and me a little edge, the curriculum would most likely have consisted of six periods of PE along with a couple of study halls to cram for the urine drug tests.

Today, no matter the reason for starting a charter school, the process to form one is extremely complicated. First, the school needs a name, preferably something fancy sounding like Academy, Institute, Conservatory—you know, the more British or ancient Greek sounding the better. Just plain old "School" simply won't do. "My Kid is an Honor Student at The Oracle at Delphi School of the Classical Arts"—now that would be an impressive bumper sticker on a mini-van, don't you think?

Next you need a location—like a building made out of bricks or wood with four walls and a roof—which is a critical step frequently overlooked when groups brainstorm their charter school proposal. Due to this oversight, often, at the last minute, just as the students step off the bus on opening day all decked out in their brand spankin' new purple and green paisley uniforms, in a panic the founders desperately route the kids to a vacated Jamba Juice stand at the mall where a makeshift classroom has been hastily set up.

Despite such complications, it comes as no surprise that since Superintendent Luna made his one-charter-school-per-student proposal public the innovative ideas have come pouring in from far and wide throughout the state.

For example one group of parents who are tired of their school bully sons being singled out for constant unfair criticism have submitted an idea for a charter school just for bullies. Despite a number of delays caused by constant name calling, put downs and noogie attacks at the organizational meetings, the parents finally submitted a proposal for the Biff and Scut Charter School where all of the students will be encouraged to pick on one another and to explore new techniques to aggravate their peers.

Another recent application was submitted by a couple named Dark Lord and Queen of Darkness. Their school will cater to "Victorian era cyber punks", or Goths. Its proposed name and mascot is the Voodoo High Ravens. The school uniform consists of, you guessed it, black on black, and all students will receive a Raven tattoo on their forehead in place of a student ID card.

Voodoo High will offer the basic curriculum plus a unique list of electives including a couple of body piercing classes: "Nuts and Bolts" an introductory class, and the advanced class "Abs of Steel Rings." In a more metaphysical realm they will offer a class on reincarnation called "Oink—don't eat me! I'm your Uncle Bob!"

I hope that all of the proposed charter schools will be able to open their doors to students soon. And if none of these is a perfect fit for your child, just wait and the right one may open at a Jamba Juice stand near you soon.

What's love got to do with it?

Hold on! Hold the phone! Hold your horses! Hold anything but your partner's hand in marriage as the legal joining together of same-sex couples "is under further review" by some Supreme Court Judge somewhere.

Gay and lesbian couples argue that it is not fair to allow men and women to achieve marital bliss by proclaiming "I do" while they remain trapped in legal limbo. In other words, what's good for the goose and the gander should be good for two ganders.

Since the basic argument of same-sex marriage proponents is the matter of fairness, the simplest solution to this entire marriage debate is for the Supreme Court to declare all marriage illegal, making everyone equal.

There, that was easy. Now we can move on to more important issues like what Kim and Kanye are wearing today.

Seriously, if we simply did away with the institution of legal marriage would it really have any effect on society whatsoever? History seems to indicate it would not.

The marriage myth in our culture today implies that a man and a woman meet "in the misty moonlight, by the flickering firelight," fall madly in love, and are joined for eternity, or at least what seems like an eternity even if it's only for a year, and live happily ever after.

To support this belief, some quote the Bible, written back when people used fancy sounding words like "therefore." It states "Therefore what God has joined together, let no one separate." But what if the writer is referring to Siamese twins? If so, I'd say some surgeons are in mighty big trouble.

Does the early history of this nation support the notion that if two people are in love they must marry before they can have sex? First of all, in early Jamestown settlement men outnumbered women four to one which sounds like paradise for the gals until one considers that the men had names for their pet pubic lice.

Nonetheless, women eventually succumbed to their advances as men showered them with gifts of Pepe Le Pew Perfume and moccasin-leather jerky. So it was down with the bundling boards and on to bundles of joy.

Marriage retained its utilitarian role even after the more religious-motivated Puritans started arriving on our shores. People married for wealth and power, as well as out of necessity since 30-40% of the women were pregnant when they tied the knot. And here I thought the Puritans were like, you know, pure.

Around this same time the Christian pilgrims were mystified by the Native American concept of marriage. It was common for a man to have more than one wife. In some tribes, women had more than one man. Most shocking was the fact that the Indian women were treated equal to the men—a fact totally contrary to the Christian "wives submit yourselves to your husbands" concept which has been carried to the extreme today by a number of NFL players.

236

In addition, the Native Americans had no type of formal divorce. They simply split up their personal property and went their separate ways. Boy, wouldn't that arrangement drive lawyers crazy today!

Recent statistics clearly indicate that the necessity and the desire for traditional marriage are on the decline. In the U.S. the marriage rate for young adults is at its lowest point ever. Does this imply that they are not falling in love and, thus, are not having sex? The answers are "Maybe" and "Ha!"

The reasons for the decline in marriage are varied. One is that the motivation for it as a mode of survival simply no longer exists. Sure, marriage was great when a guy actually needed a wife to cook and serve him dinner. But now he has fast-food drive-up windows for all that—and no dishes to wash! And as far as reasons why women ever needed men, I really can't think of any.

Another reason for the decline in marriage is that people are living a lot longer now, so that "till death do us part" vow is a very serious commitment. It's just not the same as when Captain John Smith could declare his love for Pocahontas one minute and possibly get his head bashed in with a large rock the next minute due to a rather fickle father-in-law.

Plus, whereas marriage back then was a means of survival or economic gain, today, according to Hallmark, it is based on romance, and, let's face it, one can only keep that passionate fire burning just so long without adding some new lighter fluid.

Ultimately, the demise of marriage, like lots of traditions, will result from technological advances. Guys, just imagine the advantages of being married to a robot. If she proves to be incompatible, you simply remove her batteries and head to Burger King.

Where is global warming when you need it?

As I gaze out the window I see that it is snowing again. The white stuff continues to pile up to the point that, even if I did go temporarily insane and decide to shovel it, I can no longer determine where the sidewalk is located. In addition, there is a mountain of snow in the driveway which could challenge Borah as the highest point in Idaho. As far as my getting around outdoors on the rare occasions when I venture out, I have a great system. I simply go out to the garage, crawl onto my ATV and plow my way to the F350 pickup parked on the front lawn, or what use to be the lawn. For short trips, say to the mailbox, I step out the backdoor, straddle my snowmobile and I'm there in a jiffy.

I must admit that during the winter months I, a normally energetic, active male, turn into a victim of seasonal atrophy. At the mere thought of shoveling the walk, I begin to perspire and gasp for breath. Sure, some people might call me lazy, irresponsible, un-neighborly, unpatriotic, etc. To such a harangue I say...uhhh ... actually I'm not sure what to say since I don't really know what harangue means. I thought it was some sort of lemon flavored pie.

So as the wind howls and the temperature plummets, I sit and debate risking a search and rescue mission for my poodle Muffy who disappeared beneath the white blanket three days ago while attempting to find solid footing so he could go wee-wee after being forced to hold it throughout the month of January.

Besides, eventually it will all melt. Granted, until that occurs sometime in mid-July, my sidewalk will remain a no man's land where school children sink out of sight, joggers slip and slide while cursing the homeowner, and penguins march merrily along confusing my walk with an ancient Antarctic migration route.

To be totally honest, despite not lifting a finger to shovel the walk, I have made various other pathetic attempts to exercise this winter. Why only yesterday I nearly broke a healthy sweat working out to my newest exercise video "Abs of Flab," and let me assure you that this particular exercise routine is a lot more strenuous than you might think. Just try to eat a Krispy Kreme baker's dozen then wash it down with a gallon of Ben and Jerry's Mocha Tangerine Marshmallow Ice Cream. And to add to the pain, I only had an hour to cool down before heading out to dinner. One thing for sure, it's a lot better than my Richard Simmons video – all I got from it was some funky looking striped shorts and curly hair.

It has become increasingly obvious to me that one has to be creative and try to discover new ways to get in a workout during the winter. An inspiration that I had last week resulted in a visit to the Golden Corral for Sirloin Night. During the course of the evening I waddled through the buffet line three times! In addition to that cardio-vascular stress, I also got a heck of an upper body workout as I carried my over flowing surf-board sized plate back and forth, although I think the dining experience would be more enjoyable if they would simply deliver the food to my table with a forklift. Now, throw in the mental exercise of geometrically organizing the food to allow the whole fried chicken and the one pound sirloin steak to remain untainted by the Watergate salad, and I was so drained that I gave up trying to choose between the chocolate sundae and the caramel-fudge pudding and just scooped up a quart of each.

As I wedged my way towards the cash register, a glance at my GPS indicated that I had walked 102 steps and burned up 35 calories! All I can say is that it's a good thing that I packed along a pocket full of Power Bars or I may not have been able to complete the workout.

Alas, despite all of my ingenious and valiant attempts to stay in shape during the winter, I always somehow manage to end up back on the couch staring wistfully out the front window, straining to hear the howls of Muffy as the penguin caravan carries him away to the Great White North. And I wish that I could rescue him, but my stomach tells me that it is time for the breakfast buffet, and I must answer the call of the wild.

Yes, I believe that humans were meant to hibernate during the winter, and, only when absolutely necessary, roll out of our electric blanket-swaddled cavern like a hippo-sized Punxsutawney Phil, and rumble to the fridge for a feeding frenzy which we can top off by eating our shadow. Then, to the symphonic sound of our neighbors' scrapping shovels, slowly drift back to slumber land for six more weeks.

Women are from Venus; men are from Hell

It's a good thing that Mother Nature has arranged it so that wives outlive their husbands. Without my wife, Thanksgiving would be a complete bust since I am not even sure which end of the turkey to stuff. Besides I wouldn't be able to find the stove under the greasy pyramids of dirty dishes.

Who am I trying to kid? Without my wife, I would simply starve to death. Or I would suffocate beneath a pile of unwashed sheets. Or I would succumb to a weird medical condition because I did not see a doctor about the baseball-sized red lump on my nose which I thought was just a pimple.

In other words, I would not be around by Thanksgiving, or even this coming Friday for that matter.

It seems obvious to me that males, along with a XY chromosome, also have a ZZZZ chromosome resulting in excess sleeping and overall laziness.

Now I know that girls can be negligent when it comes to not picking up their clothes, but when I enter the house that my son rents along with his buddies it reminds me of the Chamber of Horrors ride at the amusement park. In contrast to the local Museum of Clean, my son's house is the Museum of Filthy.

You couldn't pick up the clothes from the floor if you tried since there are large dogs lying on top of them, each one having set up permanent residency on "his pile" and will only depart it if bribed with a petrified pizza crust. That is, if you can manage to wrestle the crust away from a platoon of ants just before they slide under the kitchen door with it.

Truthfully, I have never entered the house and seen another human being, so I'm beginning to wonder if the dogs have taken over the lease. Come to think of it, I have noticed that the lawn looks better recently.

If you really want to witness the wide gap between males and females concerning neatness and effort, attend a garage sale. In fact, if you analyze garage sales as a microcosm of the U.S.

economy, it is no wonder it tanked, since the business world is dominated by men.

First of all, a woman is running the sale 99% of the time because the man is a) still in bed b) fishing, hunting, or watching an old Chuck Norris film or c) simply "ran off several years ago."

Women will mark a price on every item—and it's legible. But if a man is in charge, he will say, "How much do you want to give me 'cuz I just want to get rid of it." Or if a man does quote a price, the woman will rush in and double it.

Women will separate clothes into neatly folded piles on tables: jeans, shirts, jackets, etc. Men will toss all the clothes into one pile . . . on the lawn . . . just after watering it. . . and where the dog loves to go potty.

The one exception to this is the man's personal ball cap collection which is organized on a table in perfectly straight rows. But then the man will actually discourage you from buying any of them: "Oh, you don't want that greasy old NAPA Auto cap do you?" Or he will just snatch it from you and say, "Did she put this out here? I told her not to," and proceed to slap it on top of the other three already on his head.

Women, who I'm sure had the best intentions when they purchased them, will sell their barely used bun-buster, stomach tucker, or leg toner devices. While the men reluctantly offer for sell their KISS memorabilia collection or NASCAR stein set.

At a garage sale, one can also clearly observe differences in the female and male shoppers. First of all, the woman will get out of the car and look for what they need while the man will sit in the car with the air conditioner running listening to the radio since he has no clue what they need.

The woman will attack the merchandise very aggressively while, eventually, the man will drag himself out of the auto and just sort of saunter around the perimeter before he moseys over to look at a 1958 Edsel tail light or a mounted moose head.

By the time they are all done shopping, the woman will have her arms full of practical stuff like bed sheets, silverware, etc. Whereas, the guy will be tickled pink because he got an Ernest

Tubbs 8-track tape for 50 cents, forgetting that he no longer owns a player.

There may be some truth to the expression "It's a man's world," but that world sure runs a lot smoother when a woman's in it.